文化艺术篇

游学在中国

A STUDY TOUR IN CHINA

暨南大学华文学院 编

主编：周健

编写：萧思齐 胡建刚 刘刚
文雁 萧文茵 周健

翻译：周健 余惠芬 胡建刚
章恒珍 印妮 罗晓英
梁辉元

外语教学与研究出版社
北京

图书在版编目(CIP)数据

游学在中国. 文化艺术篇／周健主编. —北京：外语教学与研究出版社,2003.9
ISBN 7-5600-2179-4

Ⅰ. 游… Ⅱ. 周… Ⅲ. 中国—概况—对外汉语教学—教材 Ⅳ. H195.4

中国版本图书馆 CIP 数据核字(2003)第 074156 号

出 版 人：李朋义
责任编辑：赵晓晖 李彩霞
封面设计：王 琳
出版发行：外语教学与研究出版社
社 址：北京市西三环北路 19 号 (100089)
网 址：http://www.fltrp.com
印 刷：北京大学印刷厂
开 本：787×1092 1/16
印 张：20.25
版 次：2005 年 8 月第 1 版 2005 年 8 月第 1 次印刷
书 号：ISBN 7-5600-2179-4
定 价：55.00 元（附赠光盘一张）

＊ ＊ ＊

前言

　　《游学在中国》分为"语言文字篇"和"文化艺术篇"两册，是专门为外国人短期学习汉语和中国文化而编写的实用型语言文化综合教材。

　　中国改革开放以来，经济、文化日趋繁荣，来华学习、经商、考察、观光、旅游和进行各种文化交流的外国朋友越来越多，其中参加夏令营、冬令营，就读于各种短期班的人数迅速增长。您来到中国，一定渴望了解中国和中国文化，迫切希望能在很短的时间内尽可能高效率地接触、了解和学习中国文化。除了学习汉语之外，您可能还想了解中国的历史、地理概况，学点儿中国的书画剪纸，练练中国功夫，唱一两首中国歌曲，做几道中国的家常菜，购买一些中国的土特产，游览中国最有代表性的名胜古迹。为了适应外国朋友们多方面的要求，填补短期语言文化综合教材的空缺，我们组织编写了这套教材。

　　本书由暨南大学华文学院长期从事汉语短训班教学的专家执笔编写。力求简明生动，实用易学。许多内容均自出机杼，特色鲜明。

　　"语言文字篇"内容包括"汉字入门"、"汉语初阶"、"常用交际语"三个部分。"汉字入门"通过巧妙的提示解说，使您能在短短的几个小时内轻松地掌握100个最基本的汉字；"汉语初阶"（附有录音带）重在日常口语的训练，介绍了一些最基本的交际文化知识，还编写了三则小话剧，可用于提高和表现您的汉语水平。如想扩大会话的范围，您可以参考"常用交际语"。您如果想在中国的大学继续深造，附录"中国留学指南"为您提供了60所中国著名高等学府及教学机构的通讯地址、网址及相关的信息。这些大学的对外汉语教学机构都具有丰富的经验和相当的规模。

　　"文化艺术篇"内容包括"中国概况"、"中国书画ABC"、"剪纸入门"、"学中国功夫"、"学做中国菜"、"学唱中国歌"、"中国导游"及"中国特产"八个部分。"中国概况"介绍中国的史地常识和基本国情，学了之后您一定能对中国的自然地理、历史发展、人口、民族、节日、风俗、国家机构、行政区划和台湾问题有一个大概的了解；"中国书画ABC"通过简要的说明和步骤图示，引导您跨进中国传统书法与绘画的门槛；学了"剪纸入门"，一剪在手您就能剪出惟妙惟肖的人物花鸟；"学中国功夫"能使您在亲友面前显露身手；"学做中国菜"能使爱吃中华美味的您受用终生；"学唱中国歌"精选了十首脍炙人口的中国歌曲；"中国导游"则通过一条S形的线路，带领您饱览中国的历史文化名城与自然风光名胜之精华；"中国特产"除了介绍中国各地著名的土特产之外，还提供了主要城市的购物地点，相信您一定会满载而归的。

外语教学与研究出版社的英文专家凌原先生、陈海燕女士认真审校了全书的英文翻译，北京外国语大学熊德輗教授、何其莘博士，美国朋友马克先生也审校了部分英译，谭桂英老师为文稿的电脑输入付出了辛勤的劳动。国务院侨务办公室、外语教学与研究出版社、广东省侨务办公室、亚加达外语专修学院大力支持并资助了本书的编写出版，在此一并致谢。

周　健
2003 年 5 月

PREFACE

A STUDY TOUR IN CHINA comes in two volumes, *Chinese Language and Writing* and *Chinese Culture and Arts*. It is a practical textbook that helps foreigners learn Chinese language and culture in a short period of time.

Since China adopted the policy of reform and opening up to the outside world, both its economy and culture have been thriving. Foreigners are arriving in droves for academic pursuits, trade and business, discovery, cultural exchanges and sightseeing. There is also an increasing number of students who come for summer or winter camps or short-term training programs of various kinds. While you are here, you inevitably will want to know more about the country and its unique culture. Besides the Chinese language, you may also want to have some elementary knowledge of Chinese history and geography, learn calligraphy, traditional Chinese painting and paper-cutting, practice Chinese martial arts, sing Chinese songs, cook Chinese family dishes, buy native products, or visit famous places of historical interest and scenic beauty. To meet the needs of foreign visitors and make up for the shortage of textbooks for short-term language and cultural training, we decided that it would be worth our while to bring out a book like what you have now before you.

This book was written by professors and experts from the College of Chinese Language and Culture of Jinan University, who have rich experience in teaching Chinese. The language and cultural materials selected for this book are simple and interesting, easy to learn, and of practical use. You will find this book quite original.

Volume I, *Chinese Language and Writing*, includes three parts: "The Rudiments of Chinese Characters," "Basic Chinese," "Say It in Chinese." "The Rudiments of Chinese Characters" enables you to master 100 basic characters in just a few hours by clear explanations. "Basic Chinese" (with cassette tapes attached) trains you in basic skills of listening and speaking. There are also three short plays in this part, which can improve and display your language skills. If you want to extend your language skills in communication, "Say It in Chinese" will come in handy. The appendix "Chinese Language Programs for International Students" offers a brief introduction to Chinese programs for international students at 60 famous Chinese universities that operate large and well-established institutions for teaching Chinese as a second language.

Volume II, *Chinese Culture and Arts*, consists of eight parts: "A Survey of China," "The ABC of Traditional Chinese Calligraphy and Painting," "Paper-Cutting for Beginners," "Basic Chinese Martial Arts," "Cooking Chinese Dishes," "How to Sing Chinese Songs," "Tourist Highlights in China" and "Native Produce of China." "A Survey of China" offers a brief introduction to Chinese history, geography and national conditions, and gives a general idea about China's geography, historical development, population, ethnic groups, festivals, social customs, state structure, administrative divisions and the Taiwan issue. "The ABC of Traditional Chinese Calligraphy and Painting" teaches the basic skills in traditional handwriting and painting. From "Paper-Cutting for Beginners" you will learn how to cut beautiful flowers, birds, animals and human figures out of paper. You can show off what you have learned from "Basic Chinese Martial Arts" in front of your relatives and friends. If you love Chinese food, you will benefit from learning "Cooking Chinese Dishes" for the rest of your life. The ten songs in "How to Sing Chinese Songs" are carefully chosen popular pieces. "Tourist Highlights in China" takes you on an itinerary of famous historical and cultural cities and spectacular sights along an S-shaped route. You will be acquainted with China's well-known special products and local delicacies as well as shopping places in major cities in "Native Produce of China." You will get plenty of best buys by following this guide.

Mr. Ling Yuan and Ms. Chen Haiyan from Foreign Language Teaching and Research Press have checked and revised the English translation very carefully. We are also grateful to Professor Xiong Deni, Dr. He Qixin from Beijing Foreign Studies University and my American friend Mr. Mark E. Roth, who have read the translation. Thanks are also due to Ms. Tan Guiying, who has done much paper work. We are also indebted to our friends at the Office of Overseas Chinese Affairs under the State Council, Foreign Language Teaching and Research Press, the Overseas Chinese Affairs Office of Guangdong Provincial People's Government and Alcanta College of Foreign Languages, who have given us great help and support in the publication of this book.

Zhou Jian
May 2003

总 目 录
General Contents

中国概况

A SURVEY OF CHINA

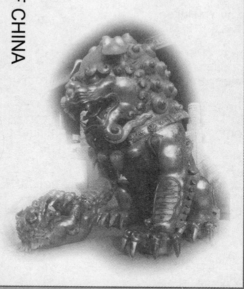

中国概况

周　健　编写
余惠芬　翻译

A Survey of China

Compiled by Zhou Jian

Translated by Yu Huifen

第一课　自然地理

欢迎大家来到中国。先请大家回答几个问题，看看你们对中国了解多少。

这几个问题是：

1. 中国的全名叫什么？
2. 中国的面积有多大？在世界上占第几位？
3. 中国最有名的两条河流叫什么名字？
4. 中国最有名的野生动物是什么？

这些问题我来给大家讲一讲。（图1：中国的国旗和国徽）

中国，全名叫中华人民共和国，位于亚洲东部。中国陆地面积约960万平方公里，

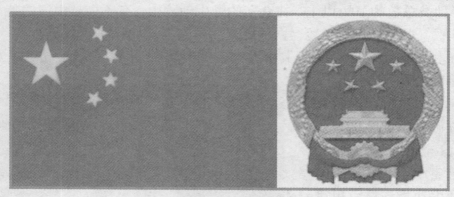

图1　中国的国旗和国徽

居世界第三位，仅次于俄罗斯和加拿大。中国大陆的东部和南部濒临渤海、黄海、东海和南海。在辽阔的中国海域上，分布着约6,500个岛屿，其中，最大的是台湾岛，面积约3.6万平方公里；其次是海南岛，面积约3.4万平方公里。这两个岛各为中国的一个省。

从高空俯瞰中国大地，可以看到她的地势像四级阶梯，由西而东，逐级下降。

最高的一级是青藏高原，平均海拔4,000米以上，号称"世界屋脊"。

第二级阶梯由内蒙古高原、黄土高原、云贵高原和塔里木盆地、准噶尔盆地、四川盆地构成，平均海拔1,000米至2,000米。

第三级阶梯地势下降到海拔500米至1,000米以下，自北而南分布着东北平原、华北平原、长江中下游平原和珠江三角洲平原。平原的边缘镶嵌着低山和丘陵。

再向东是中国大陆架浅海区，也就是第四级阶梯。这里水深大都不足200米，堆积着河流入海带来的大量泥沙。

中国山脉众多，闻名于世。位于青藏高原西南端的喜马拉雅山的主峰珠穆朗玛峰，

海拔 8,848 米，为世界第一高峰。

中国的河流大多数由西向东流入太平洋。长江是中国第一大河，全长 6,300 多公里，流域面积 180.9 万平方公里，是中国内河运输的大动脉。黄河是中国第二大河，全长 5,464 公里。黄河流域是中国古代文明的发祥地之一，那里有许许多多的古迹文物。

另外，中国还有一条著名的人工河，那就是北起北京、南至杭州的大运河，全长 1,800 公里，已经通航 1,000 多年了。

中国拥有众多的湖泊，多分布在中国南方。最大的淡水湖是位于江西省的鄱阳湖，最大的咸水湖是位于青海省的青海湖。

中国大部分地区处于温带，南方部分地区处于热带和亚热带，北部则靠近寒带。因此各地气温差异很大。总的来说，中国的气候属于大陆季风性气候，四季分明，夏季炎热多雨，冬天寒冷干燥。

中国是世界上拥有野生动物种类最多的国家之一，仅陆栖脊椎动物就有 2,000 多种，占世界种类总数的 10% 以上。在众多的野生动物中，有不少是中国的特产，如大熊猫、金丝猴、白唇鹿、扭角羚、白鳍豚、扬子鳄等。（图 2：大熊猫）

中国有木本植物 7,000 多种，其中乔木 2,800 多种。水杉、水松、银杉、杉木、金钱松等树种为中国所特有。

为了保护和拯救中国特有的动植物资源和濒危物种，截至 1999 年底，全国已建立 1,146 处（未计台湾省）自然保护区来保护森林和野生动物，总面积达 8,815 多万公顷。

练习

1. 请你在中国地图上找到黄河、长江和珠江。
2. 请你在地图上找出中国的 14 个邻国。
3. 想想看，为什么中国的大多数河流都是从西向东流?

图 2　大熊猫

Lesson One   Physical Geography

Welcome to China. Please answer the following questions first, so that we can find out how much you know about China.

1) What is the full name of China?
2) How much is the total area of China and how high is it ranked internationally in terms of territorial size?
3) What are the names of the two best known rivers in China?
4) What is the most famous wild animal in China?

Now, let me give you a brief introduction of China. (Illustration 1: The National Flag and Emblem of China)

The full name of China is the People's Republic of China. China is situated in the eastern part of Asia. It has a total land area of 9.6 million square kilometers, next only to Russia and Canada, ranked number three in the world. The Chinese mainland is flanked by the Bohai Sea, the Yellow Sea, the East China Sea and the South China Sea in the east and south. Almost 6,500 islands are scattered over China's vast territorial seas, the largest being Taiwan Island with an area of 36,000 square kilometers, and the second largest, Hainan Island with an area of 34,000 square kilometers. Taiwan and Hainan are two provinces of China.

A bird's-eye view indicates that China's terrain descends in four steps from west to east.

At the top step of the "staircase" is the Qinghai-Tibet Plateau, with an average elevation of over 4,000 meters and known as the "Roof of the World."

The second step encompasses the Inner Mongolia Plateau, the Loess Plateau, the Yunnan-Guizhou Plateau and the Tarim Basin, the Junggar Basin as well as the Sichuan Basin, with an average elevation of 1,000 to 2,000 meters.

The third step, about 500 to 1,000 meters above sea level, contains, from north to south, the Northeast Plain, the North China Plain, the Middle and Lower Yangtze Valley Plain, and the Pearl Delta Plain. Interspersed along the plains' edges are hills and foothills.

Stretching further east into the shallow sea less than 200 meters deep, with massive accumulation of sediments from river estuaries, is the continental shelf that forms the fourth step of the "staircase."

China is famous for its numerous mountains. Rising 8,848 meters above sea level on the southwest tip of the Qinghai-Tibet Plateau is Mount Qomolangma, the main peak of Himalayas and the world's highest.

Most of China's rivers flow east into the Pacific. The Yangtze River, over 6,300 kilometers long, is the largest river in China. It has a drainage area of 1,809,000 square kilometers, and is the major inland-river transport artery in China. The Yellow River, stretching over 5,464 kilometers, is China's second largest. The Yellow River Valley was a cradle of the ancient Chinese civilization and a veritable repository of historic sites and relics.

In addition to these natural rivers, China has a famous man-made river—the Grand Canal. Running from Beijing in the north to Hangzhou in the south for 1,800 kilometers, it was open to navigation over 1,000 years ago.

China has many natural lakes, most of them scattered in the south. The largest freshwater lake is Poyang Lake in Jiangxi Province and the largest salt lake is Qinghai Lake in Qinghai Province.

China is situated mostly in the temperate zone. Some parts of south China are in tropical and subtropical zones while the northern part is near the frigid zone. The temperature varies greatly in different parts of the country. In general, China has a continental monsoon climate. The four seasons are quite distinct. It is hot and moist in summer, and cold and dry in winter.

China is one of the countries that have the greatest diversity of wildlife in the world. It has more than 2,000 species of terrestrial vertebrates, accounting for more than 10% of the world's total. Many wild animals are found only in China, including the giant panda, the golden monkey, the white-lipped deer, the takin, the white-flag dolphin and the Chinese alligator. (Illustration 2: The Giant Panda)

China has more than 7,000 species of woody plants, of which 2,800 are arbors. The metasequoia, the China cypress, the silver fir, the China fir and the golden larch etc. are found only in China.

In a concerted effort to protect the nation's unique zoological and botanical resources and endangered species, China had established 1,146 nature reserves of forests and wildlife by the end of 1999 (Taiwan not included), with a total area of more than 88.15 million hectares.

Exercises

1) Please point out the Yellow River, the Yangtze River and the Pearl River on the map of China.
2) Please indicate China's 14 neighboring countries on the map.
3) Please answer this question: Why do most rivers in China flow from west to east?

第二课　人口与民族

中国是世界上人口最多的国家，截至2005年初，中国人口已超过13亿（不含港澳台地区人口）。

中国的人口密度为每平方公里130人，但人口分布很不均匀，东部沿海地区人口稠密，密度高达每平方公里400人以上；在中部地区，每平方公里约为200人；在人烟稀少的西部高原，每平方公里不足10人。

中国城市人口占30.4%，农村人口占69.6%；从性别看，男性占50.8%，女性占49.2%；从年龄看，14岁以下的占25.7%，15岁至64岁的占67.6%，65岁以上的老年人占6.7%。

1949年新中国成立以后，人口迅速增长，阻碍了社会和经济的发展。中国政府从70年代开始采取了计划生育政策，即"晚婚、晚育、少生、优生"，提倡每对夫妇只生一个孩子；但在少数民族地区和农村地区，采取了比较灵活的政策。自从实行计划生育政策以来，人口出生率逐年下降，已从1969年的34.11‰下降到2002年底的12.83‰。人口自然增长率也从26.08‰下降到6.45‰。目前，中国人口已基本实现了向低出生、低增长的人口再生产类型的转变。

中国现有3.4亿个家庭，每个家庭平均人口为3.63人。多数家庭由夫妇和孩子组成，但也有不少由三代人或更多代人组成的家庭。在中国家庭里，夫妻都能支持对方的工作，并与其他家庭成员一起协商解决家庭的问题，分担家务工作。中国人有尊老爱幼的传统，尽管许多年轻夫妇不再和父母同住，但他们之间仍保持着密切的联系。长大成人的子女有责任赡养和帮助父母。中国人十分重视家庭成员之间以及亲戚之间的联系。

中国是一个统一的多民族国家，由56个民族组成。汉族人口约占92%，其余55个民族约占总人口的8%。由于汉族人口众多，习惯上把其余55个民族称为少数民族。汉族分布在全国各地，主要聚居在黄河、长江、珠江三大流域的中下游和东北平原；其他民族主要分布在西北、西南和边疆地区。

汉族有自己的语言和文字。汉语的普通话是当今中国的通用语言，也是联合国的工作语言之一。回族和满族也使用汉语。其余53个民族都使用本民族的语言，其中23个民族有自己的文字。

练习

1. 说说你所知道的中国计划生育政策。你有什么看法？
2. 在中国的少数民族中，哪三个民族的人口最多？

少数民族人口与分布表

少数民族名称	人口（万人）	主要分布地区
蒙古	480.24	内蒙古、新疆、辽宁、吉林、黑龙江、甘肃、河北、河南、青海
回	861.20	宁夏、甘肃、河南、河北、青海、山东、云南、新疆、安徽、辽宁、黑龙江、吉林、山西、北京、天津
藏	459.31	西藏、青海、四川、甘肃、云南
维吾尔	720.70	新疆
苗	738.36	贵州、湖南、云南、广西、四川、湖北
彝	657.85	四川、云南、贵州、广西
壮	1,555.58	广西、云南、广东、贵州
布依	254.83	贵州
朝鲜	192.34	吉林、辽宁、黑龙江
满	984.68	辽宁、吉林、黑龙江、河北、北京、内蒙古
侗	250.86	贵州、湖南、广西
瑶	213.70	广西、湖南、云南、广东、贵州
白	159.80	云南、贵州
土家	572.50	湖南、湖北
哈尼	125.48	云南
哈萨克	111.08	新疆、甘肃、青海
傣	102.54	云南
黎	111.25	海南
傈僳	57.40	云南、四川
佤	35.20	云南
畲	63.47	福建、浙江、江西、广东
高山	0.29	台湾、福建
拉祜	41.15	云南
水	34.71	贵州、广西
东乡	37.37	甘肃、新疆
纳西	27.78	云南、四川
景颇	11.93	云南
柯尔克孜	14.35	新疆、黑龙江
土	19.26	青海、甘肃

少数民族名称	人口（万人）	主要分布地区
达斡尔	12.15	内蒙古、黑龙江、新疆
仫佬	16.06	广西
羌	19.83	四川
布朗	8.24	云南
撒拉	8.75	青海、甘肃
毛南	7.24	广西
仡佬	43.82	贵州、广西
锡伯	17.29	新疆、辽宁、吉林
阿昌	2.77	云南
普米	2.97	云南
塔吉克	3.32	新疆
怒	2.72	云南
乌孜别克	1.48	新疆
俄罗斯	1.35	新疆
鄂温克	2.64	内蒙古、黑龙江
德昂	1.55	云南
保安	1.17	甘肃
裕固	1.23	甘肃
京	1.87	广西
塔塔尔	0.51	新疆
独龙	0.58	云南
鄂伦春	0.70	内蒙古、黑龙江
赫哲	0.43	黑龙江
门巴	0.75	西藏
珞巴	0.23	西藏
基诺	1.80	云南

Lesson Two   Population and Ethnic Groups

China is the most populous country in the world. Its population totalled 1.3 billion at the beginning of 2005, which did not include Hong Kong, Macao and Taiwan.

中国概况

The population density in China is 130 people per square kilometer. This population, however, is unevenly distributed. Along the densely populated east coast there are more than 400 people per square kilometer. In the central region, about 200 per square kilometer. And in the sparsely populated plateaus in the west, there are less than 10 people per square kilometer.

Urban dwellers account for 30.4% of the Chinese population, and rural dwellers 69.6%; males make up 50.8% of the population and females 49.2%. People 14 years old or younger make up 25.7%; those from 15 to 64, 67.6%; and those of 65 or older, 6.7%.

After the People's Republic of China was founded in 1949, rapid population growth became a major impediment to the nation's economic and social development. In the 1970s, the Chinese government introduced a family planning policy, advocating late marriage and late childbirth, fewer but healthier babies, especially one child per couple. The policy, however, is rather flexible for rural people and ethnic minorities. Since then, China's birth rate has been steadily declining year by year. The birth rate dropped from 34.11‰ in 1969 to 12.83‰ at the end of 2002, and the natural growth rate decreased from 26.08‰ to 6.45‰. Thus the population of this country has basically accomplished the transition to a reproduction pattern that is characterized by low-birth and low-growth rates.

China has 340 million families, with 3.63 people per household on average. Most families are composed of a couple and their child/children, but there is no lack of big families with three or more generations living under the same roof. In most Chinese families, husband and wife support each other's work, handle family affairs through consultation, and share housework with other family members. The Chinese have a tradition of respecting the old and loving the young. Though many young couples do not live with their parents, they maintain close contact with them. Grown-up children are duty-bound to support and help their parents. The Chinese attach due importance to relations between family members and between relatives.

China is a united multi-ethnic nation of 56 ethnic groups. The Han people make up 92% of the country's total population, and the other 55 ethnic groups, 8%. As the majority of the Chinese population is made up of the Hans, the other ethnic groups are customarily referred to as minorities. The Han people are found throughout the country, though most of them inhabit the middle and lower Yellow, Yangtze and Pearl river valleys, and the Northeast Plain. The minorities are also widely scattered, but they are mainly distributed in the northwest, the southwest, and the border regions.

The Han people have their own spoken and written language. Chinese is the official language of China; it is also one of the working languages of the United Nations. All China's minority peoples use their own languages except the Huis and Manchus, who use Chinese; 23 of them have their own written forms.

Exercises

1) Please tell us what you know about China's family planning policy and comment on it.
2) Please name the three most populous minority groups in China.

China's National Minority Population and Their Distribution

Ethnic group	Population	Major Areas of Habitation
Mongol	4,802,400	Inner Mongolia, Xinjiang, Liaoning, Jilin, Heilongjiang, Gansu, Hebei, Henan, Qinghai
Hui	8,612,000	Ningxia, Gansu, Henan, Hebei, Qinghai, Shandong, Yunnan, Xinjiang, Anhui, Liaoning, Heilongjiang, Jilin, Shanxi, Beijing, Tianjin
Tibetan	4,593,100	Tibet, Qinghai, Sichuan, Gansu, Yunnan
Uygur	7,207,000	Xinjiang
Miao	7,383,600	Guizhou, Hunan, Yunnan, Guangxi, Sichuan, Hubei
Yi	6,578,500	Sichuan, Yunnan, Guizhou, Guangxi
Zhuang	15,555,800	Guangxi, Yunnan, Guangdong, Guizhou
Bouyei	2,548,300	Guizhou
Korean	1,923,400	Jilin, Liaoning, Heilongjiang
Manchu	9,846,800	Liaoning, Jilin, Heilongjiang, Hebei, Beijing, Inner Mongolia
Dong	2,508,600	Guizhou, Hunan, Guangxi
Yao	2,137,000	Guangxi, Hunan, Yunnan, Guangdong, Guizhou
Bai	1,598,000	Yunnan, Guizhou
Tujia	5,725,000	Hunan, Hubei
Hani	1,254,800	Yunnan
Kazak	1,110,800	Xinjiang, Gansu, Qinghai
Dai	1,025,400	Yunnan
Li	1,112,500	Hainan
Lisu	574,000	Yunnan, Sichuan
Wa	352,000	Yunnan
She	634,700	Fujian, Zhejiang, Jiangxi, Guangdong
Gaoshan	2,900	Taiwan, Fujian
Lahu	411,500	Yunnan
Shui	347,100	Guizhou, Guangxi
Dongxiang	373,700	Gansu, Xinjiang

中国概况

Ethnic group	Population	Major Areas of Habitation
Naxi	277,800	Yunnan, Sichuan
Jingpo	119,300	Yunnan
Kirgiz	143,500	Xinjiang, Heilongjiang
Tu	192,600	Qinghai, Gansu
Daur	121,500	Inner Mongolia, Heilongjiang, Xinjiang
Mulao	160,600	Guangxi
Qiang	198,300	Sichuan
Blang	82,400	Yunnan
Sarla	87,500	Qinghai, Gansu
Maonan	72,400	Guangxi
Gelo	438,200	Guizhou, Guangxi
Sibo	172,900	Xinjiang, Liaoning, Jilin
Achang	27,700	Yunnan
Pumi	29,700	Yunnan
Tajik	33,200	Xinjiang
Nu	27,200	Yunnan
Ozbek	14,800	Xinjiang
Russian	13,500	Xinjiang
Ewenki	26,400	Inner Mongolia, Heilongjiang
De'ang	15,500	Yunnan
Bonan	11,700	Gansu
Yugur	12,300	Gansu
Jing	18,700	Guangxi
Tartar	5,100	Xinjiang
Derung	5,800	Yunnan
Oroqen	7,000	Inner Mongolia, Heilongjiang
Hezhen	4,300	Heilongjiang
Monba	7,500	Tibet
Lhoba	2,300	Tibet
Jino	1,800	Yunnan

第三课 节日与风俗

中国法定节日有：新年（1月1日），全国放假一天；春节（农历新年），全国放假三天；国际妇女节（3月8日）；植树节（3月12日）；国际劳动节（5月1日），全国放假三天；中国青年节（5月4日）；国际儿童节（6月1日）；中国人民解放军建军节（8月1日）；教师节（9月10日）；国庆节（10月1日），全国放假三天。

中国重要的传统节日有春节、元宵节、清明节、端午节、中秋节和重阳节。

春节是中国最重要的传统节日。过去，中国人使用农历，春节就是"新年"，它定在农历正月初一，新的一年开始之际。辛亥革命之后，中国采用了公历，为了区别农历新年和公历新年，人们把前者改称为春节。春节，通常在公历1月下旬或2月上中旬。春节前一夜叫"除夕"，是家庭团聚的重要时刻。全家人欢聚在一起，吃一顿丰盛的"年夜饭"。饭后，全家人围坐欢叙，或做游戏，或观赏中央电视台的"春节晚会"节目，许多人通宵不眠，称作"守岁"。次日清晨，大家就到亲朋好友家拜年，相互祝贺在新的一年里万事如意。春节期间，各地都有当地传统的文娱活动，以舞狮子、舞龙灯、划旱船、踩高跷、看花会最为普遍。（图3：舞狮子）

农历正月十五为元宵节，也叫"灯节"，这是春节后第一个月圆之夜，也标志着春节活动的结束。过元宵节，有吃元宵和观灯的习俗。元宵以糯米粉为皮，内裹糖馅，圆形，是"团圆"的象征。元宵节观灯的习俗始于公元1世纪，沿至当代仍在各地盛行。每到元宵节之夜，许多城市举办灯会，展出种种彩灯，造型新奇，千姿百态；在农村则举行文娱活动。

每年4月5日前后为清明节。清明节原是祭祀祖先的节日，如今除了祭奠逝去的家人外，人们也开展祭扫烈士陵墓、悼念先烈的活动。人们还常常结伴到郊外踏青、放风筝、欣赏春光。所以清明节也被称作"踏青节"。

图3 舞狮子

农历五月初五是端午节。一般认为它是为纪念古代楚国爱国诗人屈原而形成的。屈原，战国时楚国的政治家和大诗人，他多次向楚王提出整治政治腐败的改革建议，后遭奸人诬陷，被楚王流放。公元前278年，秦兵攻陷楚都，屈原于这年五月初五投汨罗江自尽。江边群众得知后，纷纷驾舟打捞屈原尸体，并用竹叶包裹糯米做成粽子投入江中，以保护屈原尸体不被鱼虾吞食，后来演变为用竹叶或苇叶来包糯米。以后逐渐形成了端午节划龙舟、吃粽子的习俗。

农历八月十五为中秋节。八月十五居于秋季之中，故名"中秋"。中秋时节，秋高气爽，圆月十分明亮。在皎洁的月光下，全家人坐在一起，一边赏月，一边吃着香甜可口的月饼，别有一番情趣。圆圆的月亮和月饼都是全家人团圆的象征。唐代大诗人李白所作的"床前明月光，疑是地上霜。举头望明月，低头思故乡"的诗句，至今仍为人们传诵。

农历九月初九是重阳节，按照中国传统说法，"九"是最大的阳数，一个吉祥的数字，而九月九日则是最吉祥的日子。到了重阳节的时候，中国人的习俗是登山、饮酒、赏菊。到了20世纪80年代后期，重阳节逐渐演变成老人节，这一天全国各地都举行各种敬老爱老的活动。

在长期的历史发展过程中，中国各民族在衣、食、住等方面形成了各自独特的风俗习惯，以适应所处的自然环境、社会条件和经济发展程度。就汉族而言，南方人爱吃米饭，北方人爱吃面食。汉族人喜欢吃蔬菜、豆类、猪肉、鸡、鱼、蛋和水果。他们特别讲究烹调方法。蒙古族人爱吃牛羊肉，喝奶茶。藏族爱吃糌粑，喝酥油茶、青稞酒。维吾尔族、哈萨克族和乌孜别克族喜爱吃烤羊肉串、抓饭和馕。朝鲜族爱吃打糕、冷面和泡菜。黎族、京族、傣族、布朗族和哈尼族都爱嚼槟榔。

在服饰方面，过去满族妇女最典型的衣服是旗袍，蒙古族习惯穿蒙古袍和马靴，藏族爱穿藏袍、系腰带、着藏靴，维吾尔族爱戴四棱绣花帽，朝鲜族爱穿船形胶鞋，彝、苗、瑶族妇女爱穿褶裙，佩戴金银饰品。

居住方面，汉族聚居地区普遍采用院落式住宅，内蒙古、青海、甘肃等地牧区的民族大多住蒙古包，傣、壮、布依等南方民族爱住"吊脚楼"式楼房等。在城市里，由于人烟稠密，绝大多数居民都住在公寓式楼房内。（图4：四合院）

图 4　四合院

中国是一个有多种宗教的国家，佛教、道教、伊斯兰教、天主教和基督教在中国都有人信仰，信仰者约有上亿人。回、维吾尔、哈萨克等民族信仰伊斯兰教。藏、蒙古等民族信仰喇嘛教（也称"藏传佛教"）。傣、布朗等民族信仰小乘佛教。苗、瑶、彝等民族中有相当一部分人信仰天主教或基督教。汉族中有些人信仰佛教、道教、基督教和天主教，但绝大多数人都不信仰宗教。

练习

1．中国全国放假的节日有哪几个？一共放假多少天？

2．中国最重要的传统节日有哪些？

3．比较一下你们国家的新年风俗与中国春节的风俗。

Lesson Three   Festivals and Customs

Official holidays in China are New Year's Day (January 1), a national one-day holiday; the Spring Festival (New Year's Day by the lunar calendar), a national three-day holiday; International Women's Day (March 8); Tree Planting Day (March 12); International Labor Day (May 1), a national three-day holiday; Chinese Youth Day (May 4); International Children's Day (June 1); Anniversary of the Founding of the Chinese People's Liberation Army (August 1); Teacher's Day (September 10); and National Day (October 1), a national three-day holiday.

Major traditional festivals include the Spring Festival, the Lantern Festival, Pure Brightness Festival, the Dragon Boat Festival, the Mid-Autumn Festival and the Double Ninth Festival.

The Spring Festival is the most important traditional festival in China. In the past, the Chinese used the lunar calendar, and the Spring Festival was their "New Year's Day." It falls on the first day of the first lunar month, the beginning of a new year. After the Revolution of 1911, China adopted the Gregorian calendar. To distinguish the lunar New Year from the New Year by the Gregorian calendar, the lunar New Year was called the Spring Festival, which generally falls between late January and mid-February. The evening before the Spring Festival, the lunar New Year's Eve, is an important time for family reunion. The whole family get together for a sumptuous dinner, followed by an evening of pleasant talk or watching the Spring Festival Gala Party on China Central Television (CCTV) . Some families stay up all night, "seeing the old year out," as the saying goes. The next morning, people pay New Year calls on relatives and friends, wishing each other good luck. During the Spring Festival, traditional recreational activities are enjoyed in various parts of China, notably the lion dance, the dragon lantern dance, the land-boat rowing competition, stilt-walking, and the flower show. (Illustration 3: Perform a Lion Dance)

The Lantern Festival falls on the fifteenth day of the first lunar month, the night of the first full moon after the Spring Festival. It also means the ending of all the Spring Festival activities. Traditionally, people eat *yuanxiao* (sweet dumpling) and enjoy watching lanterns during this festival. Sweet dumplings, round balls of glutinous rice flour with sugar fillings, symbolize reunion. Displays of lanterns of all colors and designs are held in many cities at night, hence the name "Lantern Festival." This custom began in the first century and is still popular in many places now. In rural areas, people hold evening parties and play games.

Pure Brightness Festival falls around April 5 every year. Traditionally, this is an occasion for people to make offerings of sacrifice to their ancestors. They also visit tombs of revolutionary martyrs to pay their respects. It is also an occasion for going on outings in the

中国概况

suburbs, flying kites and appreciating the seasonal beauty of spring. That is why Pure Brightness Festival is also called "Walking amid Greenery Day."

The Dragon Boat Festival falls on the fifth day of the fifth lunar month. It is generally believed that this festival was originally dedicated to the memory of Qu Yuan, a patriotic poet and great statesman of the State of Chu during the Warring States Period (475-221 BC). He put forward many proposals of political reform to punish corruption, but, framed by treacherous court officials, he was sent into exile by the king of Chu. He committed suicide by drowning in the Miluo River in modern Hunan Province on the fifth day of the fifth lunar month, after the capital of Chu fell to the State of Qin in 278 BC. After Qu Yuan's death, people living by the river went out in their boats to try to find the corpse, and threw *zongzi* (pyramid-shaped dumplings made of glutinous rice wrapped in bamboo or reed leaves) into the water to feed the fishes and crayfishes so as to protect his corpse. Today, holding dragon boat races and eating *zongzi* during the Dragon Boat Festival have become part of the Chinese folklore.

The Mid-Autumn Festival falls on the fifteenth day of the eighth lunar month, which comes right in the middle of autumn, hence its name. The sky in mid-autumn is clear and the air bracing, and the full moon is especially bright. The whole family sit together eating moon cakes while admiring the moon in its perfect splendor. The round moon and round moon cakes are both symbols of family reunion. The poem of the great Tang-dynasty poet Li Bai is often recited on such evenings even today:

> *Beside my bed a pool of moonlight,*
> *Is it hoarfrost on the ground?*
> *I lift my eyes and see the bright moon;*
> *Bowing my head, I think of my old hometown.*

The Double Ninth Festival falls on the ninth day of the ninth lunar month. According to Chinese tradition, "nine" is an auspicious number; and the ninth day of the ninth lunar month is the most auspicious. On this day, the Chinese often climb mountains, drink wine and admire the chrysanthemums. Since the late 1980s, the Double Ninth Festival has become a festival for elderly people. Various kinds of activities to show respect and concern for the elderly are held throughout the country.

During the long course of historical development, the Chinese of different ethnic backgrounds have developed unique customs regarding food, clothing and housing that are adapted to local environments, social conditions and level of economic development. In general, the Hans living in the south prefer to eat rice while those living in the north prefer wheaten food, but all of them love to eat vegetables, beans, pork, chicken, fish, eggs and fruits, and are particular about cooking techniques. The Mongols often eat beef and mutton, and drink tea with milk. The Tibetans take *zanba* (roasted *qingke* barley flour), buttered tea or *qingke* barley wine as their staple food. The Uygurs, Kazaks, and Ozbeks enjoy roast mutton kebabs, crusty pancakes and rice cooked with mutton, carrot, raisins etc. and eaten with hands. The Koreans like sticky rice cakes, cold noodles and *kimchi* (hot pickled vegetables), while the Lis, Jings, Dais, Blangs and Hanis enjoy chewing betel nuts.

The typical costume of Manchu women used to be the *qipao* (a close-fitting dress with high neck and slit skirt). The Mongols wear traditional robes and riding boots. The Tibetans love to wear Tibetan robes, waistbands and boots. The Uygurs wear diamond-shaped embroidered skullcaps. The Koreans are known for their boat-shaped shoes. Yi, Miao and Yao women wear pleated skirts, and are often bedecked with gold or silver ornaments.

Quadrangle dwellings are traditionally the rule in Han areas. Most minority herdsmen in Inner Mongolia, Qinghai and Gansu live in yurts. The Dais, Zhuangs and Bouyeis in south China often live in *Diaojiaolou* (multiple-storied houses raised on stilts). In the densely populated cities these days, most people live in apartment buildings. (Illustration 4: Quadrangle Dwelling)

China is a country with a diversity of religions, with over 100 million followers of various faiths. The main religions are Buddhism, Islam, Christianity, Catholicism and China's indigenous Taoism. The Huis, Uygurs, Kazaks and some other peoples adhere to Islam; the Tibetans, Mongols to Tibetan Buddhism, and the Dais, Blangs to Theravada Buddhism. Quite a few Miaos, Yaos and Yis are Christians or Catholics. Some Hans tend to practice Buddhism, Christianity, Catholicism or Taoism, but the majority of them are not followers of any religious faith.

Exercises

1) Which holidays in China are national holidays and altogether, how many days are there for these holidays?
2) What are the most important traditional festivals in China?
3) Please compare the customs of New Year's Day in your country with that of the Spring Festival in China.

第四课　行政区划与台湾问题

中国现行的行政区划，基本上是省、县、乡三级建制。全国分为省、自治区、直辖市；省或自治区分为自治州、县、自治县、市；县、自治县分为乡、民族乡、镇。

全国共分为23个省、5个自治区、4个直辖市、2个特别行政区（见文后附表）。

台湾自古以来就是中国领土不可分割的一部分。现在给大家简单地介绍一下。

台湾位于中国大陆东南的海面上，西隔台湾海峡与福建省相望，总面积3.6万平方公里。台湾古称夷洲、流求、琉球、琉求。大量的史书和文献记载了中国人民早期开发台湾的情况。中国历代政府在台湾先后建立了行政机构，行使管辖权。台湾社会的发展始终延续着中华文化的传统，即使在被日本侵占的50年间，这一基本情况也没有改变。1945年中国人民抗日战争胜利后，中国政府重新恢复了台湾省的行政管理机构。1949年中华人民共和国成立前夕，原在大陆的国民党当局退踞台湾；1950年朝鲜战争爆发，美国派遣第七舰队侵入台湾和台湾海峡，并于1954年同台湾当局签订非法的《共同防御条约》，造成了台湾同祖国大陆分离的状况。

1972年2月，美国总统尼克松访华，中美两国发表《上海公报》。1979年1月1日中美两国正式建立外交关系，美国承认中华人民共和国政府是中国的唯一合法政府，台湾是中国领土的一部分，并声明与台湾当局"断交"，废除《共同防御条约》以及从台湾撤军。在这样的历史条件下，中国政府出于对整个国家民族利益与前途的考虑，本着尊重历史、尊重现实、实事求是、照顾各方利益的原则，提出了"和平统一，一国两制"的方针。

这一方针的基本点是：

一个中国：世界上只有一个中国，台湾是中国不可分割的一部分，中央政府在北京。

两制并存：在一个中国的前提下，大陆的社会主义制度和台湾的资本主义制度实行长期共存，共同发展。

高度自治：统一后，台湾将成为特别行政区，享有高度的自治权。

和平谈判：通过接触谈判，以和平方式实现国家统一。但不承诺放弃使用武力，这决不是针对台湾同胞的，而是针对外国势力干涉中国统一和搞"台湾独立"的图谋的。

1997年7月1日和1999年12月20日，中国政府已先后恢复对香港和澳门行使主权，解决台湾问题、完成祖国统一大业的历史使命更加突出地摆在了全体中国人民面前。

练习

1. 中国的直辖市有哪几个？
2. 中国哪个省的人口最多？有多少人？
3. 哪个自治区的面积最大？有多大？
4. 中国政府解决台湾问题的原则立场是什么？

中国行政区划表

名称	政府所在地	面积(万平方公里)	人口(万人)
北京市(首都)	北京	1.68	1,240
天津市	天津	1.13	953
河北省	石家庄	19.00	6,525
山西省	太原	15.60	3,141
内蒙古自治区	呼和浩特	118.30	2,326
辽宁省	沈阳	14.57	4,138
吉林省	长春	18.70	2,628
黑龙江省	哈尔滨	46.90	3,751
上海市	上海	0.62	1,457
江苏省	南京	10.26	7,148
浙江省	杭州	10.18	4,435
安徽省	合肥	13.90	6,127
福建省	福州	12.00	3,283
江西省	南昌	16.66	4,150
山东省	济南	15.30	8,785
河南省	郑州	16.70	9,243
湖北省	武汉	18.74	5,873
湖南省	长沙	21.00	6,465
广东省	广州	18.60	7,051
广西壮族自治区	南宁	23.63	4,633
海南省	海口	3.40	743
重庆市	重庆	8.20	3,042
四川省	成都	48.80	8,434
贵州省	贵阳	17.00	3,606
云南省	昆明	39.40	4,094
西藏自治区	拉萨	122.00	248

续 表

名称	政府所在地	面积(万平方公里)	人口(万人)
陕西省	西安	20.50	3,570
甘肃省	兰州	45.00	2,494
青海省	西宁	72.00	496
宁夏回族自治区	银川	6.64	530
新疆维吾尔自治区	乌鲁木齐	160.00	1,718
香港特别行政区	香港	0.1092	650
澳门特别行政区	澳门	0.0023	45
台湾省	台北	3.60	2,152

(根据2000年第五次全国人口普查数据，未包括解放军现役军人。)

Lesson Four　Administrative Divisions and the Taiwan Issue

China is currently under a three-level administrative system dividing the nation into provinces, counties, and townships. At the provincial level there are provinces, autonomous regions, and municipalities directly under the Central Government. A province (or an autonomous region) is divided into autonomous prefectures, counties (or autonomous counties) and cities. A county (or an autonomous county) is subdivided into townships (or minority townships) and towns.

China has 23 provinces, 5 autonomous regions, 4 municipalities directly under the Central Government, and 2 special administrative regions. (See the table on page 22.)

Taiwan has been an inseparable part of China's territory since antiquity. Let us discuss it briefly.

Located to the southeast of the mainland and opposite Fujian Province across the Taiwan Straits to the west, Taiwan covers an area of 36,000 square kilometers. It was known variously as Yizhou or Liuqiu in old times. Its early development by the Chinese has been recorded in many historical books and documents. The Chinese governments through the ages set up administrative organizations to exercise jurisdiction over Taiwan. Traditional Chinese culture has been continuously passed on during the social development of Taiwan, even during the 50 years of Japanese occupation. After the Chinese people won the War of Resistance Against Japan in 1945, the Chinese Government restored its administrative organs of Taiwan Province. On the eve of the founding of the People's Republic of China in 1949, the Kuomintang authorities retreated to Taiwan from the mainland. In 1950, the Korean War broke out and the United States dispatched its Seventh Fleet to invade Taiwan and the Taiwan Straits. In 1954, the government of the United States and the Taiwan authorities signed the illegal "Mutual Defense Treaty," bringing about the separation of Taiwan from the mainland.

In February 1972, President Richard Nixon of the United States visited China, and the two sides issued the "Shanghai Communique." On January 1, 1979, the United States established official diplomatic relations with China, formally recognizing the government of the PRC as the sole legitimate government of China and Taiwan as a part of China. At the same time, the U.S. announced the cessation of "diplomatic relations" with the Taiwan authorities, the annulment of the "Mutual Defense Treaty" and the withdrawal of all its military personnel from Taiwan. Under these historical conditions, the Chinese Government, out of consideration for the interests and future of the whole nation, put forward the policy of "peaceful reunification of the country, and one country, two systems" in accordance with the principle of respecting history and reality, seeking truth from facts, and taking into account the interests of all the parties concerned.

The basic points of this policy are as follows:

One China. There is only one China in the world, and Taiwan is an inseparable part of China. The Central Government is in Beijing.

Coexistence of two political systems. On the premise of one China, the socialist system of the mainland and the capitalist system of Taiwan will coexist for common development.

A high degree of autonomy. After the reunification of China, Taiwan will be a special administrative region, enjoying a high degree of autonomy.

Peaceful negotiations. National reunification will be realized through peaceful means, through contacts and talks. Our not undertaking to give up the use of force is not directed against our compatriots in Taiwan, but against the schemes to interfere with China's reunification on the part of foreign forces and to bring about the "independence of Taiwan."

On July 1, 1997 and December 20, 1999, the Chinese Government resumed the exercise of sovereignty over Hong Kong and Macao respectively. For the entire Chinese people, the solution to the Taiwan issue and the realization of reunification of China have become a more important historical mission than ever before.

Exercises

1) How many municipalities are there in China? And what are they?

2) Which province in China has the biggest population? And what is the population?

3) Which autonomous region has the largest area? And how big is it?

4) What is the principled stand of the Chinese Government to solve the Taiwan issue?

A Table of Administrative Divisions in China

Name	Seat of Government	Area (sq. km.)	Population
Beijing Municipality (the Capital)	Beijing	16,800	12,400,000
Tianjin Municipality	Tianjin	11,300	9,530,000
Hebei Province	Shijiazhuang	190,000	65,250,000
Shanxi Province	Taiyuan	156,000	31,410,000
Inner Mongolia Autonomous Region	Hohhot	1,183,000	23,260,000
Liaoning Province	Shenyang	145,700	41,380,000
Jilin Province	Changchun	187,000	26,280,000
Heilongjiang Province	Harbin	469,000	37,510,000
Shanghai Municipality	Shanghai	6,200	14,570,000
Jiangsu Province	Nanjing	102,600	71,480,000
Zhejiang Province	Hangzhou	101,800	44,350,000
Anhui Province	Hefei	139,000	61,270,000
Fujian Province	Fuzhou	120,000	32,830,000
Jiangxi Province	Nanchang	166,600	41,500,000
Shandong Province	Jinan	153,000	87,850,000
Henan Province	Zhengzhou	167,000	92,430,000
Hubei Province	Wuhan	187,400	58,730,000
Hunan Province	Changsha	210,000	64,650,000
Guangdong Province	Guangzhou	186,000	70,510,000
Guangxi Zhuang Autonomous Region	Nanning	236,300	46,330,000
Hainan Province	Haikou	34,000	7,430,000
Chongqing Municipality	Chongqing	82,000	30,420,000
Sichuan Province	Chengdu	488,000	84,340,000
Guizhou Province	Guiyang	170,000	36,060,000
Yunnan Province	Kunming	394,000	40,940,000
Tibet Autonomous Region	Lhasa	1,220,000	2,480,000
Shaanxi Province	Xi'an	205,000	35,700,000
Gansu Province	Lanzhou	450,000	24,940,000
Qinghai Province	Xining	720,000	4,960,000
Ningxia Hui Autonomous Region	Yinchuan	66,400	5,300,000
Xinjiang Uygur Autonomous Region	Urumqi	1,600,000	17,180,000
Hong Kong Special Administrative Region	Hong Kong	1,092	6,500,000
Macao Special Administrative Region	Macao	23	450,000
Taiwan Province	Taipei	36,000	21,520,000

(According to the Fifth National Census data in 2000, which did not include active PLA men.)

第五课　国家机构

中华人民共和国的一切权力属于人民。人民行使国家权力的机关是全国人民代表大会和地方各级人民代表大会。所以，人民代表大会制度就成为中国的根本政治制度。

中国是一个多民族多党派的国家。每当要作出有关国计民生的重大决策时，执政党中国共产党都会与各民族、各党派、各界人士和无党派民主人士进行协商，以取得共识，然后再形成决策。中国共产党领导的多党合作和政治协商制度，是中国的一项基本政治制度。

多党合作和政治协商的主要形式有两种：

一、中国人民政治协商会议；

二、中共中央和各级地方党委召开的民主党派和无党派民主人士协商会、座谈会。

中国的国家机构包括：

国家权力机关——全国人民代表大会和地方各级人民代表大会；

国家主席；

国家行政机关——国务院和地方各级人民政府；

国家军事机关——中央军事委员会；

国家审判机关——最高人民法院，地方各级人民法院和专门人民法院；

国家法律监督机关——最高人民检察院、地方各级人民检察院和专门人民检察院。

最后，我们简单谈一谈中国的问题与希望。

中国是一个拥有13亿人口的大国，是一个发展中的国家，经济基础比较薄弱，工农业和科学技术的发展水平还不高，旧的经济体制还在阻碍着社会主义市场经济的发展；东西部之间、贫富之间的差距比较悬殊；按人均计算，中国的水、土地和矿产等资源相对贫乏；环境污染的问题也比较严重。

虽然面临着种种问题，但是中国的社会主义现代化事业充满了希望。1979年，在邓小平的领导下，中国实行了改革开放的政策，二十几年来，中国的经济建设取得了举世瞩目的成就。许多重要的工农业产品产量已跃居世界第一位。目前，中国正全面建设"小康"社会。只要我们坚定不移地执行科教兴国和可持续发展的战略方针，到本世纪中叶，中国一定能够实现现代化，人均国民生产总值达到中等发达国家水平，人民过上比较富裕的生活。古老的中国正焕发着青春，并将为人类的和平与进步作出更大的贡献。

练习

中国取得了哪些成就？还存在哪些问题？谈谈你对中国的看法。

Lesson Five   The State Organs

All power in the People's Republic of China belongs to the people. The organs through which the people exercise state power are the National People's Congress and the local people's congresses. Therefore, the people's congress system is China's fundamental political system.

China is a multi-ethnic and multi-party country. Before making important policy decisions on issues that bear on the national economy and the people's livelihood, the Communist Party of China (CPC), as the party in power, makes a point of consulting representatives of all ethnic groups, political parties, and all walks of life and nonparty democrats in order to reach a common understanding. The system of multi-party cooperation and political consultation under the leadership of the Communist Party of China is one of the basic political systems of the PRC.

The multi-party cooperation and political consultation system adopts two main forms. One is the Chinese People's Political Consultative Conference (CPPCC) and the other is the consultative meetings and forums of democratic parties and nonparty personages held by the CPC Central Committee or its local committees at different levels.

The state organs of China include:

State power organs — the National People's Congress and the local people's congresses;

Chairman of the state;

State administrative organs — the State Council and the local people's governments;

State military organ — the Central Military Commission;

State judicial organs — the Supreme People's Court, local people's courts at different levels and special people's courts;

State procuratorial organs — the Supreme People's Procuratorate, local people's procuratorates at different levels and special people's procuratorates.

Finally let's talk about China's problems and promise.

China is a large developing country with a population of 1.3 billion. The foundation of national economy has been relatively weak and the development of industry, agriculture, science and technology is still of a low level. The old economic system is still impeding the growth of the socialist market economic system. The gap between the east part and the west part of the country and the gap between the rich and the poor are quite large. China's per capita natural resources of water, land and minerals are quite poor. Environmental pollution is another severe problem.

Dispite all the odds, China has great promise in her cause of socialist modernization.

Substantial success has been achieved in its economic development since the implementation of the policy of reform and opening up in 1979 under the leadership of Deng Xiaoping. China today leads the world in the output of many major industrial and agricultural products. The Chinese people are going full steam ahead to build a well-off society. So long as we firmly implement the strategy of rejuvenating China through science and education and adhere to the policy of sustainable development, we are bound to achieve modernization, and our per capita GNP is bound to reach that of intermediate-level developed countries. As a result, our people will achieve a well-off life. China has a venerated history, but it is radiating the vigor of youth, and will make still greater contributions to peace and progress.

Exercises

What great achievements has China made? What are the main problems China is facing? What is your view on China?

第六课　古代历史概述

考古发现表明，大约在100万年以前，在今天被称为中国的这片土地上，生存着原始人群。中国是世界上历史最悠久的国家之一，文字记录的历史大约有4,000年之久。

"自从盘古开天地，三皇五帝到如今"，盘古是传说中开天辟地的英雄，而"三皇五帝"也都是古代传说中的人物。不少人认为"三皇"是指伏羲、神农和黄帝。伏羲是中国人的始祖，人头蛇身，跟他妹妹女娲结成夫妇，生儿育女，形成了人类。神农也称炎帝，是中国南方部落的首领。黄帝是中国西北部一个部落的领袖。炎帝和黄帝的部落联合起来，打败了蚩尤部落，在中国的中原地带定居下来。他们与其他部落一起，逐渐形成了中华民族。所以直到今天，全世界的华人都说自己是"炎黄子孙"。

黄帝以后又出现了三个有名的首领：尧、舜、禹。"大禹治水"的故事至今仍广为传颂。传说古代黄河年年发生水灾，禹带着很多人治水，克服了许多困难。他走过许多地方，三次经过自己家门都没有进去看看。他采用疏导的办法，经过了13年，才把水治好。

公元前21世纪，禹的儿子启建立了中国第一个朝代夏朝，中国也由此进入了奴隶制时代。关于夏朝的历史，我们知道的还不多。

公元前17世纪，商朝取代了夏朝。商朝的文字通常称为甲骨文，是现在可以看到的中国最古的文字。甲骨文的发现只有100多年的历史，传说1899年北京的一位大学者王懿荣得了疟疾病，医生开的中药里有一味叫"龙骨"，他偶然发现"龙骨"上刻有一种歪歪扭扭的他不认识的文字。王懿荣不仅买下药店里全部带字的"龙骨"，还派人到"龙骨"出土的地方河南安阳小屯村高价买回了大量带字的"龙骨"。后来发现这些所谓的"龙骨"都是龟甲和兽骨，上边刻的文字是商代使用的文字。商代还有大量的青铜器流传至今，这些青铜器十分精美，可见当时的铸造技术已经达到很高的水平了。（图5：商朝青铜器——四羊方樽）

商朝最后一个统治者纣王十分残暴，全国各地的人都起来反抗他。公元前11世纪，商朝灭亡，周朝建立了。

周朝的前200多年，国都在现在的西安，历史上叫西周。公元前770年，周朝迁都洛阳，这以后就叫东周。为什么要东迁呢？有这样一个故事。

周幽王的妃子褒姒特别不爱笑。有一天，幽王为

图5　商朝青铜器——四羊方樽

了让她笑一笑，就叫人点起烽火。诸侯们看见烽火，以为敌人来了，就立刻带兵前来救援。褒姒在城墙上看见许多兵马跑来跑去，果然笑了。不久，敌人真的来了，但大家看见烽火，谁也不愿再来。结果，敌人杀了幽王，国都也被破坏了。幽王的儿子只好把国都迁到了东边的洛阳。

东周时期，诸侯国的势力一天比一天大，他们互相争权夺利，历史上把这一段称为春秋战国时期。

那时候人们的思想非常活跃，出现了很多有名的思想家、政治家和军事家。

孔子，春秋时期鲁国人，是中国历史上最伟大的哲学家和教育家。他的弟子有3,000多人，其中著名的有72人。他和弟子的一些见解及谈话，由弟子们记录整理成《论语》，是儒家思想的集中反映。儒家文化在中国历史上产生了非常深远的影响。

儒家的代表人物除了孔子外，还有荀子、孟子等；道家学派的代表人物有老子和庄子；墨家的代表人物是墨子；法家代表人物是韩非子；军事家孙武的《孙子兵法》至今还被应用在军事、经济领域。这是一个"百家争鸣"的时代。（图6：孔子）

图6　孔子

图7　兵马俑

战国时期还剩下秦、齐、楚、燕、韩、赵、魏七个大国，最后秦王嬴政灭了六国，统一中国，于公元前221年建立了中国历史上第一个中央集权的国家，就是秦朝。

秦始皇是中国历史上最有争议的人物之一。他统一了文字、货币和度量衡，废除了分封制，实行郡县制，促进了中国经济文化的发展。另一方面，他集权力于一身，焚书坑儒，加强思想统治。他还无休止地征用全国的人力财力，伐匈奴，建长城，开驰道，造宫殿，修陵墓，最终激起了人民的反抗。秦帝国仅存在了15年，到了二世即宣告灭亡。（图7：兵马俑）

公元前206年，汉朝建立。汉朝是中国历史上最强盛的两个朝代之一，一共经过了400多年。汉朝刚建立的时候，北方的匈奴常常来侵扰，到了汉武帝，国家力量强大了，才打败了匈奴。汉武帝还发展了和中亚各国的友好往来，打通了去西域的道路。欧洲人特别喜欢中国的丝绸，所以人们就把汉朝和西域通商的这条路叫做"丝绸之路"。

由于汉朝特别强盛，所以"汉人"、"汉语"这些词汇一直使用到今天。汉朝的司马迁写的《史记》，记载了中国从黄帝到汉武帝约3,000年的历史，最主要部分是人物传记，他写的人物形象、生动。《史记》既是伟大的历史著作，又是优秀的文学著作。

东汉末年是魏、蜀、吴三国争霸时期，其中最著名的政治人物有曹操、诸葛亮和孙权。曹操是魏国的奠基人，他不仅是杰出的军事家，也是优秀的诗人。诸葛亮是蜀国的丞相，是中国古代智慧的化身。千百年来，他"鞠躬尽瘁，死而后已"的崇高精神一直激励着中国人民。著名的小说《三国演义》中记载了有关他们的故事。

中国封建社会另一个鼎盛时期是唐朝。从汉末到唐的400年间，经历了三国、晋、南北朝和隋四个时代，此时中国以分裂状态为主。

隋朝时修建了从北京到杭州的京杭大运河，全长1,800公里。

唐朝初年的唐太宗李世民，是中国历史上最杰出的帝王之一。贞观时期他采取了一系列改革的措施，使封建王朝走向空前的繁荣。唐朝水陆交通相当发达，中国与日本、朝鲜、印度、波斯、阿拉伯地区进行了广泛的经济、文化交往。唐朝的文学尤其是诗歌达到了创作高峰，出现了李白、杜甫、白居易等大量杰出的诗人。唐朝接纳了日本、朝鲜等国派来的留学生，总数超过五万人。唐朝的高僧玄奘也不远万里到印度去取佛经。

强盛的唐朝在世界历史上产生了深远的影响，至今海外还有人用"唐人"代表中国人，把中国人的饭菜、衣服称为"唐餐"、"唐装"，把华人聚居的地方称为"唐人街"。（图8：唐三彩马）

唐代以后的王朝主要有宋、元、明、清。宋朝是中国历史上外患最多的一个汉族政权。宋朝政治腐败，打不过北方的少数民族，只好年年给人家送银子、丝绸等。公元1127年，北方的金国占领了宋朝的国都开封，北宋灭亡。皇帝的一个弟弟逃到江南，在杭州又建立了一个王朝，历史上称为南宋。南宋时期出现了一位著名的抗金英雄，名叫岳飞。

1206年，成吉思汗统一了蒙古的各个部落，建立蒙古国。1271年，他的孙子忽必烈征服中原，建立了元朝，建大都（今北京）作为首都。来自威尼斯的马可·波罗在中国到处旅行，后来在他那本著名的《马可·波罗游记》中描述了元朝的繁荣景象。中国古代的"四大发明"，即造纸、印刷术、指南针和火药，在宋元时期有了进一步的发展。

1368年，汉人朱元璋在南京建立了明朝，他的儿子朱棣继位以后，把首都迁到了北京。明朝的时候，中国是世界上一个富强的国家，农业、手工业、商业都非常发达，和许多国家都进行贸易。明朝皇帝派郑和带领很大的船队到南洋去，郑和先后航海七次，到过南洋、印度洋等三十

图8　唐三彩马

多个国家和地区，最远到过非洲。

明朝末年，李自成领导的农民起义军攻占了北京，明朝最后一个皇帝崇祯在景山的一棵树上吊死，明朝的统治结束。

后来中国东北地区的一个少数民族女真族镇压了这次农民起义，建立了满清政权，开始了对中国长达260多年的统治。在清朝的皇帝中，最有作为的是康熙和乾隆。

宋元明清时期，中国文学也有了新的发展。宋代的词、元代的戏曲、明清的小说都是当时文学成就的标志。

18世纪后期，西方殖民主义者千方百计要打开中国的大门，掠夺中国的财富。英国商人把大批鸦片卖到中国，给中国带来了灾难。清朝大臣林则徐实行禁烟政策，在广东虎门销毁了外国商人的鸦片。1840年，英国对中国发动了侵略战争，史称"鸦片战争"。

鸦片战争是中国历史的一个转折点。从此，腐败的清政府一次又一次地向外国侵略者投降，1842年被迫和英国签订了丧权辱国的《南京条约》，向英国赔偿军费，割让香港。

鸦片战争以后，英、美、法、俄、日相继迫使清政府签订了一系列不平等条约。中国开始沦为半殖民地半封建社会。

练习

1．说出中国古代最强盛的两个朝代名。

2．"丝绸之路"是什么时候开始打通的？

3．中国古代的四大发明是什么？

4．你知道"汉人"、"汉语"、"唐人街"这些词语的由来吗？

中国古代历史年代简表

朝 代	起止时间
夏	约公元前 21 世纪—前 17 世纪
商	约公元前 17 世纪—前 11 世纪
西周	约公元前 11 世纪—前 771 年
东周（春秋、战国）	公元前 770 年—前 221 年
秦	公元前 221 年—前 206 年
西汉	公元前 206 年—公元 25 年
东汉	公元 25 年—220 年
三国（魏、蜀、吴）	公元 220 年—280 年
西晋	公元 265 年—317 年
东晋	公元 317 年—420 年
南北朝	公元 420 年—589 年
隋	公元 581 年—618 年
唐	公元 618 年—907 年
五代	公元 907 年—960 年
北宋	公元 960 年—1127 年
南宋	公元 1127 年—1279 年
元	公元 1271 年—1368 年
明	公元 1368 年—1644 年
清	公元 1644 年—1911 年

Lesson Six   A General Survey
of Ancient History

Archaeological findings have dated primitive human habitation to some 1 million years ago in the region now known as China. China is one of the oldest countries in the world with a chronicled history of about 4,000 years.

"Since Pangu separated heaven and earth, the three sovereigns and five emperors were the earliest lords." Pangu was the hero in Chinese mythology who separated heaven and earth. The three sovereigns and five emperors were also legendary heroes. Many believe that the three sovereigns were Fuxi, Shennong, and Huangdi. Fuxi was the first ancestor of the Chinese. He had a human head but a snake body. He married his younger sister, Nüwa, and their descendants became human beings. Shennong, the Divine Husbandman who is also called Yandi, was a tribe leader in south China. Huangdi, or the Yellow Emperor, was a leader of a tribe living in northwest China. The two tribes united to defeat the tribe led by Chiyou. They settled down in central China, and allied themselves with other tribes, and the Chinese nation formed. That is why the Chinese living all over the world call themselves "descendants of Yandi and Huangdi."

The other three emperors, Yao, Shun and Yu, came forth after Huangdi. The tale of Yu taming the rivers is still on everybody's lips. Legend has it that the Yellow River was prone to floods every year in ancient times. Determined to harness the river, Yu led his men in dredging the river and digging channels to divert the floods into the sea. He overcame a lot of difficulties and put the river under control after 13 years of continuous efforts. It is said that he was so dedicated that he had three times refrained from entering the door of his home when passing by.

In the 21st century BC, Qi, son of Yu, established the Xia, the first dynasty in Chinese history, which heralded the beginning of a slave society in China. However, little has been known about that dynasty so far.

The Shang Dynasty took the place of the Xia in the 17th century BC. The inscriptions on tortoise shells and bones which were the form of script prevalent in the Shang Dynasty provided the first written evidence of Chinese history. The oracular inscriptions, however, were not discovered until one hundred years ago. It was said that, in 1899, a well-known philologist in Beijing named Wang Yirong was taken ill. In the medicine prescribed for him by a doctor of traditional Chinese medicine there was something called "dragon bones," on which he discerned by accident some unknown inscribed figures. Wang Yirong not only bought the whole lot of bones that bore inscribed figures from the drugstore but also sent men to Xiaotun Village in Anyang County of Henan Province where the bones were excavated and bought at a considerable price large quantities of "dragon bones" with inscriptions. These so-called "dragon bones" were later found to be tortoise shells and animal bones, and the inscribed figures were the form of script prevalent in the Shang Dynasty. From the Shang Dynasty we also have fine bronze ware, which testifies to the fact that the technology of bronze casting then had already attained a relatively high level. (Illustration 5: Shang-Dynasty Bronze Vessel with Four Carved Sheep Heads — *Siyangfangzun*)

The last emperor of the Shang Dynasty, King Zhou, was so cruel and ferocious that people all over the country rose against him. In the 11th century BC, the Shang Dynasty was toppled by the Zhou Dynasty.

The Zhou Dynasty in its first 200 or so years was called the Western Zhou, with its capital in present-day Xi'an. In 770 BC, the seat of power was moved to today's Luoyang, thereupon the dynasty was called the Eastern Zhou. Why was the capital moved eastward? The story was like this:

King You had a favorite concubine named Baosi who seldom smiled. One day, in order to make her smile, King You asked his men to light the beacon-fire. Seeing the beacon-fire, which signaled the arrival of an enemy army, the dukes rushed to help with their soldiers. As expected, Baosi, who was on the city wall, smiled as she watched so many soldiers and horses running back and forth. Before long, the enemy really came, and all the dukes saw the beacon-fire, but none of them came to help. As a result, the enemy killed King You and sacked the capital. His son had to move the capital eastward to Luoyang.

During the Eastern Zhou, some of the vassal states under the dukes were becoming increasingly strong and scrambled for power and territory. It was known as the Spring and Autumn Period and Warring States Period historically.

At that time, people's minds were very active. There emerged many famous thinkers, politicians, and strategists. Among them was the greatest philosopher and educator of China, Confucius. Confucius had more than 3,000 students in his life, of whom 72 became outstanding scholars. His disciples recorded Confucius and his students' ideas and remarks, sorted through their own thoughts, and compiled them into *The Analects*, a classic that gives concentrated expression to Confucianism. Confucianism has exerted a tremendous and lasting impact on Chinese history.

Apart from Confucius, Xunzi and Mencius were also representatives of the Confucian School. Laozi and Zhuangzi were the leading exponents of Taoism. Mozi was the representative of the Mohist School. Han Fei was the chief representative of the Legalist School. *Sunzi's Art of*

War, by the strategist Sun Wu, is still applied in the military and economic areas nowadays. The Warring States Period was indeed an age of "Contention of a Hundred Schools of Thought." (Illustration 6: Confucius)

In the Warring States Period there were only seven powerful states left. They were the states of Qin, Qi, Chu, Yan, Han, Zhao and Wei. In 221 BC, after eliminating the six rival states, the king of Qin, Ying Zheng, unified the country and established the first centralized state in Chinese history, the Qin Dynasty (221-206 BC).

Qinshihuang, the First Emperor of Qin, was one of the most controversial figures in Chinese history. During his reign, the emperor standardized the currency, script, weights and measures, abrogated the system of enfeoffment, introduced the system of prefectures and counties, and therefore accelerated economic and cultural development in China. On the other hand, he centralized state power and ordered to burn books and bury Confucian scholars alive in an attempt to consolidate his rule over ideology. He continuously requisitioned human and financial resources from all over the country to fight the Xiongnu, build the Great Wall, construct public roads, and build palaces and a mausoleum for himself. All these had stirred up intense popular hatred and revolts. The feudal autocracy of the Qin Dynasty, which had lasted for barely 15 years, was swept away during the rule of its second emperor. (Illustration 7: Terracotta Warriors and Horses)

In 206 BC, the Han Dynasty (206 BC-AD 220) was founded. As one of the two most powerful and prosperous dynasties in Chinese history, it lasted more than 400 years. In the early years of the Han Dynasty, the Xiongnu in the north made frequent incursions along the northern border. It was not until the reign of Emperor Wu that the Han Dynasty was powerful enough to defeat them. The emperor developed friendly relationship with countries in Central Asia, and opened a road to the Western Regions, which greatly boosted China's export of silk goods, a favorite among Europeans. Hence the name, "Silk Road."

As the Han Dynasty was very powerful and prosperous, such expressions as "Hanren" (Chinese people), "Hanyu" (Chinese language) are still in use today. Sima Qian, a well-known historian and writer in the Han Dynasty, wrote the world-famous classic, *Records of the Historian*, which covers about 3,000-year history of China from the legendary times of Huangdi down to the reign of Emperor Wu of the Han Dynasty. "Biographies of Historical Figures," for their graphic images and vivid accounts, make the most important chapter of this work, which is hailed as a great work of history and literature.

In the last years of the Eastern Han Dynasty (AD 25-220), the three kingdoms, Wei, Shu and Wu, contended for hegemony, and for this reason the period was known as the "Three Kingdoms." Among the most famous politicians at that time were Cao Cao, Zhuge Liang and

Sun Quan. Cao Cao, the founder of the kingdom of Wei, was not only an outstanding strategist but also an excellent poet. Zhuge Liang, the Prime Minister of the kingdom of Shu, is an embodiment of intelligence and wisdom of ancient China. For hundreds of years, his noble spirit of "giving my all till my heart ceases to beat" has been inspiring the Chinese people. Their stories are recorded in the famous novel *Romance of the Three Kingdoms*.

The other period of great prosperity in feudal China was the Tang Dynasty (AD 618-907). During the 400 years from the collapse of the Han Dynasty to the establishment of the Tang Dynasty, China went through the Three Kingdoms Period and the Jin, Northern and Southern and Sui dynasties, and was torn by internal conflicts.

The Grand Canal that runs 1,800 kilometers from Beijing to Hangzhou was built in the Sui Dynasty.

Li Shimin, who reigned the Tang Dynasty in its early years as Emperor Taizong, was one of the most outstanding emperors in Chinese history. During his reign of Zhenguan, he introduced a series of reform measures that brought unprecedented prosperity to the empire. Efficient land and water transport furthered economic and cultural contacts between Tang and many countries such as Japan, Korea, India, Persia and the Arab region. The development of literature, especially poetry, reached its climax and a lot of excellent poets such as Li Bai, Du Fu and Bai Juyi emerged in succession. Moreover, more than 50,000 students from Japan, Korea and other countries made their way to China to study Chinese culture. Xuanzang, the famous monk of the Tang Dynasty, went all the way to India to acquire Buddhist scriptures.

The powerful and prosperous Tang Dynasty exerted a great influence on the world history. Today, some foreigners still refer to local Chinese residents as "Tangren" (people of the Tang Dynasty), the district where the Chinese live as "Tangrenjie" (Chinatown). They call Chinese food "Tangcan" (the food that people in the Tang Dynasty had) and the Chinese-style clothing "Tangzhuang." (Illustration 8: Tang Tricolor Horse)

The major dynasties following Tang are the Song, Yuan, Ming and Qing dynasties. Song suffered more aggression by ethnic minorities than any other Han-ruled dynasties in Chinese history. Too enfeebled by political corruption to keep the minorities in the north at bay, the Song emperors had to appease its enemies by sending silver and silk to them every year. In 1127, the Jin Dynasty (1115-1234) took the Song's capital, Kaifeng, and the Northern Song (960-1127) fell. One of the emperor's younger brothers fled across the Yangtze River to Hangzhou, where he built a new capital and that period is known as the Southern Song Dynasty (1127-1279). The famous hero of the Southern Song who resisted the Jin was Yue Fei.

In 1206, Genghis Khan united the nomadic Mongol tribes into a new nation, the Great Mongolia. In 1271, his grandson Kublai conquered the Central Plains of China and founded the Yuan Dynasty (1279-1368), taking Dadu (today's Beijing) as its capital. Marco Polo from Venice traveled widely during his 17-year stay in China. In his well-known *Travels of Marco Polo*, he vividly described the thriving scene of the Yuan Dynasty. The four great inventions of ancient China, papermaking, movable type, the compass and gunpowder, gained further development during the Song and Yuan dynasties.

In 1368, Zhu Yuanzhang, a man of Han ethnic background, founded the Ming Dynasty (1368-1644) in Nanjing. His son, Zhu Di, moved the capital to Beijing after he ascended the throne. During the Ming Dynasty, China was a rich and advanced country in the world. Agriculture, handcraft industry and commerce came a long way, and the country developed trade relations with many foreign countries. By order of the emperor, the great navigator Zheng He led a vast fleet on seven voyages that brought him across the South China Sea and the Indian Ocean to more than thirty countries. One such voyage brought him as far as Africa.

In 1644, the last year of the Ming Dynasty, the peasant uprising troops led by Li Zicheng took Beijing. The Ming Dynasty came to an end when its last emperor, Chongzhen, hanged himself on Jingshan Hill.

Later, the Manchus, a minority people from northeast china, put down the peasant uprising and established the Qing Dynasty (1644-1911). The Qing rule lasted more than 260 years and among its emperors, Kangxi and Qianlong were the ablest rulers.

During the dynasties of Song, Yuan, Ming and Qing, Chinese literature gained new development. For instance, the *ci* poetry of the Song, the drama of the Yuan and the novel of the Ming and Qing dynasties represented the heights of the literary achievements of their times.

In the late 18th century, the Western colonialists tried in a thousand and one ways to break the door of China in order to plunder the wealth. The British merchants sold large quantities of opium to China and in this way brought disasters to the country. Lin Zexu, the imperial commissioner of the Qing Dynasty, banned the opium trade and burned the opium confiscated from foreign merchants in Humen, Guangdong Province. In retaliation, Britain launched a war of aggression against China in 1840, which is called the "Opium War" in Chinese history.

The Opium War was a turning point in Chinese history. Since then the corrupt Qing Court had made repeated concessions to the foreign aggressors. In 1842, the Qing Court signed the humiliating *Nanjing Treaty* that provided for the war indemnities and the cession of Hong Kong to Britain.

After the Opium War, a series of unequal treaties with Britain, the United States, France, Russia and Japan followed, and China was turned step by step into a semi-feudal and semi-colonial society.

Exercises

1) Please name the two most powerful dynasties in ancient China.
2) When did the "Silk Road" begin to get through?
3) What are the four great inventions of ancient China?
4) Do you know the origin of these terms: Hanren, Hanyu and Tangrenjie?

A Brief Chronology of Ancient China

Dynasty	Date
Xia	21st century BC - 17th century BC
Shang	17th century BC - 11th century BC
Western Zhou	11th century BC - 771 BC
Eastern Zhou (Spring and Autumn Period and Warring States Period)	70 BC - 221 BC
Qin	221BC - 206 BC
Western Han	206 BC - AD 25
Eastern Han	AD 25 - AD 220
Three Kingdoms (Wei, Shu and Wu)	AD 220 - AD 280
Western Jin	AD 265 - AD 317
Eastern Jin	AD 317 - AD 420
Southern and Northern Dynasties	AD 420 - AD 589
Sui	AD 581 - AD 618
Tang	AD 618 - AD 907
Five Dynasties	AD 907 - AD 960
Northern Song	AD 960 - AD 1127
Southern Song	AD 1127 - AD 1279
Yuan	AD 1271 - AD 1368
Ming	AD 1368 - AD 1644
Qing	AD 1644 - AD 1911

中国概况

第七课　现代历史概述

　　1911年10月10日爆发了武昌起义，这一年是旧历辛亥年，所以把这次革命叫做辛亥革命。孙中山领导了这次革命，提出了三民主义的革命纲领。这次革命推翻了清朝，结束了中国长达2,000多年的君主制，建立了中华民国。但是它并没有完成反帝反封建的历史任务，所以孙中山临终前说："革命尚未成功，同志仍须努力。"（图9：孙中山塑像）

　　辛亥革命爆发不久，北洋军阀夺取了政权。第一次世界大战结束，中国也是战胜国，德国在中国山东的特权本该废除，可是帝国主义列强却把它交给了日本。这样，五四运动就爆发了。1919年5月4日，北京的学生们到天安门广场集会。在这场由爱国学生领导的反帝反封建革命运动中，中国无产阶级第一次登上了政治舞台。在俄国十月革命影响下爆发的五四运动标志着中国新民主主义革命阶段的开始。

图9　孙中山塑像

　　五四运动促进了马克思列宁主义在中国的传播。1921年，毛泽东、董必武、陈潭秋、何叔衡、王尽美、邓恩铭、李达等代表各地共产主义小组在上海举行第一次全国代表大会，中国共产党诞生了。1924年，共产党和孙中山领导的国民党合作，一起北伐（历史上也称为"大革命"），打败了北洋军阀。不久，孙中山去世了，以蒋介石为首的国民党右翼在1927年发动了反革命政变，屠杀共产党人和革命群众，并在南京建立了国民党政权。共产党人在1927年8月1日发动了南昌起义，朱德把起义军带上井冈山。在那里，朱德和毛泽东一起建立了革命根据地和中国工农红军。

　　1931年9月18日，日本对中国发动了侵略战争，他们想先占领东北，再占领全中国。红军在反击国民党的第五次"围剿"失败后，从1934年10月到1935年10月，经过25,000里长征，从江西来到北方抗日前线。为了抗日，国共两党进行了第二次合作。经过八年艰苦抗战，1945年8月，中国人民终于把日本侵略者赶出了中国。

　　解放战争是从1946年开始的。1949年4月，解放军渡过长江，占领南京，蒋介石和他的军队退到了台湾，并带走了全国的黄金储备和剩余的海、空军力量。中国共产党领导的解放军赢得了解放战争的胜利。

　　1949年10月1日，毛泽东在北京天安门城楼庄严宣告了中华人民共和国的诞生。

中国结束了半殖民地半封建社会的黑暗历史，开始了社会主义社会的新阶段。（图10：开国大典）

图10　开国大典

　　历经战乱的中国民生凋敝，百废待兴。中华人民共和国成立后的头三年是国民经济恢复时期。1953年至1956年，中国基本实现了农业、手工业和资本主义工商业的社会主义改造，确定了生产资料的公有制，实现了从新民主主义社会到社会主义社会的转变。从1953年起，中国开始了第一个五年计划，并在许多领域取得了成功。

　　从1957年到1966年的十年间，中国开始了大规模的社会主义建设。尽管也曾出现过"大跃进"那样严重的冒进错误，但总的来说，这十年的经济建设取得了巨大的成就。从1956年到1966年全国工业固定资产增加了4倍，国民收入增长了58%，一些重要的工业产品的产量，如钢铁、煤炭、原油、发电、机床等分别增加了几倍到十几倍。此外，还发展了一些新的工业，如电子、石油化工等。在科学技术领域，原子能、喷气式飞机、电子计算机、半导体、自动化控制设备等方面的研究进展迅速。

　　1966年开始的"文化大革命"使全国大乱，一切正常的生产、文化和社会活动都陷于停顿。20世纪六七十年代正是全世界经济蓬勃发展的黄金时期，中国的经济却处于大倒退的阶段。

　　1976年10月，中共中央粉碎了"四人帮"，举国欢庆，历时十年的"文化大革命"结束。

　　1978年底，中国共产党召开了十一届三中全会，以邓小平为首的党和国家领导人确立了改革开放的方针，做出了"把工作重点转移到社会主义现代化建设上来"的战略决策。在农村，实行了"联产承包责任制"，允许农民和生产单位在自由市场出售他们的农副产品。在中国沿海城市深圳（毗邻香港）、珠海（毗邻澳门）、汕头和厦门（均与台湾隔着台湾海峡相望）及海南岛建立了经济特区。1990年又建立了上海浦东新区和沿长江开放区。

　　改革开放二十多年来，中国经济取得了巨大成就，令世人瞩目。新世纪伊始，中国人民正在按照中国共产党"十六大"提出的要求，朝着全面建设小康社会的目标迈进。

练习

1. 中华人民共和国是什么时候诞生的？
2. 谈谈你所了解的经济特区。

Lesson Seven   A General Survey of Modern History

On October 10, 1911, the Wuchang Uprising took place under the leadership of Sun Yat-sen, who put forward the revolutionary program of the "Three Principles of the People." Because it was the year of Xinhai by the Chinese lunar calendar, the Revolution of 1911 was also known as Xinhai Revolution, which overthrew the Qing Dynasty, bringing an end to the two-millennia feudal monarchy in China. And then the Republic of China was founded. But the revolution failed to accomplish its historical mission of fighting against imperialism and feudalism. Therefore, Sun Yat-sen said on his deathbed: "As the revolution has not yet succeeded, comrades need to work harder." (Illustration 9: A Statue of Sun Yat-sen)

Shortly after the 1911 Revolution, the Northern Warlords seized power. When the First World War ended, China was one of the victorious nations. The privileges of Germany in Shandong Province of China should have been abolished, but the imperialist powers transferred them to Japan. This gave rise to the May Fourth Movement of 1919, when students in Beijing held a mass rally at Tian'anmen Square. In this revolutionary movement against imperialism and feudalism led by the patriotic students, the Chinese proletariat made its debut on the political arena. The May Fourth Movement, which took place under the influence of the October Revolution of Russia in 1917, marked the beginning of the New Democratic Revolution in China.

The May Fourth Movement promoted the spread of Marxism and Leninism in China. In 1921, delegates representing Communist Groups from all parts of China including Mao Zedong, Dong Biwu, Chen Tanqiu, He Shuheng, Wang Jinmei, Deng Enming and Li Da met in Shanghai at the first National Congress and proclaimed the founding of the Communist Party of China. In 1924, the Party cooperated with the Kuomintang headed by Sun Yat-sen and waged the Northern Expedition (also known as the Great Revolution, i.e. the First Revolutionary Civil War in Chinese history), and defeated the Northern Warlords. Sun Yat-sen passed away shortly afterwards. In 1927, the Kuomintang right-wingers led by Chiang Kai-shek staged a counterrevolutionary coup. They butchered the Communists and revolutionary masses and set up the Kuomintang regime in Nanjing. On August 1, 1927, the Communists launched the Nanchang Uprising. Zhu De led the insurrectionary army up to the Jinggang Mountains, where he joined Mao Zedong in establishing a revolutionary base area and founding the Chinese Workers' and Peasants' Red Army.

On September 18, 1931, Japan launched an aggressive war to China in an attempt to take the Northeast and then occupy the whole country. In October 1934, after its counterattack against the Kuomintang's fifth encirclement failed, the Red Army began the 25,000-*li* Long March from Jiangxi Province, and arrived at the northern anti-Japanese front in October 1935. To resist the Japanese aggressors, the Communist Party and the Kuomintang cooperated for the second time. In August 1945, after eight years of arduous resistance against Japan, the Chinese people eventually drove away the Japanese aggressors.

In 1946, the War of Liberation began. In April 1949, the Chinese People's Liberation Army crossed the Yangtze River and captured Nanjing. Chiang Kai-shek fled to Taiwan with all the gold reserve of the country and his remaining navy and air forces. The Liberation Army under the leadership of the Chinese Communist Party won the War of Liberation.

On October 1, 1949, Mao Zedong mounted the rostrum atop the Tian'anmen Gate Tower of Beijing and proclaimed the founding of the People's Republic of China. The nation ended its dark history of a semi-colonial, semi-feudal society and entered a new era of socialism. (Illustration 10: The Founding Ceremony of the PRC)

War and turmoil left the people in dire poverty, and all the neglected tasks had to be picked up once again. The first three years of the People's Republic thus became a period of economic rehabilitation. During the 1953-1956 period, the socialist transformation of agriculture, the handicraft industry, and capitalist industry and commerce was basically accomplished, public ownership of the means of production was established, and the transition from a new democratic society to a socialist society realized. In 1953, China began its First Five-Year Plan for socio-economic development, and was a success in many fields of endeavour.

During the 1957-1966 decade, large-scale socialist construction came under way. That decade was crowned with major achievements despite serious mistakes resulting from such premature actions as the "great leap forward" in economic construction. The nation's total volume of industrial fixed assets quintupled from 1956 to 1966, and the national income increased by 58%. The output of some essential industrial products, such as steel, coal, crude oil, generated electricity, and machine tools, rose by several or even a dozen times, and new industries such as electronics and petrochemicals were established. Science and technology, particularly in the development of atomic energy, jet planes, computers, semiconductors and automatic control equipment, progressed rapidly.

The "cultural revolution" that began in 1966 plunged the nation in great turmoil, and brought production and all cultural and social activities to a standstill. The 1960s and 1970s were a golden age for the thriving world economy; for China, it was a period of massive economic recess.

In October 1976, the Party Central Committee smashed the "gang of four". The entire nation was elated when the news came. The move signalled the demise of the decade-long chaos of the "cultural revolution."

At the Third Plenary Session of the Eleventh Party Central Committee held towards the end of 1978, the Party and government leadership headed by Deng Xiaoping instituted the policy of reform and opening up to the outside world, and made the strategic decision to shift the emphasis of the nation's work to the socialist modernization drive. In rural areas, a contract system of responsibility linking remuneration to output was introduced, and farmers and producers were allowed to sell farm and side-line products on the open market. In coastal areas, Special Economic Zones (SEZ) were established at Shenzhen (next to Hong Kong), Zhuhai (next to Macao), Shantou and Xiamen (both facing Taiwan across the Taiwan Straits), as well as Hainan Island. In 1990, the Shanghai Pudong New Area and the open area along the Yangtze River were established.

The Chinese economy has made remarkable achievements over the past 20 years of reform and opening-up. With the beginning of a new century, the Chinese people are working hard to build a well-off society in an all-round way according to the objectives set at the Party's Sixteenth National Congress.

Exercises

1) When was the People's Republic of China born?
2) What is your view on the Special Economic Zones?

中国书画ABC

THE ABC OF TRADITIONAL CHINESE CALLIGRAPHY AND PAINTING

中国书画 ABC

萧思齐 编著
章恒珍 翻译

The ABC of Traditional Chinese Calligraphy and Painting

Compiled by Xiao Siqi

Translated by Zhang Hengzhen

第一课　习字入门三法

中国传统书法是用毛笔写汉字的艺术。本课教授初学写楷书者应掌握的基本技法。

一、姿势

用毛笔写楷书，要讲究姿势，包括坐的姿势和站的姿势。

写字时坐的姿势正确，有利于运用柔软的毛笔把字写好。这是因为，楷书是由各种不同的基本笔画组成的形象各异的字形，笔画纵横交错，字与字之间有互相照应的密切关系，充满着美的变化和规律。如果坐的姿势不正，运笔写字时必定中心不稳，左右失调，字行歪斜，效果不好。学生初学时，不少人坐的姿势不正，或歪头扭身，或左腿压右腿，或纸放不正，习作效果不好，进度缓慢。因此，这些不正确的姿势，一定要及时纠正。

正确的坐姿，概而言之，就是：头正、身直、臂开、足安。（图1）

头正　写字时头正，稍向前倾，两眼凝视笔端。

身直　全身放松，腰和背稍直，微向前倾，两肩放平，胸部距桌沿约10厘米或一个拳头左右，笔在距胸前约30厘米处运行。

臂开　两臂自然撑开，成均衡对称姿势。右手执笔，左手按纸。这样，写起字来，神怡情舒，笔画能达到横平竖直之妙。

足安　两足自然分开，足底稳贴地面，以保持全身的平稳。不要两腿相压或两腿前伸。

这种坐的姿势一般适合写2~5厘米的小楷和中楷，要写6~12厘米以上的大字，就要站起来写。站的姿势是两腿前后分开，右腿向前跨出半步。上身微向前倾，左手轻按桌面上的纸，使人站得安稳，并能提领全身，右手悬腕[①]

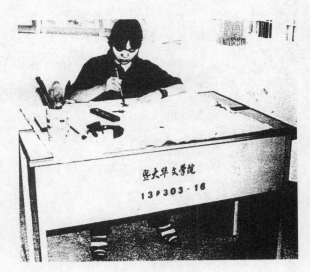

图1　坐姿

写字，把腕力、臂力乃至全身的力气都调动起来。（图2）

图2　站的姿势

二、执笔

用毛笔写楷书，掌握正确的执笔方法非常重要。

正确的执笔方法是：指实掌虚。

这里介绍一种常用的五指执笔法，此法分两步走。

第一步　是把拇指和食指（第二指）、中指（第三指）的第一指节紧握笔管，这叫"三指并拢"；（图3）

第二步　是把无名指（第四指）和小指（第五指）置于笔管后，紧贴中指，把笔管微微向前推，让笔管竖直。这样，五指齐用力，掌心自然空虚。（图4）

这就是"指实掌虚"的执笔方法。用此法执笔写字，就能随心所欲，上下左右推动着笔管，书写出形态各异的笔画来。

执笔的高低问题，据笔者体验：一般1~2厘米的小字，笔要执得低些，拇指距笔尖约6~7厘米左右；写3~4厘米的中字，拇指距笔尖约10~11厘米左右。写6厘米

图3　三指并拢

图4　五指齐用力

以上的大字，笔要执得高些。这些仅供参考。究竟执笔要多高，要看字的大小而定。总的原则是字写得越小，执笔就越低；字写得越大，执笔就越高。可在实践中灵活掌握。

三、运笔

运笔是指如何运动毛笔书写楷书笔画的方法。写字时，五指紧握笔管，全靠手腕发出的力量使手活动，驱使笔管带动笔尖在纸上写出点画来。这样运笔时，手腕一定要离开桌面，悬空运笔，才能挥洒自如，写出优美的点画来。如果手腕紧贴桌面，写点尚可，要写横、竖、撇、捺诸画就有困难了。这是由于手腕在活动时受阻，写出的笔画呆板无力。这里介绍两种运笔法。

提腕法 写字时将右手肘骨放在桌面上，腕部提起来写字，指力和腕力并用。写1～2厘米左右的小字，腕离桌面约1厘米左右。此法适宜写小字和中字。（图5）

悬腕法 写字时，执笔的右手离开桌面，悬起腕关节，指和腕关节一起作适当程度的运笔。（图6）这是难度比较大的运腕法，也是写字的基本功。悬腕写字，挥洒自如，笔画长短曲直，得心应手。写6厘米左右的大字，一定要运用此法。尤其是写6厘米以上的大字或更大的字时，一定要站起来，把笔管执得较高，让指、腕、肘和肩都悬空，甚至全身一起运动挥毫。（图2）

运笔法的另一个问题是如何运用有弹性的毛笔写出形态各异的笔画线条。要解决这个问题，

图5 提腕法

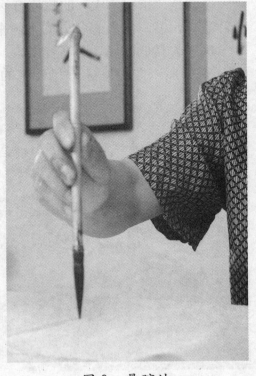

图6 悬腕法

关键是在运笔过程中要掌握按、提、顿、转四种方法。按笔是下按笔毛，使笔画线条增大；提笔是适当提高笔毛，使笔画线条变细；顿笔是将笔毛停住并带按的过程，使笔画线条涨大；转笔是转换笔毛运动方向，从而写出转折圆滑的线条。

按、提、顿、转是学楷书的基本运笔法，如音乐的旋律，高低抑扬，富有节奏感。不少外籍学生初学写楷书时，你叫他们用毛笔写一个"一"字，他们不假思索，大笔一挥，出现左右均衡的一条粗线。如懂得按、提、顿、转方法，写出来的"一"字就富有节奏感了。因此，当掌握了姿势和执笔两种方法，进入笔画练习时，一定要下工夫，学会这四种运笔方法。

练习

1. 写楷书时正确的坐姿是什么？请你坐在桌前，按课文提示，做一个写楷书的正确姿势。

2. 要写好楷书，掌握正确的执笔方法非常重要。请你按课文提示，拿一支笔，反复练习"五指执笔法"，并做到指实掌虚。

3. 什么是提腕法？请你运用已学会的执笔方法，用提腕法写一个"一"字，做到按、提、顿、转四个动作。反复练习，写10～20次。

注释

① 悬腕：这里提到的悬腕写字，本课第三部分将作详细的介绍。

Lesson One　Three Basic Techniques in Learning Chinese Calligraphy

Chinese traditional calligraphy is an art in which Chinese characters are written with a brush. This lesson deals with the basic techniques of regular script strokes as required of beginners.

1. Posture

It is important for a student to have a correct posture, whether sitting or standing, when writing the regular script with a brush.

A correct sitting posture helps write Chinese characters with a soft brush. The reason is that characters in regular script are composed of various basic strokes crisscrossing with each other and full of beautiful changes according to certain rules. There must be good coordination between words and lines of a character. A poor sitting posture throws your body off balance, resulting in slant lines and poorly written characters. Some beginners fail to get good results or make progress mainly because of their incorrect sitting postures. Therefore, poor postures must be put right at the very beginning.

What is the correct sitting posture? In short, you must keep your head upright, your body erect, your arms open and your feet firmly placed on the ground. (Illustration 1)

Upright head	Keep your head upright with a slight bent forward and keep both eyes fixed on the tip of the brush.
Erect body	Keep your body relaxed with your waist and back upright and slightly bent forward, and your shoulders level. The distance between the chest and the desk is about 10 centimeters or about the width of your fist, and that between your chest and the brush is about 30 centimeters.
Open arms	Hold your arms naturally in an open and symmetrical position. Your right hand holds the brush while your left hand keeps the paper in place. In this way, you can write in a relaxed way with well-executed strokes, which means keeping horizontals level and verticals straight.
Firm feet	Hold your feet naturally apart on the floor so as to keep your whole body balanced. Do not put one leg on the other or stretch them forward.

This sitting posture applies to the writing of small and medium-sized regular scripts (2 to 5 square centimeters). One should stand up when writing large characters (6 to 12 square centimeters): keeping your two feet apart with your right foot half a step forward; the upper part of the body slightly bent forward with the left hand pressing the paper down on the table. This standing posture will help you stand firmly. Writing with your right hand suspended (Note ①: *xuanwan*) enables you to make good use of the strength from your wrist, arm and your whole body. (Illustration 2)

2. How to hold the brush

How do you hold a writing brush? It is a very important question in writing. The correct way is to hold the brush with firm fingers and a hollow palm.

The method of holding the brush with five fingers is introduced here in two steps.

First, hold the shaft of the brush with the thumb, the forefinger and the middle finger, which is called "three fingers holding position." (Illustration 3)

Second, place the ring finger and the little finger behind the shaft and against the middle finger in order to make the shaft erect by pressing the shaft slightly forward. In this way your palm is kept hollow. (Illustration 4)

This way of holding the brush is called "fingers at work and the palm hollow." Held correctly, the shaft can be moved up and down, left and right as you please when you execute the strokes to create characters of different structures.

How high should you place your fingers on the shaft? According to the author's experience, the distance between the thumb and the brush tip is about 6 to 7 centimeters for characters of 1 to 2 square centimeters, 10 to 11 centimeters for those of 3 to 4 square centimeters, and still higher for characters at least 6 square centimeters. Remember, the position of your fingers on the shaft depends on the size of the characters you wish to write. Generally speaking, the smaller the characters you write, the lower the position of your fingers on the shaft and vice versa. Remember, practice makes perfect.

3. How to wield a writing brush

Brush wielding refers to the methods you use to write the regular script with a writing brush. When writing, you must hold the shaft firmly with your five fingers to produce dots and lines by moving the brush-tip with the force coming from your wrist. Only in this way can you write with facility and produce beautiful characters. If you rest your wrist on the desk, it is possible for you to write dots, but difficult to write the horizontal, vertical, left-falling and right-falling strokes etc., because the movement of your wrist is constrained. The strokes written in this way look lifeless and weak. The following are two ways of holding your wrist.

Wrist-raised   Place your right elbow on the desk, raise your wrist and write with the force from both your fingers and wrist. Your wrist is kept about 1 centimeter above the desk top for writing characters of 1 to 2 square centimeters. This method applies to the writing of small and medium-sized characters. (Illustration 5)

Wrist-suspended   Lift your right hand from the desk, hold the brush with your wrist hovering over the desk while exerting your fingers and wrist. (Illustration 6) This method, more difficult than the one with your wrist raised, is a basic skill of writing Chinese characters with a brush. With your wrist hovering over the desk, you can hold the brush easily to write long, short, curved and straight strokes. Your must stand up and use this method to write characters about 6 square centimeters. You should place your fingers higher on the shaft, with your fingers, wrist, elbow and shoulders hanging over the desk, and use all the strength you have to move the brush. (Illustration 2)

How to produce different strokes with an elastic brush is another question regarding brush execution. The answer is to master four ways in which the brush is wielded: *an*, *ti*, *dun* and *zhuan. An,* means pressing the brush down to make thick strokes; *ti,* raising the brush to make a stroke look a little thinner; *dun,* holding the brush firmly while pressing it down to make a stroke thicker; *zhuan,* changing the direction of the brush tip to produce smooth curving strokes.

An, ti, dun and *zhuan* are basic methods for moving the brush in the writing of regular script. They are full of rhythm, like different notes in a melody. Some foreign learners, when asked to write the character 一 with a brush, wave the brush and write a thick horizontal line offhand, which looks like an even scale. If you have mastered the methods of *an, ti, dun* and *zhuan,* your handwriting of Chinese characters will look rhythmic. You have got to make an effort to learn these methods after you have mastered the correct body posture and the two brush-holding methods.

Exercises

1) What is the correct sitting posture when writing the regular script? Try and hold a correct body posture for writing the regular script at the desk according to what you have learned in this lesson.

2) To hold the writing brush properly is very important for writing the regular script. Get a brush and practice "holding the brush with five fingers" repeatedly as the text tells you and make sure that your fingers hold the brush firmly while your palm is hollow.

3) What is the wrist-raised method? Use the method to write the character 一. Make sure that the four actions of *an, ti, dun* and *zhuan* are used. Practice repeatedly for 10 to 20 times.

Note

① *Xuanwan* means writing with a suspended wrist, which will be explained in the third part of this lesson.

第二课　楷书基本笔画运笔法

本课分为六节。重点教授楷书的点、横、竖、撇、捺、钩、挑和折等8种基本笔画的运笔法。

本课采用唐代大书法家柳公权的楷书为范本。为了方便同学们学习，简化其运笔动作，如柳体的起笔用藏锋，[图示]，按图所示的三个动作书写，本课文为露锋，两个动作[图示]。同学们可先理解课文中每种笔画的运笔图解，用一般的白纸或旧新闻纸，反复运笔练习，熟记其运笔步骤，扎实练好基本功。然后，用附录3《楷书基本笔画运笔法字帖》摹写（为了便于练习，也可把字帖放大摹写）。其方法是：用透明的薄纸（如毛边纸、宣纸或打字纸），蒙在范字帖纸上，按每个字的笔顺①进行单勾②，整张范字帖单勾完后，取下摹纸，对照范字帖，用毛笔蘸墨，循着单勾的细线摹写，写出与范字的线条相似的墨字。注意一笔写好，不要补笔。这样做的目的是训练运笔书写笔画的准确。这是初学楷书最佳的方法。

摹写到熟练时，可对着范字帖纸临写。方法是用一张白纸折成几个正方格，每个字都在正方格里面。所临写的字要比原帖字稍大一些。

在摹与临③的过程中，要学会默字。默字是不看字帖，把字的形象按字帖的样子默写出来。然后对着字帖进行比较，纠正不好的笔画。开始时，可选自己喜爱的一个字进行默写，不要贪多。第一天默写一个字；第二天再默写一个字，复习第一天学的一个字；第三天再默写一个字，复习已写过的两个字……这样，逐步积累，把已默过的每一个字的笔画、结体④都牢牢地记住。

现在，我们来学习楷书基本笔画的运笔法。

一、点的运笔法

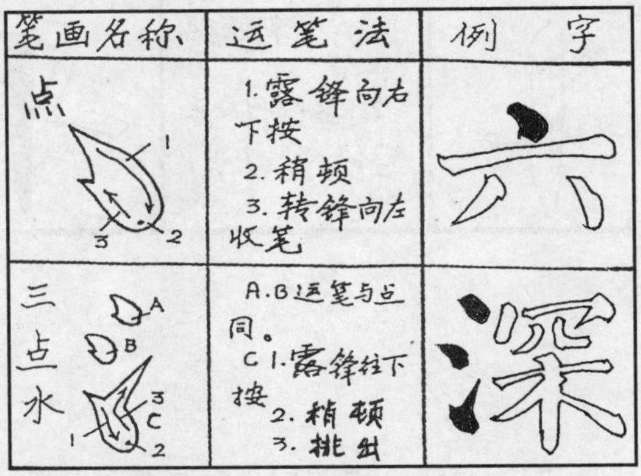

图 7

练习

1. 对照课文，练习"点"与"三点水"的运笔法，理解后，默写20个"点"与"三点水"。

2. 用一张薄纸，蒙在"点"的范字帖纸上，先单勾，后用毛笔蘸墨摹写1～2张。

二、横的运笔法

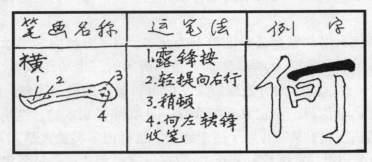

图 8

练习

1. 对照课文，练习"横"的运笔法，理解后，默写20个横画。

2. 用一张薄纸，蒙在"横"的范字帖纸上，先单勾，后用毛笔蘸墨摹写1～2张。

三、竖的运笔法

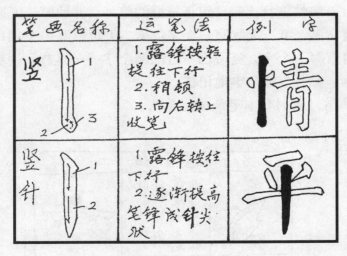

图 9

练习

1. 对照课文，练习"竖"的运笔法，理解后，默写20个竖画。

2. 用一张薄纸，蒙在"竖"的范字帖纸上，先单勾，后用毛笔蘸墨摹写1～2张。

四、撇和捺的运笔法：

笔画名称	运笔法	例字
短撇 ⟍	露锋往左下撇	作
平撇	1.露锋往下顿笔 2.转锋往左快撇	千
长撇 丿	露锋稍顿往左下快撇	左
捺	1.轻起笔右下斜行 2.逐渐增加力度 3.稍顿 4.轻提往右撇	尺
平捺	1.露锋向右平行 2.逐渐加大力度 3.稍顿 4.转锋上撇	道

图 10

练习

1. 对照课文，练习"撇"和"捺"的运笔法，理解后，默写20个撇画和捺画。

2. 用一张薄纸，蒙在"撇"和"捺"的范字帖纸上，先单勾，后用毛笔蘸墨摹写1～2张。

五、钩的运笔法

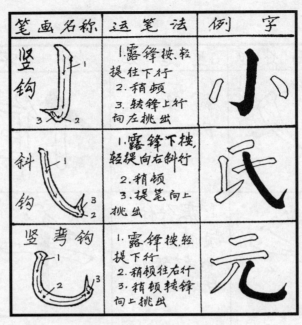

笔画名称	运 笔 法	例 字
竖钩	1.露锋按,轻提往下行 2.稍顿 3.转锋上行向左挑出	小
斜钩	1.露锋下按,轻提向右斜行 2.稍顿 3.提笔向上挑出	氏
竖弯钩	1.露锋按,轻提下行 2.稍顿往右行 3.稍顿转锋向上挑出	元

图 11

练习

1. 对照课文,练习"钩"的运笔法,理解后,默写20个钩画。

2. 用一张薄纸,蒙在"钩"的范字帖纸上,先单勾,后用毛笔蘸墨摹写1～2张。

六、挑和折的运笔法

笔画名称	运 笔 法	例 字
挑	1.露锋按稍顿 2.提笔即往右上挑	均
折	1.露锋按轻提右行 2.稍顿 3.转锋向下行收笔	香

图 12

练习

1. 对照课文,练习"挑"和"折"的运笔法,理解后,默写20个挑画和折画。

2. 用一张薄纸,蒙在"挑"和"折"的范字帖纸上,先单勾,后用毛笔蘸墨摹写1～2张。

注释

① 笔顺：楷书笔画的书写顺序。

② 单勾：是初学楷书的方法。用毛笔尖蘸墨，跟着范字笔画的线条的中间，勾出细的线条来，目的是逐步认识范字的形象。

③ 摹与临：这是学习楷书的两种方法，可参考附录2《临摹方法举例》。

④ 结体：是指每个笔画的粗、细、疏、密的设计，组成一个字的形象美，这好比人的身体，如果每个部位都很匀称，就会给人以美的印象。

Lesson Two   Basic Techniques for Writing the Strokes of Regular Script

This lesson is composed of six sections, with emphasis on how to wield the writing brush when writing the eight basic regular script strokes.

In this lesson, we use Liu Gongquan's regular script characters as the model. Liu Gongquan was a famous calligrapher of the Tang Dynasty. To make it easier for you to learn the ropes, we have simplified Liu's three brush movements with the *cangfeng* technique to two with the *lufeng* technique.

Students should first try to understand the diagram of every stroke in this lesson. Practice repeatedly until you can know the sequence of each written stroke by heart. It is very important to have a thorough training in basic skills. You should then trace the characters in Appendix III. (For your convenience, you may get the model script enlarged.) First, put a thin piece of transparent paper (for example, writing paper made from bamboo, *xuan* paper or typing paper) on the model script, sketch (Note②: *dangou*) each character according to its stroke sequence (Note①: *bishun*), and then take the model script away and write with a brush by tracing the lines and imitating the model script. Do not retouch the same stroke back and forth to make it look better, and make sure to finish each stroke accurately at one go. This is the proper way for beginners.

When you can trace the characters deftly, you can go further to copy the model script. The steps are: fold a sheet of paper into squares, unfold it, and write a character in the middle of each square. Make sure the characters you write are a little larger than the models.

While tracing and copying (Note ③: *mo* and *lin*), you should memorize the structure of each character, which means to write from memory without looking at the model book, and then compare the characters you write with the models and correct the wrongly or poorly executed strokes. To begin with, choose one character that you like best to write from memory. Do not write more than you can remember. On the first day, just write one character. On the second day, write another one and review the character you wrote the day before. On the third day, write a new character from memory and review the two characters you wrote on the first and second days, and so on. Thus, day after day, week after week, you will be able to memorize the strokes and structure of each character (Note ④: *jieti*) you have written.

Now let us practice the brush-wielding techniques for the basic regular script strokes.

1. Dot strokes

(Illustration 7)

The dot stroke

1) Press the tip of the brush down to the right with the *lufeng* technique.

2) Pause.

3) Turn the brush tip up to the left to end the stroke.

Three dots

A and B as above.

C 1) Press the brush down with the *lufeng* technique.

2) Pause.

3) Turn the tip of the brush up to the right and end the stroke.

Exercises

1) Practice writing the single dot and the three dots according to the steps described in the text. When you have familiarized yourself with the strokes, write each of them from memory 20 times.

2) Use a thin sheet of paper to cover the dots on the model script, sketch the dots and then trace them on one or two sheets of paper.

2. Horizontal stroke

(Illustration 8)

The horizontal stroke

1) Press the brush down with the *lufeng* technique.

2) Lift the brush lightly and move it to the right.

3) Pause for a while.

4) Turn the tip to the left and end the stroke.

Exercises

1) Practice writing the horizontal stroke according to the steps described in the text. When you

have familiarized yourself with the wielding steps, write the stroke from memory 20 times.

2) Use a thin sheet of paper to cover the horizontal stroke on the model script, sketch the stroke and then trace it on one or two sheets of paper.

3. Vertical strokes

(Illstration 9)

Vertical stroke

1) Press the brush with the *lufeng* technique, lift it lightly and move it downward.

2) Pause for a while.

3) Turn the tip slightly to the right and then upward to end the stroke.

Vertical stroke with a downward sharp end

1) Press the brush with the *lufeng* technique and move it downward.

2) Raise the brush gradually while moving it downward to get a pin-shaped ending.

Exercises

1) Practice writing the vertical stroke according to the steps described in the text. When you have familiarized yourself with the wielding steps, write each of them from memory 20 times.

2) Use a thin sheet of paper to cover the vertical strokes on the model script, sketch them and then trace them on one or two sheets of paper.

4. Left-falling and right-falling strokes

(Illustration 10)

Short left-falling stroke

Press the brush with the *lufeng* technique and move it down to the left.

Flat left-falling stroke

1) Press the brush down with the *lufeng* technique and pause.

2) Turn the tip to the left and write the stroke quickly.

Long left-falling stroke

Press the brush with the *lufeng* technique, pause, and then move it down to the left quickly.

Right-falling stroke

1) Start the brush gently down to the right.

2) Increase the force gradually.

3) Pause for a while.

4) Lift the brush slightly to the right to end the stroke.

Flat right-falling stroke

1) Start the brush movement with the *lufeng* technique, move it to the right and a little downward.

2) Increase the force gradually.

3) Pause for a while.

4) Turn the tip upward to the right to make a sharp ending.

Exercises

1) Practice writing the left-falling and right-falling strokes according to the steps described in the text. When you have familiarized yourself with the wielding steps, write each of them from memory 20 times.

2) Use a thin piece of paper to cover the left-falling and right-falling strokes on the model script, sketch them and then trace them on one or two sheets of paper.

5. Hook strokes

(Illustration 11)

Vertical stroke with a hook

1) Press the brush with the *lufeng* technique, lift it a little and move it downward.

2) Pause for a while.

3) Turn the tip upward to the left to make an ending.

Slant stroke with a hook

1) Press the brush with the *lufeng* technique, lift it a little and move it slantwise to the right.

2) Pause for a while.

3) Turn the tip upward to make a hook ending.

Vertical bend stroke with a hook

1) Press the brush with the *lufeng* technique, lift it a little and move it downward.

2) Pause for a while and move the brush to the right.

3) Pause and turn the tip upward to make a hook ending.

Exercises

1) Practice writing the hook strokes according to the steps described in the text. When you have familiarized yourself with the wielding steps, write each of them from memory 20 times.

2) Use a thin sheet of paper to cover the hook strokes on the model script, sketch them and then trace them on one or two sheets of paper.

6. Rising and turning strokes

(Illustration 12)

Rising stroke

1) Bring the brush down with the *lufeng* technique and pause.

2) Lift the tip and move it upward to the right to make a sharp ending.

Turning stroke

1) Press the brush with the *lufeng* technique, lift it a little and move it to the right.

2) Pause for a while.

3) Bring the tip of the brush downward and then upward a little to the left to make an ending.

Exercises

1) Practice writing the rising and turning strokes according to the steps described in the text. When you have familiarized yourself with the wielding steps, write each of them from memory 20 times.

2) Use a thin piece of paper to cover the rising and turning strokes on the model script, sketch them and then trace them on one or two sheets of paper.

Notes

① *Bishun* refers to the stroke-writing sequence of characters in regular script.

② *Dangou* is the way for beginners to learn regular script. Steps: dip the brushtip into the ink, sketch the characters with thin lines by following the example. The purpose is to understand the structure of the model characters.

③ *Mo* and *lin* (tracing and copying) are two techniques in writing regular script. Refer to Appendix II "Illustrations of Tracing and Copying."

④ *Jieti* (structure and style) refers to the design of thickness and density of strokes, and the proportional structures of characters that convey harmonious beauty.

第三课　楷书基本笔画综合练习①

　　本课重点复习楷书八种基本笔画的运笔法,使学生能理解每个字的笔画的正确运笔法。

　　同学们经过对楷书八种基本笔画的练习,已经初步掌握了每个字的笔画的运笔方法。现在,我们看唐代诗人王之涣的一首诗,共20个字,通过摹写来复习运笔法。(图13)摹写的范字帖见附录4。在摹写前,同学们先将这首诗的每一个字认真地看几遍,默记每个字的运笔方法,看看每个字的外形怎样,哪些笔画要写粗些,哪些笔画要写细些,哪些地方的笔画组合要密些,哪些地方的笔画组合要疏些,做到心中有数。然后进行单勾,最后用毛笔蘸墨摹写。

楷书基本笔画综合练习

图13

练习

1. 你能够把范字帖纸中每一个字的笔画名称说出来吗?每个字怎样运笔?用一张白纸,折好方格,对着范字帖,边认边练,进行临写。每个字临写5遍。

2. 用一张白纸,折好方格,对着范字帖纸临写1～2张。

注释

① 本书选用的范字是唐代大书法家柳公权的代表作《玄秘塔碑》真迹。字的结体端正,用笔劲秀,充满力度,具有阳刚之美。当代书法家在创作书法作品时,往往采用繁体字书写。为了便于初学者学习,本书在注释中标注了与繁体字对应的简体字。

盡—尽　　窮—穷

層—层　　樓—楼

Lesson Three   Comprehensive Practice of Regular Script Strokes ^①

This lesson reviews the brush wielding steps of the eight basic strokes for the regular script to help you understand the correct ways to execute these strokes when writing characters.

By now you have had a preliminary mastery of the brush-wielding skills of every stroke. Now let us review these skills by tracing a 20-character poem written by Wang Zhihuan, a poet of the Tang Dynasty. (Illustration 13) Before tracing, read carefully every word of the poem and memorize the brush-wielding steps of each character. Pay attention to the structures of the characters to see which strokes are thick, which are thin, which have compact structures and which are sparse, so that you can have a clear idea of the structures of the characters used. Then sketch the characters and trace them with a brush.

Exercises

1) Can you tell the names of the strokes used in every character in the model script? How is each character written? Fold one or two sheets of paper into squares and copy each model character five times while reading them aloud.
2) Fold one or two sheets of paper into squares, unfold them, and copy the model characters in the middle of the squares.

Note

① The model characters featured in this book are chosen from the inscriptions of *Xuanmita Stele*, in the genuine handwriting of Liu Gongquan, a celebrated calligrapher of the Tang Dynasty. His writing is statuesque of structure and both vigorous and elegant of style. His works of calligraphy are imbued with the beauty of dynamics. Most contemporary calligraphers write the original complex form of characters in their creative works. The simplified forms of these characters are presented in the notes for the convenience of the beginners.

▲ 中国书画 *ABC*

第四课　中国画的基本知识

本课讲述有关中国画的用具、材料、执笔、用笔、设色和表现方法等问题。目的是使初学中国画的同学在教师的讲解和示范下，了解中国画的特点，为学好中国画找到入门的钥匙。

一、作画工具和材料

笔　笔是画中国画的主要工具，有柔毫、硬毫和兼毫三类。羊毫属柔毫类，毛软，吸水量较大，可以画花和叶、蘸水染色，如大、小提笔，染色笔等。狼毫属硬毫，有弹性，可作勾勒或画山石、树干，如大、中、小兰竹笔，叶筋笔，点梅笔等。兼毫笔头中兼有狼毫和羊毫，笔性柔软而富有弹性。兼毫笔用途很广，适宜画人物、花卉和山水，如大、中、小白云，七紫羊，兼鬃提笔等，另外，还有底纹笔、排笔等，可作染天地和大面积的底色用。

选笔时，因新笔头外面有胶，要把笔头压在拇指的指甲上，看笔锋的毛是否齐。用手指按一按笔肚，不要太充实，一般要瘦于笔管为佳；否则，笔肚太大，影响笔锋的使用。再看笔管是否圆。把笔平放在玻璃板上，用手掌按着转一转便知。新笔在使用前，要用冷水或温水浸开，切不要用开水或热水浸洗。笔用后要洗干净，理顺笔毛，挂起或插在笔筒中晾干，这样，可使笔耐用。

初学者要备五支笔：大提笔、大兰竹笔、小白云、叶筋笔和底纹笔（刷子），这样就够用了。

墨　现在画写意画，很多人都喜欢使用书画墨汁，用起来很方便，如北京产的"一得阁"书画墨汁，质量甚佳。另备一条油烟墨块。这种墨块黑而有光泽，淡墨也很柔和。如墨汁不够浓时，可倒在砚中用墨块磨一磨。

纸　中国画用纸以宣纸为主。宣纸有生宣和熟宣之分。生宣纸质柔软，吸水性能好，最适宜画写意画。常用的如"夹江宣"，有单宣和夹宣（比较厚的）两种。初学者用单宣就可以了。熟宣是在纸面上涂上胶矾，纸质比较坚实，作画时不吸水，可画工笔画。宣纸要包好，放在柜里，不要吹风和见光，以防变质。

砚　绘画用的砚池（又称墨海），以广东省肇庆产的端砚和安徽省歙县产的歙砚最好。这两种砚石质比较坚硬，磨墨时容易把墨磨稠。作画的砚台要大些，墨海要深些，并要有盖，以保持清洁。墨一次用完，用完后要将砚台洗干净。初学者可用盘子或碟子代替砚台。

调色盘　用以调颜色的小碟或大盘，以白瓷盘为最佳，以便辨别调用的颜色是否正确。不宜用有颜色或有花纹的盘或碟子。

笔洗　是洗笔的罐子，要备三个。为了节约空间，笔者自制了一个三级笔洗，如图14：①是大碗，②是中碗，③是玻璃瓶或易拉罐。全盛水。作画时换换颜色，先将着色的笔在1号碗中洗去颜色，然后在2号碗中将余色洗净，最后到3号瓶中蘸清水调需要的颜色。发现水脏要勤换水，以保证画面颜色的清新。

颜料　用12色软管装的"中国画颜料"比较方便。

笔帘　是用竹枝织成的软帘子，可卷起来（书画文具店有售）。上课或外出作画，画笔可卷在笔帘里，既可保护笔头，又不玷污其他物品。

垫毡　作画时垫在宣纸下面。如有旧毡子，也可代替，效果比新画毡还好。初学者作小品，最方便的是用旧报纸作垫。

印章、印盒和印泥　印章以石章为佳。可各刻一方名章和闲章①。印泥有朱膘、朱砂二色，均可选用。印章用后要用废宣纸擦净置盒内，可自制或找一合适的盒子放置，目的是保护印章不被碰损。

图14　笔洗

二、笔法

以指执笔，靠腕的运动，使笔锋接触纸面而出现各种点和线，这叫做用笔。用笔的方法叫笔法。笔法是画好中国画的重要手段。要掌握用笔方法，首先要懂得如何执笔和运笔。

1. **执笔**　画物象的细部可用书法执笔方法。画大块面和较长的线条，要用作画的执笔方法。（图15）第一步仍是按书法执笔——三指（拇指、食指和中指）并拢，这三指的第一个指节紧执笔管。第二步是让无名指（第四指）的第一指节紧靠中指并稍着笔管，小指（第五指）微靠无名指，这种执笔法的优点是让拇指和食指起握笔和转动笔管的作用，中指和无名指起拨和挑的

图15　作画的执笔法

作用，小指微护无名指。做到五指齐用力，指实掌虚，画时感到用笔十分灵活。执笔时，精神要十分集中，凝神笔锋，把力运到腕和手指上，画出的点和线就有力度了。（图16）

图16　执笔作画

关于执笔的高低问题，应视笔与画的大小和技法而定。一般是执笔的中间处。大笔执住笔管的上半部；小笔执住笔管的下半部。作小幅画，执笔宜低；作大幅画，执笔宜高。作工细的画或画物象的细部，执笔稍低；画写意画，执笔稍高。

2. **运笔**　作画的运笔道理和书法基本相同，都是用手指和腕运动写出点画和画出点线，从而组成字和物象的。画物象的细部，可用书法的提腕法。但画长线和大块面，一定要用悬腕法，站起来，让指、腕、肘和肩都悬空，甚至发动全身力量挥写。因此，作画的运笔比书法更灵活自由，为了画面的美，可任意挥写。灵活运用按、提、顿、转的运笔方法，画出刚柔相济而多彩多姿的线条，产生气韵生动[②]的艺术效果。

3. **笔锋**　前面说过，形象是靠笔锋接触纸面而出现的。这里，要讲一讲什么叫笔锋，笔锋有什么作用。笔锋指笔头的腹部到尖端的一段。它依靠画者执笔时的正、侧、逆等运动而画出变化多样的点和线，塑造千姿百态的物象。这里介绍三种常用的笔锋的运笔方法：（图17）

中锋　运笔时笔管与纸面垂直，画面线时，笔锋在线中间运行。由于笔尖容易渗水，因此画出来的线圆浑光滑。这是勾线的主要方法。

侧锋　运笔时，笔管倒向一侧，笔锋露在侧面。侧锋的线粗细、浓淡、干湿有变化，同时能画出线和面，可表现粗细不平的形象。如画树的枝干和山石以及点叶、皴擦、渲染等时，多用侧锋。

逆锋　运笔时，笔管向上或向左方向运行，故意让其不顺手，让笔锋在运行时碰到阻力。画出的线条变化多姿，有力量，有动感。以此法画树干和山石更具美感。

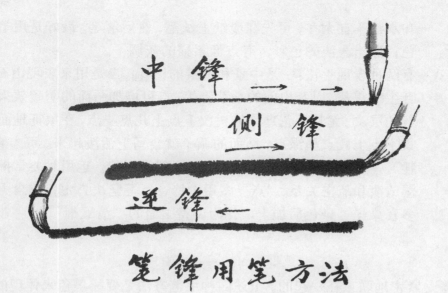

图 17　笔锋用笔法

4.用笔方法　运用上述三种笔锋，可表现出丰富多彩的绘画效果。常见的用笔表现物象的方法有勾、皴、擦、点四种方法。（图18）

勾法　勾是中国画的基础，即用各种线条来画物象的轮廓，然后进行渲染。勾法也可独立成画。如中国画"白描"（一切物象完全用线条勾画）和外出写生记录景物的速写。勾法多中、侧锋并用。

皴法　皴本义是指皮肤受冻而裂开的样子。以此引申到对山石、树皮纹理、质感、光暗的描绘。皴法用笔多样，中、侧、逆锋并用，并要求"见笔"③，可有面有线，有长线和短线、单线和复线等，根据不同的形象，采用不同的方法，灵活运用。

擦法　有两种方法：一是先皴后带擦。趁皴时墨色将尽，用笔根擦出淡淡的墨迹。色彩很调和；二是皴后待纸干再擦。此法是为了增强物象的质感和体积感。无论是勾、皴、擦，画时蘸墨

图 18　几种不同用笔方法

和水都不宜太多，可先在废纸上试笔，然后落笔。最好是用笔根少量余色，擦出淡淡的色彩，有点像素描的灰调子。

点法 有两种表现手法：一是中景和远景的树叶；二是用来表现山石、树木上野生的霉苔，以及山间的杂草等等。点可增加画面的明暗效果和加强山石的层次。尤其在花鸟画的树杈上点上几点墨点，在象征地面的白色背景上点上几点墨绿点，画面的调子就会马上活泼起来。可参看范画《野趣》。（图35）点有横、直、圆、尖、斜等形状。运用时要掌握墨色的干湿浓淡和疏密关系。"点"多用中锋，行笔坚决肯定，饱含力度。"点"多在染墨、染色后加上，作为调整画面的"清醒剂"。

三、墨法

笔和墨是紧密地联系在一起的。上述四种用笔方法是要靠墨色来体现的。打个比方：笔是骨，墨是肉。笔用来画出物体的形象，墨用来使形象更具有质感和体积。因此，中国画家历来非常讲究用墨的方法——包括墨的不同色阶和使用技法。

1. **墨的色阶** 墨即是色，"墨分五彩"，即焦、浓、重、淡、清。（图19）

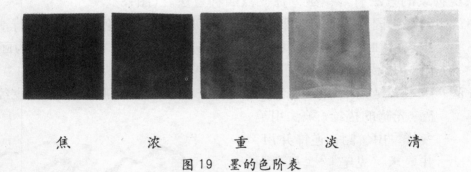

焦　　　　浓　　　　重　　　　淡　　　　清

图19　墨的色阶表

焦墨 即把墨汁磨得很浓。这样画在画面上黑而有光泽。一般作为主要物象的点缀，让物象更具有神采。

浓墨 其黑度比焦墨稍淡。是表现主要物象的重要墨色。有突出物象、增强气氛之效。

重墨 其黑度比浓墨淡。比例为4分墨汁加6分水。

淡墨 其黑度比浓墨更淡。比例为3分墨汁加7分水，成为灰色。重墨和淡墨是交替使用的，目的是让画面的墨彩更富有变化。

清墨 黑度极淡之灰色。比例为1分墨汁加18分水。在纸上干后，灰色隐约可见，适宜表现远山、远水、远云和晨昏、夜雨等朦胧的景物。

2. **墨的使用技法**（图20）

泼墨法 著名画家张大千把墨泼在绢或宣纸上，然后依照墨色的浓淡、形状进行勾、填、皴、擦，画出雄奇的山水和生动的花卉。历来一些有成就的画家都用此法作画，称为泼墨法。本文要讲的泼墨法是作画时一次性地用墨完成干、湿、浓、淡的墨彩效果，不需要二次或多次。如画竹竿、花叶、树干和鸟类的羽毛等。

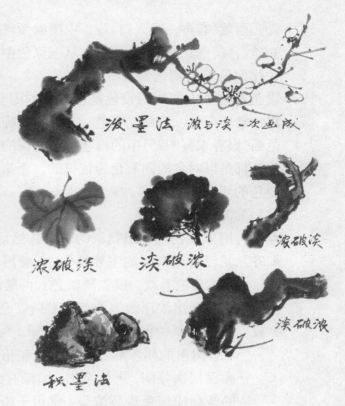

图 20　用墨技法

破墨法　二次用墨。第一次用墨后，稍停，趁湿进行第二次用墨。方法可用浓墨点画在淡墨上，这叫"浓破淡"，如以淡墨画花叶，用浓墨画叶脉。另一方法是用淡墨点画在浓墨上，这叫"淡破浓"，目的是使浓重的墨色中有变化。

积墨法　是使用多层墨渲染之法。一般由淡到浓。第一遍墨色干后再染第二遍。在进行第二遍渲染时，要适当保留第一遍的部分墨色，不要全部覆盖。

3．用墨应注意的问题

1）墨要磨浓。

2）蘸墨作画时笔与水要清洁。

3）下笔时要大胆而慎重，掌握好浓淡干湿的变化。初学者下笔前最好用画过的废纸试一下，看墨度恰当才下笔。

4）墨需要用多少就磨(倒)多少，一次用完，不留"宿墨"④。

5）用墨效果要洁净、生动、光泽、滋润、饱和。忌太重、太湿、太燥以及死和浊(死墨是墨色重复太多，毫无光彩；浊墨是墨不洁净或被色掩盖)。

四、设色

1．中国画的颜色　分为矿物质和植物质两类。矿物质的颜色有石青、石绿、石黄、赭石、朱砂、朱膘、白粉、金、银等；植物质的颜色有洋红、胭脂、花青、藤黄(有毒，忌入口)等。中国画颜料的特点是经久不变，色泽厚重。我们知道，红、黄、蓝是三原色，从三原色中可调出各种中间色。各种中间色的调色比例见下页调色表。

2. 设色方法　中国画的设色是以对象的固有色为依据的，但不讲究光和影的作用，常用夸张、取舍、变色、以墨代色等各种手段来增强表现力。如第五课的范画《报春来》(图25)中的梅花，第七课的范画《红莲出水分外娇》(图32)中的荷花，都是以对象的固有色为依据的，而第六课的范画《劲竹凌霄》(图30)则是用变色的手段来描绘了。

3. 常用的几种着色方法

填色　用墨或色勾勒出物象的轮廓，然后在其中填色。

点写　是没骨花鸟画的主要技法，一般用来画不勾墨线轮廓的花鸟。在一笔之中，有浓有淡，或先蘸淡色，再蘸深色，然后笔尖蘸更深的色，一笔按下，现出浓深淡等均匀的色阶，色彩十分调和。

渲染　是山水画中很重要的一个步骤。画面勾、皴、擦后，通过渲染，加强山石、树木的体积感和空间感。在花鸟画中，染树干和树叶，染衬底，使画面层次分明，主体突出。渲染有大染和小染两种方法。大染用大面积的淡色或深色进行渲染，常用于染天空、云水、日月、雨雪以及花鸟画的背景。染时先用清水将纸喷湿（生宣要，熟宣不要），然后将调好的色层层加染，由浅到深，染时要将色多调一些，免得不够时再调，因为色度深浅很难相似。染天空、海面或背景，如要不显笔痕，可在颜色水中略加少许清胶或白粉（国画白色）。笔宜用羊毫，宜大不宜小。染时手要轻，一笔接一笔地横染，切不可往返拖刷！干后如要加染，仍需将纸喷湿，染时纸背要垫画毡或白吸水纸(最好用便宜的宣纸，用完晾干，下次再用)。小染指在画面的局部进行渲染。如花鸟画的树干、太湖石，山水画的前景或部分景物。染前先用干净的羊毫笔蘸清水局部刷湿，用吸水纸（如画坏的宣纸）吸去纸面上多余的水分，然后蘸色或淡墨进行渲染，由浅到深，染四、五次都可以，但不要把画面弄脏。

渗化　蘸墨或蘸色时，有意识地吸足墨或色，落笔后，让物象的轮廓稍渗出墨或色，干后仍有水分淋漓的感觉。此法花鸟画最常用。

反衬　为了使所画的形象鲜明突出，待作品完成后，在画背面涂上另一种颜色，如范画《红莲出水分外娇》(图32)在宣纸的正面画红莲花，在纸的背面染青灰色，表现莲花生在水中，同时让莲花和莲叶更加突出，层次也显得深远。用此法可反衬出山水画的天空，扩大画面的空间感。

调　色　表

调色比例／单色 调合色	花青	藤黄	赭石	墨	胭脂	洋红	朱膘	朱砂	石青	石绿	粉
草绿	5	5									
老绿	6	4									
嫩绿	3	7									
芽绿	2	8									
墨绿	3	4		3							
苍绿	4	5	1								
新绿		5								5	
油绿	5	4		1							
浓绿									5	5	
秋香色	4	4	2								
金红		5					5				
肉红			4		1	1					4
银红					2		4				4
殷红					2	2		6			
粉红						4					6
橘红		1					5	4			
土红				5				5			
老红			4					6			
金黄		7					3				
苍黄	1	4	5								
土黄		5		5							
檀香色		4	5	1							
鹅黄		9					1				
墨赭			7	3							
赭黄		8	2								
藕荷	2				3	3					2
青莲	2				4	4					
深紫	4				1	5					
酱色		5		3	1	1					
紫酱	1			4		5					
青灰	4			4							2
铁灰	2			6							2
墨青	6			4							
茶褐			5						5		
淡灰				5							5

五、中国画的表现方法

勾勒填色法　先用墨或色线勾勒出物象的轮廓，然后在轮廓线中间填上描绘的颜色。此法工笔画和意笔画都常用。如第七课范画《红莲出水分外娇》中的荷花。

没骨点写法　又称没骨点染。此法是用1～3种颜色蘸在笔头上，一笔画在画纸上，而出现物象完整的部分形象，不用线条勾勒轮廓。用此法画花鸟画，效果很好，如第八课的范画《野趣》(图35)中的小鸡。又如画红梅花，用大白云笔洗净蘸清水，先蘸曙红，然后在笔尖点少许胭脂，点一片花瓣，这时，花瓣外部呈深红色，中间颜色自然渗化，外深里浅，很有立体感。

勾勒与没骨相结合法　一幅作品中同时用勾勒填色和没骨点写两种方法。此法在人物、山水和花鸟画中都广为运用，也适合初学者学习。如范画《红莲出水分外娇》中的荷花和蜻蜓是勾勒法，而荷叶和荷梗是没骨法。

注释

① 闲章：书画家用来点缀书画的印章。其内容用简练的语言，表达作者对人生和艺术的看法。如"墨当随时代"(写字、作画要有时代精神)、"师牛堂"(师牛，学习牛辛勤劳作的精神；堂，学习工作的地方)。

② 气韵生动：形容文章、书画的形象和意境特别生动美好。

③ 见笔：中国画的一种表现手法，指在描绘物象时看到笔画的运动痕迹，好像油画的"笔触"。

④ 宿墨：指作画用不完的墨，由于有胶粒粘笔毛，不能再作画。

练习

1. 中国画非常重视笔法和墨法的运用。你能理解运笔的三种方法和"墨分五彩"的道理吗？请拿起笔来，在宣纸上练习。

2. 中国画很讲究墨的使用技法，具体地说，就是泼墨法、破墨法和积墨法。请你对照图20所示，练习上述三种技法。

Lesson Four　Basics of Traditional Chinese Painting

This lesson deals with painting tools and materials, brush wielding techniques, the use of brush uses, coloring and the different ways of expression in traditional Chinese painting. The aim is to give the beginner some ideas about the salient features of traditional Chinese painting and learn the basics through demonstrations by the teacher.

1. Painting tools and materials

Brushes

Brushes are the main painting tools in traditional Chinese painting. There are three kinds of brushes: *rouhao*, *yinghao* and *jianhao*. The *rouhao* brush is made of goat's hair; it is soft and good at absorbing water. It is used to paint flowers and leaves, and also for coloring. The *rouhao* brush comes in three types: the large and small *ti* brushes and the coloring brush. The *yinghao* brush is made of weasel's hair; it is stiff and resilient, and used to sketch or paint mountains, rocks and tree trunks. There are a variety of *yinghao* brushes, including large, medium and small *lanzhu* brushes, the *yejin* brush and the *dianmei* brush. The *jianhao* brush is made of a mixture of weasel and goat's hair; it is soft as well as resilient, and used widely to paint figures, flowers and landscapes. The large, medium and small *baiyun* brushes, the *qiziyang* brush and the *jianzongti* brush come under this category. Besides the above brushes, there are also the *diwen* brush and the broad brush, which are used to wash-color the background of a large space, such as the sky and the land.

When selecting a brush, press the tip of the brush against your thumb nail to see whether the hair is even because the tips of new brushes are coated with glue. Press the middle part of the brush to see if it is too plump. In general, the brush head should be thinner than the shaft; otherwise, the wielding will be affected. Roll the shaft on top of a glass plate to see whether it is round or not. Before using a new brush, soak it in cold or warm water. Never use boiling or hot water. After use, brushes should be cleaned, tidied, hung up or put in the brush pot .

A beginner should have five brushes: a large *ti* brush, a large *lanzhu* brush, a small *baiyun* brush, a *yejin* brush and a *diwen* brush.

Ink

Nowadays it is convenient for people to do freehand brushwork with ready-made ink. The Yidege-brand Ink made in Beijing is very good in quality for Chinese calligraphy and painting. You also need a lampblack-in-stick, which is shiny black in color. Light black made from it looks very soft. If the ready-made ink is not thick enough, pour some of it into an ink-slab and make it thicker by rubbing an ink stick against the ink-slab.

Paper

The *xuan* paper is mainly used in traditional Chinese painting. There are *shengxuan* paper (unrefined) and *shuxuan* paper (refined). The *shengxuan* paper is soft in quality and highly absorbent; it is suitable for creating freehand brushwork. The *jiajiangxuan* paper is commonly used by painters, which comes in single-layer and double-layer types. Beginners can use the single-layer type for practice. The *shuxuan* paper, glued with a film of alum, is of a strong texture and suitable for *gongbi* painting (traditional Chinese realistic painting characterized by fine brushwork and close attention to detail) because it does not blot. The *xuan* paper should be wrapped up and kept in a cabinet, because exposure to wind and light will lead to its degradation in quality.

Ink-slab

The ink-slab used for painting is also called *mohai* (ink sea). The best ones are the *duan* ink-slab made in Zhaoqing, Guangdong Province, and the *she* ink-slab made in Shexian County, Anhui Province. As these ink-slabs are made of hard rock, it is easy for painters to produce thick ink by grinding an ink stick on them. The ink-slabs for painting should be a little larger in size and deeper in depth than those for calligraphy, and they should have a lid to keep clean. Clean the ink-slab with water after use. Beginners can use a plate or a saucer to prepare the ink .

Color-mixing trays

To see whether the mixed color is right or not, white porcelain plates or saucers are preferred to those with other colors or decorative patterns.

Brush-washing jars

Prepare three jars for washing a brush. Illustrtion 14 shows a set of self-made jars. The first one is a big bowl, the second one a medium-sized bowl, and the third one a glass bottle or a tin can, all filled with water. When you need to change color while painting, you should first wash your brush in the big bowl to get rid of most of the color, then rinse it in the medium-sized bowl to get rid of remnants and finally use the clean water in the bottle or tin can for mixing the wanted color. Change the water frequently to keep the color pure and fresh on the painting.

Pigments

It is convenient to use the "Pigments for Traditional Chinese Painting," which come in 12 colors in soft tubes.

Brush wrapper

A brush wrapper is a small bamboo mat which can be rolled up to wrap brushes. When you go to a painting class or go out painting, wrap the brushes in it so that the brushes are well-protected and will not stain other things.

Felt mat

Put a felt mat under a piece of *xuan* paper before beginning a painting. Old felt is better than new one. Beginners can use old newspapers as an under mat.

Seal, seal container and seal paste

Seals made of stone are the best. Prepare two seals, one with your name carved on it (*mingzhang*) and the other carved with a motto (Note ①: *xianzhang*). Ink paste comes in two colors: dark red and bright red. You can choose either color. Clean the seal with a piece of used *xuan* paper and keep it in its container for protection.

2. Brush techniques

Hold the brush with your fingers and move the brush tip with the strength of your wrist to produce dots and lines on the paper. This is called wielding. Brush-wielding techniques are very important in the learning of traditional Chinese painting. To master these techniques, you must first know how to hold the brush and wield it correctly.

Brush holding

You can use the brush-holding techniques of calligraphy for drawing details of an object or a figure. But to do large paintings or draw long lines, you should use the brush-holding techniques of painting (Illustration 15): first, hold the shaft with the cushions of the thumb, the index finger and the middle finger the way you do in writing characters; second, put the ring finger against the middle one and touch the shaft slightly, and put the little finger against the ring finger. In this way, the function of the thumb and the index finger is to hold and move the brush, that of the middle finger and the ring finger is to turn the brush, and that of the little finger is to fix the ring finger. Thus the five fingers work together to hold the brush while the palm is hollow. Holding the brush this way enables you to paint dexterously and quickly. While painting, you should concentrate all your attention on the tip of the brush and try to wield the brush with the strength of the wrist and the fingers so as to produce forceful dots and lines. (Illustration 16)

The position of your fingers on the shaft depends on the size of the painting and on the techniques you use. Generally speaking, you should hold the middle part of the shaft. If it is a large brush, hold its upper part; and if it is a small one, hold the lower part. Hold the shaft a little lower for small paintings and for drawing details of an object or a figure, and higher for large paintings and freehand brushwork.

Brush wielding

Brush wielding in painting is similar to that in calligraphy. Both rely on the movement of the wrist and fingers to produce dots and lines of which an object or a figure is composed. You can use the wrist-raising method for calligraphy to draw details of an object or a figure. But in drawing long lines and doing large paintings, you have to stand up and use the wrist-suspending method, in which your fingers, wrist, elbow and shoulders are all suspended in order to paint with strength from all over your body. Therefore, the wielding techniques in painting are more flexible and free. You can wield the brush at will, using the techniques of *an*, *ti*, *dun* and *zhuan* to create beautiful and vivid paintings with sturdy, graceful and vivid lines, all with a unique artistic effect (Note ② : *qiyun shengdong*).

Wielding techniques of the brush tip

As mentioned above, images on paper are produced by wielding the brush tip. But what is a brush tip and what is its function? A brush tip refers to the part of the brush head from the middle down to its point. It is with this part of the brush that painters wield up and down, sideways and backward to produce a variety of dots and lines, of which numerous vivid and charming images are composed of. Three commonly-used brush-tip wielding techniques are introduced as follows. (Illustration 17)

1) *Zhongfeng* method (upright tip wielding technique)

   The shaft is perpendicular to the paper. In drawing a line, the tip moves along the middle of the line, and as the tip is full of ink and tends to exude it when pressed, the line drawn looks smooth and plump. This is the main technique for drawing lines.

2) *Cefeng* method (sideways tip wielding technique)

   The shaft turns to the side and the tip is exposed either to the left or the right side. In this way, the lines you draw can be thin or thick in shape, light or dark in color, and dry and wet in imagination. In addition, this technique enables you to draw lines and spaces at the same time to express images composed of various lines and spaces. *Cefeng* is usually used for painting tree trunks and leaves, mountain rocks, and for expressing a certain artistic effect.

3) *Nifeng* method (backward tip wielding technique)

   The shaft turns upward or leftward with a purpose of creating some resistance against the tip's forward movement. The lines drawn this way are in a variety of shapes, forceful and dynamic. Tree trunks and mountain rocks painted in this way give a more aesthetic feeling.

Brush-using methods

The three brush-tip wielding techniques mentioned above are helpful in producing rich and colorful artistic effects. Four brush-using methods are commonly used when painting objects or figures: outlining (*goufa*), chapping (*cunfa*), striking (*cafa*) and stippling (*dianfa*). (Illustration 18)

1) Outlining

   Outlining, which involves sketching the contours of objects or figures before coloring, is the basic skill in traditional Chinese painting. This technique is used in "*baimiao*" (lines drawn in traditional ink and brush style) and sketches. *Zhongfeng* and *cefeng* are usually used for outlining.

2) Chapping

Cun in Chinese means chapping of the skin. Here it refers to the technique we employ to depict the texture, the three-dimensional quality, light and shade of mountain rocks, tree barks etc. *Zhongfeng*, *cefeng* and *nifeng* methods are usually used in chapping so that traces of brush movements (dots, short and long lines, single lines and multiple lines) can be identified (Note ③ : *jianbi*). Painters use different skills according to the images they are going to create.

3) Striking

There are two kinds of striking. The first is to strike shortly after chapping. When the ink is about to dry, strike it with the root of the brush hair to make the color more harmonious. The second is to strike after the ink has dried, with the purpose of increasing the thickness and three-dimensional effect of the object or figure. Whatever method mentioned above is used, remember not to dip the brush with too much ink. Try it on a piece of used paper before starting to paint. You should strictly control the amount of ink in the brush head and use only the ink in the brush root to strike so that the color is a light gray like that in a sketch.

4) Stippling

There are two ways of stippling. First, for painting leaves in mid-distant and distant views. Second, for creating wild mosses on mountain rocks and tree trunks, weeds on hills and in the fields etc. Stippling increases the effect of light and shade and make mountain rocks look three-dimensional. A few dots on the branches of a tree or on a white background that symbolizes land in a flower-and-bird painting enliven the tone of the painting. (Illustration 35: *A Funny Scene in the Country*) Dots vary in shape: horizontal, vertical, round, pointed, slanting etc. It is important to master the use of ink and the relationship between dryness and wetness, thinness and thickness, sparseness and denseness etc. The *zhongfeng* method, which is forceful and firm, is usually used in stippling. Dots are generally added after coloring as the finishing touches to a painting.

3. Ink techniques

Brush and ink are related to each other in the making of traditional Chinese paintings. The four brush-using methods cannot be applied without the use of ink. If we compare their relationship to a human body, brush is the skeleton and ink is the flesh. Brush sketches the outlines of an object while ink makes them dynamic and three-dimensional. Therefore, traditional Chinese artists have all along attached great importance to the use of ink, including the use of different color shades of ink and the techniques in applying them.

Color shades in ink scale

There are five shades in Chinese ink scale: black-burned (*jiaomo*), thick (*nongmo*), heavy (*zhongmo*), light (*danmo*) and clear (*qingmo*). (Illustration 19)

1) Black-burned ink

Jiaomo refers to ink thickly ground in an ink-slab, and appears shiny black in a painting. It is usually used to set off the subject matter in a painting.

2) Thick ink

Nongmo, a little bit lighter in color than *jiaomo*, is used to depict the main subject. It can not only make the subject matter stand out but also heighten the atmosphere of the painting.

3) Heavy ink

Being lighter in color than *nongmo*, *zhongmo* is produced by using a mixture with 40 percent of ink and 60 percent of water.

4) Light ink

Danmo is lighter in color than *nongmo*. *Danmo* is produced by using a mixture with 30 percent of ink and 70 percent of water. *Danmo* and *zhongmo* are used alternately so as to make the shades of the paintings more colorful.

5) Clear ink

Qingmo is very light in color and looks gray. The proportion of ink to water is 1 to 18. When dried on paper, it is faintly gray and suitable for depicting misty scenes in the distance, such as mountains, rivers, clouds, the dawn, the dusk and the night rain.

Ink-using techniques (Illustration 20)

1) Ink-splashing (*pomofa*)

Zhang Daqian, a famous Chinese painter, splashed ink on silk scrolls or *xuan* paper and then applied the methods of outlining, filling, chapping and striking to his painting according to the thickness of the ink and the shape it created. Many other artists in history used the same technique, known as "ink-splashing." Here it refers to the completion of a painting by splashing the ink at one go to produce the effect of different color shades. No need to splash for a second time or more. The technique is suitable for painting bamboo, flower petals and leaves, tree trunks, feather of birds etc.

2) Dual ink-using (*pomofa*)

It means applying ink to paper twice. Wait for a while after the first splashing, then apply ink to the paper for a second time before the first ink dries. If thick ink is splashed over light ink, it is called "*nongpodan*." For instance, one paints leaves with light ink and their veins with thick ink. The other way is called "*danponong*," in which light ink is splashed over thick ink, the purpose of which is to bring about some changes in the color of the ink.

3) Multiple ink-using (*jimofa*)

This refers to applying layer upon layer of ink to paper, usually from light to thick. The second layer of ink should be applied after the first dries, and part of the previous coloring should be left intact.

Essentials for ink use

1) Ink should be produced by grinding an ink stick on an ink-slab.

2) The brushes and water to be used must be kept clean.

3) When painting, one should be both decisive and careful, and have a good knowledge of the color scales of ink. It would be better for beginners to try the color on used paper to see whether it is suitable before applying it to the painting.

4) Prepare the ink according to actual needs. Clean the ink-slab each time when you finish painting. Avoid using ink left over from the last painting (Note ④: *sumo*).

5) Ink should look clean, fresh, bright, smooth and plump on the painting. Avoid using ink which is too thick, too wet, too dry or too turbid, and try not to apply any ink to a painting a second time.

4. Color design

Colors in traditional Chinese painting

Colors in traditional Chinese painting come from mineral and vegetative pigments. Mineral pigments include azurite, malachite green, mineral yellow, ochre, cinnabar, vermilion, white, gold, silver etc. Vegetative pigments include carmine, nacarat, cyanine, gamboge (poisonous, do not eat) etc. Chinese pigments are heavy and thick enough to stand the test of time.

We all know that red, yellow and blue are the three primary colors, from which various intermediate colors are prepared. See the Color-Mixing Chart (on pages 80 - 81) for proportions in the making of intermediate colors.

Color-designing

Colors in traditional Chinese painting are mixed according to the natural color of the subject matter, not according to the effect of light and shade. Techniques like exaggerating, selecting, discoloring, coloring with black ink instead of other colors etc. are often used to strengthen the expressive force. See the plum blossoms in the model painting *Spring Is Coming* (Illustration 25) in Lesson Five, and the lotus in the model painting *Charming Red Lotus Coming out of Water* (Illustration 32) in Lesson Seven, which are both based on their natural colors. But the model painting *Vigorous Bamboo* (Illustration 30) in Lesson Six is done by

中国书画 ABC

means of discoloring.

Here are some commonly-used coloring techniques:

1) Filling (*tianse*)

Sketch the contours of an object or a figure and then fill in the color.

2) Stippling (*dianxie*)

Stippling is the major technique used in painting flowers and birds that do not have a framework and need not be outlined first. Dip the brush tip first in light color, then in dark color, and finally in even darker color before applying it to the paper. Bearing three colors at the same time, the tip can produce a harmonious patch with different shades of the same color.

3) Wash-coloring (*xuanran*)

Wash-coloring is an important step in the painting of landscapes. It can enhance the three-dimensional and spacious feeling of rocks and tree trunks after outlining, chapping and striking methods are used. Wash-coloring tree trunks and leaves, and wash-coloring the background brings the subject matter in focus and the other objects in perspective. Wash-coloring is divided into large wash-coloring (*daran*) and small wash-coloring (*xiaoran*). *Daran* means wash-coloring large areas in a painting with light or dark colors, which is often used to paint the sun, the moon, the sky, clouds, rain, snow and the background of flower-and-bird paintings. Before wash-coloring, wet the paper (use only the *shengxuan* paper rather than *shuxuan* paper) with water, then apply the prepared mixed color to the paper layer upon layer, and from light to dark. Prepare the color mixture by mixing a little more than necessary lest it be not enough and you have to prepare it again; and it is difficult to prepare the color exactly the same as the previous one. Add a little transparent glue or Chinese white to the color when wash-coloring the sky, the sea or the background so that no brush traces can be seen. It is better to use a large brush made of goat's hair in *daran*. You should paint gently, stroke by stroke, in a level way, and not in a to-and-fro way like mopping the floor. If you want to wash-color again after the paper dries, the paper has to be wetted again. Put a felt or a piece of white blotting paper (cheap *xuan* paper can be used for many times) underneath the *xuan* paper.

Small wash-coloring refers to the wash-coloring of small areas of a painting such as tree trunks and Taihu rocks in flower-and-bird paintings, and the front scene and some objects of landscape paintings. Before wash-coloring, use a clean goat-hair brush to wet the part to be wash-colored with clear water, blot the extra water with the blotting paper (waste *xuan* paper) and then use the prepared color or ink to wash-color. Wash-color four or five times and from light to dark. Take care not to mess up the painting.

4) Bleeding (*shenhua*)

Dip a brush in ink or color until it is saturated. While painting, let ink or color bleed slightly from the contours of the object or figure. There will be a feeling of wetness even after the color dries up. This method is commonly used in painting flowers and birds.

5) Contrasting (*fanchen*)

To highlight the subject of a painting, apply a different color to the back of the painting after its completion. For example, in the model painting *Charming Red Lotus Coming out of Water* (Illustration 32), the lotus on the right side of the *xuan* paper is painted red while the other side of the paper is painted grayish blue to indicate that the lotus is growing in water. The contrast of color serves to set off the lotus flowers and renders depth to the depiction. This technique can be used in landscape paintings to contrast the sky and heighten the sense of space.

5. Expressive means in traditional Chinese painting

Outlining and color-filling

First, draw the outlines of the object or figure to be depicted with ink or color, and then fill in the colors. This method applies commonly to *gongbi* and *yibi* (conception painting) painting. See the lotus in the model painting *Charming Red Lotus Coming out of Water* in Lesson Seven.

Stippling without outlining

This technique is also called dotting and washing. Dip the brush tip in one to three colors and then apply the color to the paper at one go to produce part of an image without outlining. This technique makes good flower-and-bird paintings. See the chick in the model painting *A Funny Scene in the Country* (Illustration 35) . If you paint red plum blossoms, wash a large *baiyun* brush clean and moisten it with clear water, dip it in bright red, and then add a little carmine color to the brush point. Apply the brush to the paper to paint a blossom petal at one stroke. The petal will look three-dimensional, dark red outside, red at its root, and naturally mixed color in the middle.

Outlining combined with stippling

A common practice is to combine outlining and stippling in doing a painting. The technique is widely applied in painting figures, landscapes, flowers and birds. Beginners can do this too. In the model painting *Charming Red Lotus Coming out of Water*, the lotus flowers and the dragonfly are painted by outlining while the lotus leaves and stalks are stippled.

Color Mixing Chart

color mixing ratio / primary color / mixed color	cyanine	garcinia	ochre	Chinese ink	carmine
grass green	5	5			
dark green	6	4			
light green	3	7			
yellow green	2	8			
blackish green	3	4		3	
bright green	4	5	1		
fresh green		5			
glossy dark green	5	4		1	
rich green					
charming autumn green	4	4	2		
golden red		5			
flesh red			4		1
silver red					2
rich red					2
pink					
tangerine		1			
yellow red				5	
dark red			4		
golden yellow		7			
greenish yellow	1	4	5		
soil yellow		5		5	
sandalwood yellow		4	5	1	
light yellow		9			
blackish brown			7	3	
reddish brown		8	2		
pale pinkish purple	2				3
pale purple	2				4
dark purple	4				1
dark reddish brown		5		3	1
dark brownish purple	1			4	
greenish gray	4			4	
iron oxide gray	2			6	
blackish blue	6			4	
dark brown			5		
light gray				5	

magenta	vermilion	cinnabar	azurite	malachite green	white powder	primary color / color mixing ratio / mixed color
						grass green
						dark green
						light green
						yellow green
						blackish green
						bright green
				5		fresh green
						glossy dark green
			5	5		rich green
						charming autumn green
	5					golden red
1					4	flesh red
	4				4	silver red
2		6				rich red
4					6	pink
	5	4				tangerine
		5				yellow red
		6				dark red
	3					golden yellow
						greenish yellow
						soil yellow
						sandalwood yellow
	1					light yellow
						blackish brown
						reddish brown
3					2	pale pinkish purple
4						pale purple
5						dark purple
1						dark reddish brown
5						dark brownish purple
					2	greenish gray
					2	iron oxide gray
						blackish blue
			5			dark brown
					5	light gray

Notes

① *Xianzhang* is a seal that painters use to decorate their paintings. The brevity of the wording carved in such a seal summarizes a painter's outlook on life and art, such as "Writing and painting should be imbued with the spirit of the times"and"Learn from the hard-working oxen."

② *Qiyun shengdong* refers to the artistic concept and imagery in writing and painting.

③ *Jianbi* (literally,seeing the traces of the brush movement) is an artistic concept in traditional Chinese painting, similar to the brushstroke styles of oil painting.

④ *Sumo* means the ink residue from the previous painting, which cannot be reused in painting because its fine glue granules tend to tangle up the brush hair.

Exercises

1) Traditional Chinese painting pays great attention to brush and ink techniques. Do you understand the theory about the three brush techniques and the "five ink shades"? Practice these skills on *xuan* paper with a brush.

2) Traditional Chinese painting is particular about the ink techniques, that is, splashing, dual inking and multiple inking. Practice these three techniques according to Illustration 20.

第五课　梅的画法

本课教授梅从主干、出枝到开花的作画步骤和运笔、用墨的方法。

梅，早春开花，是中国人民喜爱的花。它不怕严寒，越寒冷花开得越艳丽。它与下文的竹和荷花，都被历代的诗人和画家作为人品的写照——歌颂那些不怕困难、追求光明的人。

一、工具和材料

叶筋笔、中白云笔和大提笔各一支。墨汁。宣纸。国画色：曙红、胭脂、石绿。调色盘六个（其中两个为画红梅专用）、笔洗等。

二、画梅先学画梅花（图21）

画梅花先学圈花法，这是基础。此法适宜画白梅。

图21（1）A 和 B 是全开的梅花的正面和侧面各个部位的名称：①花瓣，②花心，③花须，④花蕊，⑤花蒂。

图21（2）是正面的梅花，分为五瓣。画时用叶筋笔蘸淡墨，中锋用笔，按图所示顺序画成花形；待墨色稍干，仍用叶筋笔蘸浓墨，中锋用笔画花心、花须，点花蕊和花蒂。

图21（3）花须是花心长出的细长的须子，画6～7根，在末端点蕊。点时不用一根对着一根地点，不要太规则，以"活"为好。

图21（4）是花蒂的画法。每朵花五个蒂。花蒂点在两瓣中间。现实的花蒂是 ♨，写意画概括为 ◡，好像汉字书法在左右相对的两点，这是侧面花朵的花蒂的画法（图22）；背面就要视其

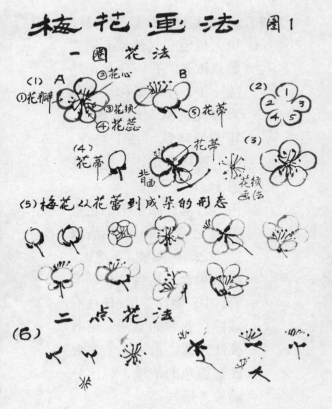

图21　梅花画法

具体方向点4～5点了。花蒂要随着花开的方向点，不能随便乱点。

图21（5）是梅花从开出花蕾到长成花朵的各种形态，供习作者参考。

其次是点花法，如图21（6）。此法是圈花法的提高，适宜画红梅。

画红色的花要用干净的笔和调色碟，画出来的花才鲜艳。用中白云笔先将曙红调少许水蘸至笔根部，再用笔尖蘸少许胭脂，一笔按下稍作圆形转动成一花瓣，画成花形后，待色稍干，用叶筋笔蘸浓墨点花心和花蒂。

三、范画《报春来》习作步骤（图23～25）

1. 用泼墨法画主干和枝（图23）

1) 用大提笔吸足淡墨，笔尖蘸点浓墨，在调色盘中略按一下，让浓墨和淡墨稍为渗化，从左向上落笔，转弯处略顿，往下斜行，中、侧锋并用，一笔完成主干。

2) 用兰竹笔在画主干的色盘中吸足余墨，笔尖蘸浓墨，按顺序画枝。运笔时，拇指和食指适当地转动笔管，中、侧锋并用，让枝有屈曲、苍劲的笔意。画时要注意留空白画花，并要注意墨色的浓淡，以区分前枝、后枝。

现实　　　　写意

图 22

图 23　画主干和枝

图 24　画花

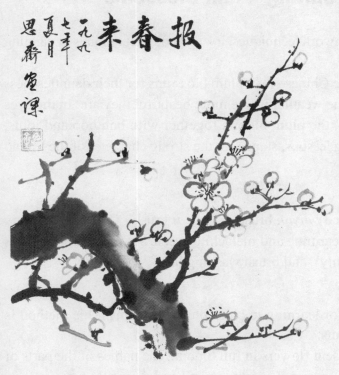

报春来

一九
九七
年月
夏
思齐笔课

图25　《报春来》

2. 画花（图24）

用叶筋笔蘸淡墨圈花。按图的顺序圈写。先圈正面的1号花，这是全图的中心。其余各朵或正向，或侧向，或相对，或相背，或聚或散，富有变化，形成一个主次分明的画面。

3. 增添笔墨，完成全图（图25）

1) 用叶筋笔蘸浓墨点花心和花蒂。仍用叶筋笔，洗净后蘸石绿（2分石绿加8分水）圈花朵外轮廓，衬出白色。

2) 用兰竹笔蘸浓墨点枝干上的梅苔，增强画面的韵律感。

3) 题款、签名、盖章。一幅《报春来》的习作就完成了。这是白梅的画法。如将梅花按点梅法画，就是一幅红梅图了。

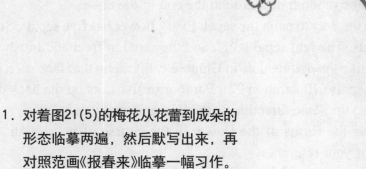

练习

1. 对着图21(5)的梅花从花蕾到成朵的形态临摹两遍，然后默写出来，再对照范画《报春来》临摹一幅习作。

2. 图26是一幅未完成的梅花图。请你给添枝、加花、题款，使它成为一幅完整的中国画。

图26　练习图

Lesson Five　Painting Plum Blossoms

This lesson deals with the steps, brushwork techniques, ink and color techniques in painting plum blossoms.

Plum trees bloom in early spring. The Chinese love plum blossoms for their dauntlessness against cold winter. In fact, the colder the weather is, the more beautiful they are. In the eyes of poets and painters through the ages, the plum bloom, together with bamboo and lotus, which will be dealt with in the following lessons, stands for the strong character of those who fear no adversity and search after truth.

1. Tools and materials

Prepare a *yejin* brush, a medium-sized *baiyun* brush, a large *ti* brush, Chinese ink, *xuan* paper, Chinese pigments of bright red, carmine and malachite green, six color-mixing trays (two for painting red plum blossoms only), and brush washing jars.

2. Techniques (Illustration 21)

Outlining the contours is the basis for learning to paint plum blossoms. This method is suitable for painting white plum blossoms.

1) In Illustration 21 (1), A and B present flowers in full bloom. The names of the parts of the flower are: ① petal, ② pith, ③ tassel, ④ stamen/pistil and ⑤ sepal.

2) Illustration 21 (2) is a flower with five petals. Dip a *yejin* brush in light ink and use it to paint the flower with the *zhongfeng* method according to the steps shown in the illustration. When the ink dries a little, paint the pith, the tassel, the stamen and the sepal with the *zhongfeng* method, using the same brush after tipping it with thick ink.

3) Illustration 21 (3) shows how to paint the tassel, which has six or a seven stems growing out from the pith. Put some random dots around the end of the tassel.

4) Illustration 21 (4) shows the way to paint the sepal. Every flower has five sepals. Stipple the sepals between petals. The real sepal is , and the sepal in freehand brush is , which looks very much like the double dots in Chinese calligraphy that face each other to indicate the sides of sepals (Illustration 22). Put four or five dots on the back of the sepals, which should face the same direction as the flower does.

5) Illustration 21 (5) shows the forms of the flower in the course of its growth, from budding to blooming, for your reference.

6) The other technigue of painting plum blossoms is stippling, which is shown in Illustration 21 (6). Stippling is more demanding than outlining for painting red plum blossoms.

Clean brushes and color-mixing trays result in bright-colored red plum blossoms. First douse the head of the medium-sized *baiyun* brush with bright red color which has been mixed with a little water, and then put a little carmine color on the brush tip. Set the brush to paper, and whirl it slightly to produce a petal. After five petals have been painted and the color becomes slightly dry, use the *yejin* brush with thick black ink to stipple the pith and the sepals.

3. Steps in painting *Spring Is Coming* (Illustrations 23 to 25)

Painting the main branch and the twigs with the ink-splashing (*pomofa*) technique (Illustration 23)

1) Fill the large *ti* brush with light ink and put a little thick ink on its tip, and let these two shades of ink mix by slightly pressing the brush in a color-mixing tray . Apply the brush to paper upward to the right, press it slightly for a pause, and then turn the brush downward using the *zhongfeng* and *cefeng* methods. You should paint the main branch at one stroke.

2) Fill the *lanzhu* brush with the ink left in the color-mixing tray and put a little thick ink on the tip. Paint the twigs according to the order shown in the illustration. When wielding the brush, turn the shaft with the thumb and the forefinger properly, and use both *zhongfeng* and *cefeng* methods at the same time. In this way, the twigs will look curved, sturdy and vigorous. Make sure to leave some space for flowers, and be mindful of the thickness of the ink so that the front twigs and the back ones can be distinguished.

Painting the flowers (Illustration 24)

Use the *yejin* brush with light ink to draw the flowers according to the order shown in the illustration. Draw the flowers in the middle first. When drawing the other flowers, let them face different directions — frontward, sideways, backward, or opposite each other — and let them be in clusters or scattered, so that the entire composition will come alive with plenty of delightful changes, with the main subject in relief.

Finishing touch (Illustration 25)

1) Use the *yejin* brush with thick ink to stipple the piths and the sepals. Wash the brush clean and dip it in light malachite green (malachite green mixed with water at the rate of 2 to 8) to draw the contours of the flowers to set off their white color.

2) Stipple the mosses with the *lanzhu* brush and thick ink to induce a rhythmic touch.

3) After inscribing, signing and sealing, the painting *Spring Is Coming* will be accomplished. The steps mentioned above are used for painting white plum blossoms. If the flowers are painted with the stippling method and red color, it will make a red-plum-blossom painting.

Exercises

1) Copy twice plum blossoms from buds to flowers according to the steps described in Illustration 21 (5), and then paint without looking at the model. After that, paint a copy of *Spring Is Coming.*

2) Illustration 26 presents an unfinished plum painting. Add twigs, flowers and inscriptions to complete it.

中国书画 ABC

第六课　竹的画法

本课教授墨竹的作画步骤和运笔、用墨的方法。

竹，终年翠绿，竿圆枝劲叶美，是历代文人画家喜欢赋诗作画的题材。

中国画以墨竹最具特色。其用笔与书法一样。画竹叶如楷书的"撇画"，故称为"撇叶"。画竹竿如写篆书，都是以中锋用笔。画竹枝如写草书。因此，画竹同书法的关系十分密切。

一、工具和材料

画墨竹要备大兰竹笔和叶筋笔各一支，调色盘三个，都要洗干净。笔洗盛足清水。墨要新磨的，或刚从罐里倒出来的书画墨汁。调好淡墨，份量要多些，浓墨适量。各盛于调色盘中，另一个调色盘为调色之用。旧报纸数张，夹江宣纸等。

二、画墨竹要理解竹叶、竹竿和竹笋的画法

可分为三个阶段练习。懂得其造型和运笔方法了，再将这三者合成——画一幅完整的墨竹习作。

1. 竹叶的画法（图27）

初学画竹叶，宜用大兰竹笔蘸墨在废纸（如旧报纸）上反复练习。

画竹叶，前人已整理出一套程式，式样颇多。为了便于学习，拟教授"四字画竹叶法"，较易掌握。"四字画竹叶法"就是写（画）"一"、"人"、"个"、"介"四个字，要求变形。画竹叶有垂叶和仰叶二种方法。垂叶下垂如A，表现老叶和经受风吹雨打的叶。仰叶挺拔向上，如B，表现嫩叶，春天的竹叶。垂叶和仰叶不能在同一幅画中出现，以保持画面格调的统一。郑板桥的墨竹，在满幅垂叶中，偶现几枝仰叶，是作为点缀的。由于他精湛的笔墨技巧，画面效果仍很协调。画竹叶是中、侧锋用笔。垂叶一笔往下斜撇；仰叶一笔向上斜撇。这个"四字画竹叶法"除

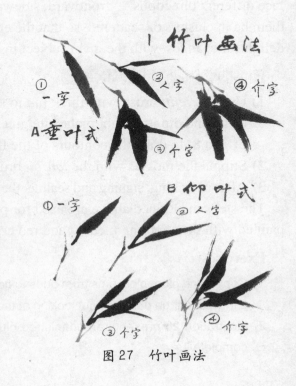

图 27　竹叶画法

"一"字外，其余三个字实际上就是三组竹叶的形态。每组竹叶中，每片竹叶都不要形态相同。如"个"字组，第一笔是正面的叶，第二笔是大侧面的叶，第三笔稍细，为侧面的叶。初学者可参照范图，用兰竹笔蘸墨，悬肘，在旧报纸上反复练习。

懂得了这"四字画竹叶法"，就可以用这四个图形进行组合，按照疏密结合的构图方法，画出变化多样的画面来。

2. 竹竿的画法（图28）

画竹竿要用泼墨法，作画时一次性地用墨色完成干、湿、浓、淡的墨彩效果。作画步骤如下（图28-1）：

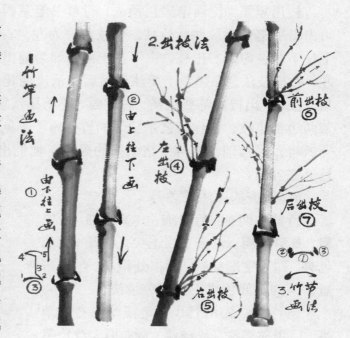

图28 竹竿和枝的画法

1) 用大兰竹笔吸足淡墨。然后用手指把笔头捻扁，在笔头一边抹浓墨，自下向上行，逆锋落笔，中锋行笔，一笔一节往上画。起笔时由于墨水较多，行笔要快些，逐步放慢。这时，由于墨色渐少，出现"飞白"①效果。这样画成的竹竿，一边灰色，另一边黑色，中间自然渗化成过渡色，色调十分柔和，好像竹竿一边受光，另一边背光，富有立体感。如要表现竹竿中间受光，可用上述方法，在笔头两边抹墨，画出来的竹竿成两边黑，中间灰的效果，此法要反复练习，才出效果。

2) 竹竿是一节一节往上长的，节与节之间稍凸出，中间修长。运笔时，每节应逆锋起笔，先左后右稍摆动，中锋上行至竹节处顿笔，左右稍摆动。共5个动作，如图28-1③。节与节之间要留一空白线。

3) 竹竿画成后，待墨色稍干，用叶筋笔蘸浓墨在空白线处画竹节。此是点睛之笔，要认真用笔。方法如图28-3。第一笔，逆锋起笔，按、提、按三个动作画中间一笔，然后点两点，要有呼应，这样用笔才活泼。如书法的草书"八"字，有笔断意连的笔意。

4) 竹竿还可以自上往下画（逆锋运笔），也可从左向右、从右向左画。但初学者还是踏踏实实地学好由下往上画的笔法。画熟了，怎么画都行。

5) 画竹竿应注意的问题：

● 两竿并排要分前后，节不要平行。
● 三竿并排距离不能相等。
● 三竿交叉不能成一点。
● 一竿各节不能一样长短。

3．出枝法（图28－2）

枝用重墨（比画竿墨色稍浓）行草书笔意画出，趁湿用小笔浓墨点竹节。初学者可用楷书笔意略放些画竹枝。出枝可分为左、右、前、后方向。图中④为左出枝，由上往下画；⑤为右出枝，由下往上画；⑥为前出枝，画法同⑤；⑦为后出枝，画法如左、右出枝法。在墨色上要注意前后的浓淡变化。枝的交错不要出现米字或井字等形象。总之，出枝用笔要流畅，忌直画，要稍具弧型，以表现竹枝的韧性。现实的竹，每节两边都出枝，但作为艺术化了的竹，为了避免对称、呆板，不要两边都出枝。细读郑板桥、吴昌硕、董寿平诸名家的墨竹，他们出枝都很讲究，不但一节只出一边枝，且形态各异。

4．竹笋的画法（图29）

竹笋有两种：竹竿细，其笋则细；竹竿粗，其笋必粗。竹笋下粗上尖。竹箨②层层包裹，作人字形交错。近根处距长，越上越短。笋的上部色重，越下色越淡。

画竹笋，先用HB铅笔或淡墨打好草稿，后用破墨法（浓破淡）画，用大兰竹笔蘸重墨或淡墨，笔头蘸点浓墨，自上往下画竹箨，一笔画完。忌对称呆板。待墨色稍干，用叶筋笔蘸浓墨画箨脉和点斑纹。斑纹深浅要与箨的墨色协调。

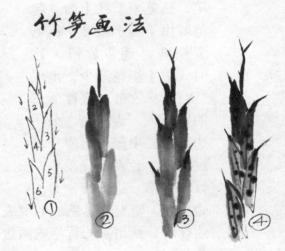

图29　竹笋画法

三、范画《劲竹凌霄》（图30）习作步骤（泼墨法）

1．先画竹竿、画节、出枝、布叶。然后补小竿，在竹叶空间补枝。主要部分完成后，画竹笋，最后题款、签名、盖章。

2．开笔的两枝竹竿，左边斜立，右边弯出。画左竿不要画直，才不会造成画面呆板。这是关键的第一笔，一定要画好，以增强习作信心。

3．以淡墨补后面之叶，要注意墨色的浓淡交错，营造空间感。每笔蘸墨色，一笔画完，自然会出现先浓后淡效果。最忌画一两片叶后就再蘸墨色画新叶。那样，墨色必然平淡无奇。

4. 大体完成后，要小心收拾。对竹叶的空隙，适当补枝；小竿末梢画仰叶。别看这淡淡的几笔，却给画面增添无限生气，故应小心为之！

注释

① 飞白：书画运笔时，由于墨色渐少，或行笔稍快，在宣纸上出现一丝丝白线或色块，与周围的色调十分谐调，这是很难得的笔墨！如画竹竿，可表现受光或斑点。图22的竹竿，就可见飞白笔意。

② 竹箨(tuò)：竹笋上一片一片的皮。

图30　《劲竹凌霄》

练习

1. 对照图27、图28和图29的竹叶、竹竿和竹笋的图例，临摹两遍，然后默画出来。
2. 运用"四字画竹叶法"画出一组好看的竹叶来。然后对照范画《劲竹凌霄》，临摹一幅习作。

Lesson Six　Painting Bamboo

This lesson deals with the steps and brush-wielding and ink-using techniques in painting bamboo. With round poles, sturdy twigs and pretty leaves, the evergreen bamboo is a favorite for poets and painters through the ages.

Traditional Chinese painting is famous for depictions of bamboo in black ink, using the same brush-wielding techniques as in calligraphy. Bamboo leaves are painted in the manner of the "left-falling" stroke (*pie*) for regular script; hence the term "*pie* leaves." Bamboo poles are painted the way seal characters are written with the *zhongfeng* technique, while the twigs are painted freehand, which resembles the cursive hand (*caoshu*) in calligraphy. Therefore, painting bamboo and writing Chinese characters are closely related in techniques.

1. Tools and materials

Prepare a large *lanzhu* brush and a *yejin* brush, three color-mixing trays and brush-washing jars, all clean for use. Fill the jar with clear water. Mix the ink, newly ground or fresh from the bottle, with water on one tray to prepare enough light ink. Pour some thick ink on another tray, and leave the third one for mixing colors. Prepare some old newspapers and *jiajiang xuan* paper too.

2. Techniques for painting bamboo leaves, poles and shoots

The painting of bamboo is practiced in three steps. When you have grasped the structure of each step and the skills needed, you can combine them to produce a complete bamboo painting in black ink.

Painting bamboo leaves (Illustration 27)

It is advisable for beginners to practice on scrap newspaper with a large *lanzhu* brush. Artists of the past created a series of ways to paint bamboo leaves. To make it easy for students to learn, the author uses the "four-character" method, that is, painting bamboo leaves the way one writes the Chinese characters一,人,个 and 介. Of course, you have to change their shapes a little. There are two kinds of bamboo leaves: the up-facing and the down-facing. The down-facing leaves shown in Illustration 21A are old or weather-beaten ones, while the up-facing leaves shown in Illustration 21B are tender ones often seen in spring bamboo. The two kinds of leaves must not appear in the same painting to keep a unified style. In the bamboo paintings by Zheng Banqiao, clusters of down-facing leaves are embellished with a few up-facing ones, but his works still look harmonious thanks to his consummate skills in brushwork and ink coloring. The leaves are depicted using the *zhongfeng* and *cefeng* techniques. Bringing the brush downward to the left at one stroke produces a down-facing leaf, and an upward brush stroke results in an up-facing leaf. Each leaf in a cluster should be in a different shape. For instance, in the 个 cluster, the first stroke is a leaf in its front, the second one in its broad side and the third one in its thin side. Beginners can refer to the model painting and practice repeatedly on used newspapers by wielding a *lanzhu* brush in the elbow-suspending way.

Having mastered the "four-character" leaf-painting method, you can combine the four shapes of leaf clusters to produce a variety of scenes by means of variegated spacing and density.

Painting bamboo poles (Illustration 28)

Use the the ink-splashing method to paint the bamboo pole. It should be done to show the visual effect of dry and wet, light and thick ink. The steps are as follows (Illustration 28-1):

1) Saturate the large *lanzhu* brush with light ink, press the tip with your fingers to make it flat and take some thick ink on one side of the tip. Use the *nifeng* method to start at the bottom of the paper and the *zhongfeng* method to move the brush upward step by step. Start quickly because the brush is full of ink, and then slow down gradually to produce a desired *feibai* effect (Note ①). Bamboo poles painted this way are gray at one side and black at the other with a subtle interim color in the middle. It looks three-dimensional,

as if the bamboo were lit on one side and dark on the other side. If you want to paint a bamboo pole lit on the middle, just put thick ink at both sides of the flattened brush tip, and you will produce a pole with the two sides black and the middle gray. You should practice a lot to master the technique.

2) Bamboo grows upward section by section with projecting joints in between. The sections are long and slim. Start the brush using the *nifeng* method for every section, shake it slightly from left to right, move the brush up in the *zhongfeng* method, pause and shake it again in the same way at the next joint. These five movements together complete one bamboo section (Illustration 28-1 ③). Leave a blank line between the sections.

3) After the ink dries a little, draw the joints in thick ink with a *yejin* brush at the blank. This is the finishing touch, so do it seriously. The steps (Illustration 28-3) are: first, begin using the *nifeng* method; second, draw the middle line using the *an, ti*, and *an* methods; and third, make two dots that face each other to appear lively and seem at once separated and connected, like the Chinese character 八 in the cursive hand style (*caoshu*).

4) Bamboo poles can also be painted from top to bottom (using the *nifeng* method), from left to right, and from right to left. But for beginners, it is better to practice from bottom to top. Once you have mastered the basic skills, you can paint the poles as you please.

5) Some points of attention:

   ● Two bamboo poles standing abreast should be arranged one in front and the other behind, with their joints at different levels.

   ● Three bamboo poles standing in a row should not be painted at equal intervals.

   ● Avoid painting three bamboo poles that cross each other at one point.

   ● Sections in one pole should differ in length.

Painting bamboo twigs (Illustration 28-2)

Use heavy ink (a little darker than that for the poles) and the freehand technique to paint bamboo twigs. While the ink is still wet, dot the joints in thick ink with a small brush. Beginners can paint the twigs the way they write Chinese characters in regular script, only a little bit more free with the brush movement. The twigs can point in all directions.

Illustration 28 ④ shows a pole branching to the left, which is wrought by moving the brush downward to the left; in Illustration 28⑤ the pole branches to the right, which is created by moving the brush upward to the right; in Illustration 28⑥ the pole branching to the front is created with the same brush movement in ⑤; and Illustration 28 ⑦ shows the pole branching to the back, which is wrought with the same skills as in ④ and ⑤. Pay attention to the thickness of the ink used to paint the twigs of different locations. Avoid painting them in the shape of 米 or 井. In short, twigs should be painted smoothly and bend slightly to show their resilience. Real bamboo branches out at both sides of the joint, but the artistic bamboo in paintings does not, in order to avoid symmetry and dullness. By studying the bamboo paintings by famous artists like Zheng Banqiao, Wu Changshuo and Dong Shouping, you will notice that the twigs at each joint branch out at one side but they come in a variety of postures and shapes.

Painting bamboo shoots (Illustration 29)

Bamboo shoots are of two kinds: thin poles with thin shoots, and thick poles with thick shoots. But all of them are thick at bottom and thin at top, and wrapped in layer upon layer of sheaths (note ②:*zhutuo*) in herringbone crossing. A bamboo shoots consists of sections that are long at bottom but get shorter and shorter upward; its color is darker at the top but becomes lighter and lighter downward.

Use a pencil with a HB hardness outline or draw the contours of a bamboo shoot. It is better to use the dual-inking method (*pomofa* or *nongpodan*) to paint bamboo shoots. First dip a large *lanzhu* brush in heavy ink or light ink and take a little thick ink on the tip, then move it downward and finish each sheath at one stroke. Avoid symmetry and dullness. Wait a while and then use a *yejin* brush with thick ink to paint the sheaths and the stripes on the sheaths. The strips should be in harmony with the sheaths in color.

3. Steps for painting *Vigorous Bamboo* (Illustration 30)

1) First, paint the bamboo poles, joints, twigs and leaves; second, the small poles and add twigs among the leaves; third, the bamboo shoots. Finally, write inscriptions, sign your name, and stamp your seal.

2) Paint the two bamboo poles with one standing on the left and the other bending to the right. Avoid painting the poles paralleled to the vertical side of the paper. This is an important step. Do it well, and you will be confident of what you are doing.

3) Add the leaves in light ink at the background, paying attention to different shades of the ink to yield a sense of space. When adding each cluster of leaves to a pole, dip the brush in ink only once, so that the leaves will have different hues. Avoid dipping the brush in ink again after adding a couple of leaves; otherwise the hues will look dull.

4) Put the finishing touches where it counts, such as a few twigs among leaves, or some up-facing leaves at the end of slim twigs, to bring the painting to life. Such touches are very important, so you have got to be careful about them.

Notes

① *Feibai* is a style of calligraphy or painting, characterized by hollow strokes done with a half-dry brush or with a light touch. It is a special style, like white threads or color patches that are harmonious with the surrounding colors. For example, bamboo poles painted in this manner can display their bright side and the speckles on them. See the effect of *feibai* in Illustration 22.

② *Zhutuo* means sheaths of bamboo shoots.

Exercises

1) Copy twice the bamboo leaves, poles and shoots after Illustration 27 to 29. Then paint them from memory.

2) Paint bamboo leaves using the "four-character" method, and then paint a copy of *Vigorous Bamboo*.

第七课　荷花的画法

本课教授荷花、荷叶和荷梗的作画步骤以及运笔、用墨、着色等方法。

荷花，又名莲花，是历来诗人画家喜欢吟画的题材。他们把荷花作为一个"出淤泥而不染"的高尚形象来颂扬。夏天荷花盛开，红花、白花映着翠绿的荷叶，在湖边、在池塘，迎风吐艳，给观赏者以清新愉快的凉意！

一、工具和材料

大提笔、大兰竹笔、中白云笔、叶筋笔和底纹笔各一支。调色盘五个(其中两个是染红色专用盘)，笔洗盛足清水。旧报纸和夹江宣纸等。墨汁、胭脂、曙红、花青、藤黄、赭石、白色等中国画颜料。调好淡墨，分量要多些，浓墨适量，各盛于调色盘中。

二、画荷花前要理解花、花苞、荷叶、花梗、叶梗及点缀物蜻蜓等要素的画法，才能够画成一幅完整的习作

同学们可对照图31，反复练习，掌握上述各部分的造型和运笔方法，画起习作来就得心应手了。

1. **画荷花的技法**(图31)　荷花是画面的眼睛，一定要画得美丽动人。因此，必须了解荷花的结构。荷花的中心是莲蓬(A)，连接花梗(B)。莲蓬下边长花蕊(C)。花蕊与花梗交接处长出一片一片的花瓣(D)，它们呈放射状向四面绽开。懂得这个规律，画荷花就心中有数了。画花瓣先从前面画起，依次画两边的侧瓣，再画对面的花瓣，最后完成整个花型。每瓣互不雷同——注意花瓣的透视变化。读者可参考"莲花透视图"(图31-1)进行练习。常画的荷花有白荷花和红荷花二种。

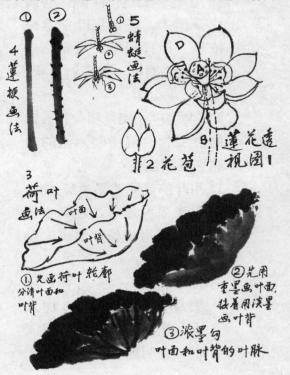

图 31　荷花画法

白荷花画法　用叶筋笔蘸淡墨勾勒花瓣（勾勒顺序如上文）。墨色干后，以淡草绿圈染花瓣外圈，托出白色。用重墨画花蕊。

红荷花画法　用叶筋笔蘸胭脂勾勒花瓣，待干后，以中白云笔蘸重曙红（曙红加一点水）染花瓣，一笔一笔自上往下染，下笔重，收笔轻，形成上深下淡色调。花瓣背面深些，正面淡些。半干时，用叶筋笔蘸曙红，笔头调少许胭脂勾背面花瓣的花纹络，或不勾。胭脂调少许墨点花蕊，莲蓬用赭墨（赭加一点墨）勾勒，待干后，上面染淡黄（藤黄加一点白色），下面染赭色。初学者可参看范画（图32）。

2. 花苞画法　与花的画法相同。

3. 荷叶画法　中国画画荷叶、叶梗和花梗多用墨色，以破墨法画（参考"竹竿画法"）。荷叶是侧面叶。先打好轮廓草稿，分清叶面和叶背，如图31-3①。用大提笔蘸重墨，笔头点浓墨画叶面，用笔要表现荷叶轮廓美和轻盈的质感。一笔接一笔画，一气呵成。要看出笔法，如油画的笔触一样；紧接着，以淡墨画叶背，用笔自上而下，成弧形，也要见笔，如图31-3②。墨色稍干，用叶筋笔蘸浓墨画正、背面叶的叶脉，如图31-3③。

4. 花梗和叶梗画法　都以大兰竹笔蘸淡墨，笔头点浓墨，中锋用笔，自上往下一笔画成，稍干，趁湿用叶筋笔蘸浓墨，中锋用笔，点刺。点刺忌两点对称，要成错落状，图31-4①②。

5. 蜻蜓画法　蜻蜓是画荷花最佳的点缀物，可增强画面的动感。其画法是：

1）用叶筋笔蘸浓墨画身体；

2）以淡墨画翅膀，趁湿在翅膀中间用浓墨点墨斑，以重墨画足；

3）待干，用石绿染身体；用染身体的石绿，再加点水，用笔轻抹翅膀，以表现其透明感（图31-5）。

图32　《红莲出水分外娇》

三、范画《红莲出水分外娇》(图33)习作步骤

1. 先画荷花，次画荷叶，再画花梗和叶梗。主要部分完成后，补画花苞、花梗，墨色干后，用浓墨和淡墨画莘草。画蜻蜓。染水。然后，题款、签名、盖章。

2. 此图以一花、一苞、一叶、数笔莘草，表现一种恬静的意境。荷花微仰，花梗轻斜，似有微风轻轻吹来，一只蜻蜓扑向荷花，似与花对话。而红花与墨叶的强烈对比，使红花显得更加突出，更加娇艳。这就是中国画中的诗情画意。

3. 几枝莘草，虽是点缀，却很不好画。先用手指在纸上按出草稿(不要用铅笔打草稿，以保持画面干净)，看好了，一笔一条，中锋用笔撇出。

4. 染水很重要。染不好，前功尽弃！墨色全干后，作"背染"①，目的是使层次深远。将画纸翻过来，下面最好垫一张宣纸(用完晾干，下次再用)，用大提笔或底纹笔蘸清水刷湿，用一张画过的宣纸盖在上面吸去多余水分。用大提笔或底纹笔蘸淡墨青(花青加一点墨再加水)，自下往上，一笔一笔横染过荷叶后，逐渐淡化至红花下部。留出上面一片空白，给人以天和水的联想。初学染法，应由淡到深。若不够理想，就趁湿加深，但不要全染，用大提笔横扫几笔即可，既增加画面的层次，又使水色有变化。

图33　荷花照片

注释

① 背染：又称反衬，是染的一种技法。染时，在纸的后面染上需要的颜色，可增强画面的空间感。

练习

1. 对照图31的图例，临摹两遍，然后对照范画《红莲出水分外娇》，临摹一幅习作。

2. 参考图33的荷花照片，运用已学过的画荷花的笔法，画一幅荷花习作。

Lesson Seven   Painting Lotus

This lesson deals with the brushwork, inking and coloring techniques and steps for painting the flowers, leaves and stalks of lotus.

The lotus flower, also called water lily, is a favorite subject for poets and painters through the ages. The lotus grows in mud but emerges unstained. In summer, red and white lotus flowers come in full bloom at lakesides and in ponds, amidst the dense foliage of green leaves, and sway in a gentle breeze, forming a scene that is most refreshing to visitors.

1. Tools and materials

A large *ti* brush, a large *lanzhu* brush, a medium-sized *baiyun* brush, a *yejin* brush, a broad brush, five color-mixing trays (two of them are only for red), brush-washing jars filled with clear water, some used newspapers and *jiajiangxuan* paper. Pigments: ink, carmine, eosine, cyanine, gamboge, ochre and Chinese white. Prepare enough light ink and a proper amount of thick ink, and put them in different trays.

2. To paint the lotus, one has to know its structure

A painted lotus consists of the flower, the bud, the leaf, the flower stalk, the leaf stalk and usually, the dragonfly as an ornament. One must first learn how to paint each of these items. Students can practice by following Illustration 31.

Painting lotus flowers (Illustration 31)

The flower is considered to be the "eye" of a lotus painting and must be painted beautifully and attractively. To achieve the purpose, you must know its structure: (A) the seedpod in the center; (B) the flower stalk, connected to the seedpod; (C) the stamen, which is beneath the seedpod; (D) the petals, which grow out of the joint of the stamen and the stalk, and radiate in four directions. Having this in mind, you should paint the front petals first, the two side ones, and then the opposite ones to complete the flower. Pay attention to the perspective shapes of the petals and paint them clearly. Refer to the lotus flower perspective (Illustration 31-1) and practice after it.

Lotus flowers are usually red and white in paintings.

1) Painting white lotus flowers. Sketch the contours of the petals using a *yejin* brush in light ink according to the steps mentioned above. When the ink dries, color the edges of the petals with a light green to contrast the white, and then paint the stamen in heavy ink.

2) Painting red lotus flowers. Sketch the contours of the petals using a *yejin* brush in

carmine color. When the pigment dries, use a *baiyun* brush to color the petals with heavy eosine mixed with a little water, stroke by stroke from top downwards. Start the stroke with a little strength and end it gently to make the color heavy at the upper part and light at the lower part. The back of a petal should be darker than its front. When the color is half dry, dip a *yejin* brush in eosine with a little carmine on the tip to draw the streaks on the back of the petals, or you may choose not to draw them. Color the stamen with carmine mixed with a little ink. Draw the seedpod with brown color mixed with a little ink. When the ink is dry, apply light yellow (gamboge mixed with a little white) to the upper part and brown to the lower part. Refer to Illustration 32.

Painting the bud

Similar to painting the flower.

Painting the lotus leaf

Dual-inking method (*pomofa*) is commonly used in doing the lotus leaf, the leaf stalk and the flower stalk in traditional Chinese painting (refer to the techniques and steps for painting the bamboo). Here let us learn how to draw a leaf on its side. First, sketch the contour of the leaf blade with a clear distinction of its front and back (Illustration 31-3①). Second, use the large *ti* brush after dipping it in heavy ink with a little thick ink on its tip to paint the leaf front to make it look gentle and lovely. Paint it stroke by stroke with only one ink dipping and with the brush-moving traces identified on the paper like those in oil painting. Third, paint with light ink the leaf back from top downward in an arc while leaving the brush's traces on the paper (Illustration 31-3②). Finally, when the ink dries a little, paint the leaf veins in thick ink on both sides with a *yejin* brush (Illustration 31-3 ③).

Painting flower and leaf stalks

Both stalks are painted with the large *lanzhu* brush dipped in light ink and a little thick ink on the tip. Wield the brush with the *zhongfeng* method from top downward and paint the stalk at one stroke. When the ink is a little dry, dot the thorns in thick ink with the *yejin* brush using the *zhongfeng* method. Avoid symmetry and dot them at random (Illustration 31-4 ① ②).

Painting the dragonfly

The dragonfly is the best ornament to a lotus painting in that it brings the entire composition to life. First, draw the body in thick ink with the *yejin* brush; second, draw the wings in light ink and put some dots in thick ink on them when they are still wet, and draw the feet in heavy ink; third, when the ink is dry, color the body malachite green. Finally, color the wings gently with malachite green mixed with some water to bring a transparent effect

(Illustration 31-5).

3. Steps in painting *Charming Red Lotus Coming out of Water* (Illustration 32)

1) First, paint the flower, leaf and stalks. Add the bud and its little stalk. When the ink is dry, paint the reeds and the dragonfly in thick and light ink, and color the water a pale green. Finally, write the inscription, sign the name and stamp the seal.

2) The painting is composed of a flower, a bud, a leaf and a few reeds, suggesting an artistic conception of tranquility. The flower is facing slightly upward with its stalk slanting a little as if it were swaying in the breeze. A dragonfly is flying towards the flower as if they were talking to each other. The striking contrast between the flower and the leaf in color serves to set off the red flower's delicate beauty. Such a poetic and picturesque scene is characteristic of traditional Chinese painting.

3) It is not easy to paint the reeds though they are only for ornament. First, make a rough sketch of them with your finger nail (avoid using a pencil so as to keep the painting clean), and then draw them with the *zhongfeng* method. Finish each reed at one stroke.

4) Coloring the water is important, too. Your previous efforts would come to nothing if you fail to do this well. When the ink is completely dry, wash-color the water on the back of the paper (Note①: *beiran*) for the purpose of increasing the depth of the scene. Turn the painting over and put it on a piece of *xuan* paper (which can be reused after it is dried by airing), wet it with a large *ti* brush or a broad brush, and blot the extra water with the used *xuan* paper. Dip the brush in light blackish green (cyanine mixed with water and a little ink) and wash-color the water horizontally from bottom up to the lower part of the red flower with a decreasingly light color, leaving the upper part of the painting uncolored to give the impression that the sky is blended with the water. Beginners should start doing this using a lighter color first, so that if you are not happy about the color, you can always increase it while the painting is still moist, but do not color the entire space. Just wield a few strokes horizontally with a large *ti* brush, which can enhance the sense of space and change.

Note

① *Beiran*, or contrasting, is a wash-coloring technique. Wash-coloring the back of the *xuan* paper with the right color can enhance the sense of space.

Exercises

1) Copy twice according to Illustration 31 and then paint a copy of *Charming Red Lotus Coming out of Water*.

2) Study Illustration 33 and do a lotus painting with the techniques and knowledge you have learned in this lesson.

第八课　小鸡的画法

　　本课教授用简练的笔墨画小鸡的步骤和运笔、用墨、着色等方法，并运用已学过的墨竹作衬景，阐述有关中国画构图的知识。

　　小鸡，毛茸茸的饱满躯体，十分惹人喜爱，使人联想到天真活泼的小孩和金色的童年。本课教授用六笔画出小鸡侧面躯体的方法，稍加点画，即成一只侧身仰视的小鸡。举一反三，画鸟类也可参照此法。

一、工具和材料

　　大提笔、大兰竹笔、叶筋笔各一支，调色盘五个。笔洗盛足清水。墨汁。国画色：花青、藤黄、赭石、朱膘等。调好淡墨，分量要多些。浓墨，汁绿（6分花青加3.5分藤黄再加0.5分石绿），各盛于调色盘中，另备1～2个调色盘作调色之用。旧报纸数张和夹江宣纸等。

二、小鸡和蜘蛛画法（图34）

1. 画小鸡步骤（破墨法）

1）用大提笔吸足淡墨，笔头点少许汁绿，在调色盘中按一下，让淡墨与汁绿稍为渗化。中锋行笔写鸡头，转笔画颈，顿笔侧锋往右斜按画腹，好像写一个"乙"字。用笔要有圆味，如图34-1；

2）理顺笔锋，如上步；调色，轻补一笔背部，如图34-2；再理顺笔锋，在腹部后横按一笔画腿，如图34-3；

3）有余色，点尾巴，如图34-3。

4）用叶筋笔蘸朱膘，笔头点赭石，中锋用笔先按后斜拖画嘴。然后画

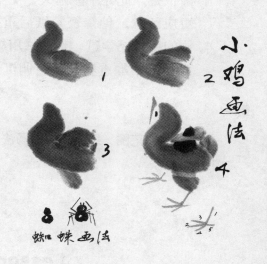

图34　小鸡和蜘蛛的画法

足，步骤如图34-4。用叶筋笔蘸焦墨点睛。这是关键之笔，笔要抹干水分，侧锋竖点，让眼睛成侧视状。不能用圆点。最后用兰竹笔蘸浓墨点翅膀。

2. 蜘蛛画法　用叶筋笔蘸重墨画头、腹，画两个圈，注意不要圈满，要留光

点。接着用浓墨点眼睛，画足。

三、范画《野趣》（图35）习作步骤

1. 习作步骤：先画小鸡，次画竹，第三步以叶筋笔蘸淡墨先画下垂的蜘蛛丝，然后在丝的末端画蜘蛛。最后点墨绿苔点。

2. 此图以小鸡与蜘蛛在竹阴下相遇，表现郊野宁静的意趣，让人联想到天真无邪、充满快乐的金色童年。构图上密下疏，留出大片空白，故意不把背景画满，让小鸡的形象十分突出。右下方疏疏落落的几点苔点，增强了画面的韵律感。

3. 小鸡的造型要反复练习。用笔宜简不宜多，要见笔，以训练笔法的简练。起笔要重按轻拖，留出弧度，作为点睛位置。此处不能画大，更不能画满——初学者用笔往往有此弊病。小腿用笔更应留意。偏锋轻着纸后重按，成为上粗下细的形象。

4. 竹的用笔已学过，色调试用墨绿。用兰竹笔先蘸汁绿，笔头点重墨挥写。绿不要太艳，加重墨是让色调沉着。

图 35　《野趣》

练习

对照图34的范图，练习小鸡的画法，到你认为满意时，对照范画《野趣》，画一幅《小鸡赏梅图》习作。

Lesson Eight　Chicks

This lesson deals with the steps and the basic brushwork, inking and coloring techniques for painting chicks. It also tells something about the composition of traditional Chinese painting by employing bamboo painted in ink as the backgroud.

Chicks, downy and plump, are pleasing to the eye. They are associated with lovely children and golden childhood. In this lesson, you will learn how to paint a chick with only six strokes. With some finishing touches, you can produce the profile of a pretty chick craning its neck to see the sky. Birds can also be painted this way.

1. Tools and materials

A large *ti* brush, a large *lanzhu* brush, a *yejin* brush, five color-mixing trays, brush-washing jars, some used newspapers and *xuan* paper. Pigments: ink, cyanine, gamboge, ochre and vermilion. Fill the jars with clean water, prepare plenty of light ink, some thick ink and jade green colors (6 portions of cyanine, 3.5 portions of gamboge and 0.5 portion of malachite green) in different trays, leaving 1 or 2 trays for mixing colors.

2. Techniques in painting chicks and the ornamental spider (Illustration 34)

Painting the chick (*pomofa*)

1) Saturate the large *ti* brush with light ink, add a little green to the tip, and press it on a tray to let the two colors mix a little. Paint the chick's head using the *zhongfeng* method, turn the brush to paint the neck, pause and press gently while moving downward to the right and using the *cefeng* method to paint the round belly that looks like the Chinese character ㄥ(Illustration34-1).

2) Wash and tidy the brush, mix the colors like the previous step and add one stroke on the chick's back (Illustration34-2). Wash and tidy the brush again, and paint the leg by pressing the brush tip slantwise below the belly (Illustration 34-3).

3) Use the remainder of the color to paint the tail (Illustration 34-3).

4) Dip the *yejin* brush in vermilion and add a little ochre at the tip, press the brush on the paper and move it downward slightly to the left using the *zhongfeng* method to paint the mouth. Paint the feet (Illustration34-4). Use the *yejin* brush to paint the eye; to execute this important finishing touch, you must squeeze water out of the brush and use the *cefeng* method to make a vertical dot instead of a round dot, so that the chick is looking sideways. Finally, paint the wings in thick ink with a *lanzhu* brush.

Painting the spider

Draw two round circles with a *yejin* brush and use heavy ink to produce the head and body of the spider (avoid making two black spots) and dot the eyes and feet with thick ink.

3. Steps in painting *A Funny Scene in the Country* (Illustration 35)

1) First, paint the chick; second, the bamboo; third, the cobweb hanging down the bamboo twigs with a *yejin* brush dipped in light ink; fourth, paint the spider hanging on the end

of the cobweb. Finally, stipple the moss in blackish green.

2) The model painting (Illustration 35) depicts a chick meeting a spider in the shade of a a bamboo cluster. The tranquility of this rural scene evokes the memory of childish innocence. The picture is composed in such a way that the upper part is dense while the lower part is spacious, leaving the chick standing out against the background. A few dots of moss at the right lower corner render a rhythm appeal to the entire composition.

3) Practice painting the chick repeatedly until you are familiar with its composition. It is better to paint it with a few strokes, the traces of which should be identified on the paper. Start the brush movement by pressing it forcefully on the paper, and then make a gentle stroke, leaving a curve where the eye belongs. Avoid painting the chick too large and all black (a mistake beginners often make). In painting the leg, apply the brush gently with the *pianfeng* method, and then press it to produce a leg that is thick at the upper part and thin at the lower part.

4) The brushwork techniques for painting bamboo have been introduced in Lesson Six. The bamboo for this painting is blackish green, a color that is achieved by dipping the *lanzhu* brush in jade green with a little heavy ink at the tip. The green color should not be too bright. The purpose of the additional heavy ink is to add some solidity to the color green.

Exercises

Practice the skills in painting the chick after Illustration 34 again and again until you are satisfied. After that, do a painting entitled *Chick and Plum Blossoms* by patterning after *A Funny Scene in the Country*.

第九课　山水的画法

本课教授山水画的作画步骤和运笔、用墨、着色的方法。

中国山水画有独特的民族风格。它非常讲究笔墨和意境。画家以大自然为师，"搜尽奇峰打草稿"（石涛语），把观察、写生所得印象，糅合自己的学养，重新安排山河，画成比现实景物更美的图画。

这一课教授的山水画，是以中国的名胜——桂林象鼻山为主景，表现宋朝大诗人苏东坡"竹外桃花三两枝，春江水暖鸭先知"的诗意，画题为《春江水暖》。

一、工具和材料

叶筋笔、中兰竹笔、白云笔和大提笔各一支。墨汁、宣纸、已写过的宣纸或面巾纸（试色和吸水之用）。国画色：花青、藤黄、石绿、赭石、朱膘、曙红和白色等。调色盘六个，笔洗等。

二、习作步骤

山水画比较难画，初学者最好先从摹画入手。

1. 摹画稿和勾勒主景象鼻山（图36）

   1）用一张与附录5山水画范画《春江水暖》一样大的宣纸，盖在范画上，用HB铅笔轻轻摹好范画每个部分的大体轮廓，不要太具体，目的是把整幅画的布局定下来。

   2）用叶筋笔（画稍大的习作用中兰竹笔）蘸浓墨，中、侧锋用笔，勾勒好主景象鼻山的墨线。中国画很重视笔墨，要认真运笔和用墨，把物象画好。这是关键的一步。

2. 皴擦和墨染（图37）

   1）用叶筋笔（画稍大的习作用中兰

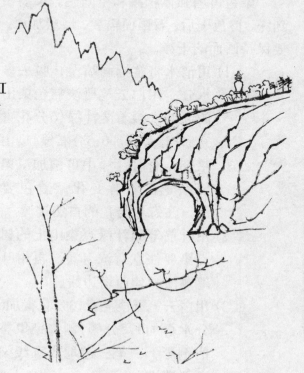

图36　摹画稿和勾勒主景象鼻山

竹笔)蘸重墨(墨和水各一半)皴擦山的暗部，皴(以点的形式)要见笔，可先淡后浓；擦要柔和，不要擦成一团黑，可借鉴素描画法。皴和擦笔头水分宜少，多时可在废宣纸上擦一下，以去余墨。

2) 墨干后，主景部分用清水喷湿，用面巾纸吸去多余水分，用中兰竹笔蘸淡墨(3分墨汁加7分水)染已皴擦过的暗部，增强体积感。然后，用叶筋笔蘸重墨画山上的树干，点树叶，画白塔。画树干和点树叶时要适当加画些淡墨的树干和树叶，以显示树的前后，增强空间感。

图 37　皴擦和墨染

3. 染色(图38)

染色可增强体积感和空间感。染要由浅到深，待色干后，看画面需要，层层加深。染要保持画面的干净。

1) 用清水将整幅画喷湿，吸去多余水分。用白云笔蘸淡赭色染山石的亮部，接着蘸汁绿(6分花青加3.5分藤黄再加0.5分石绿)染山石暗部，有时汁绿中可稍加淡墨，使颜色沉着有变化。着色要灵活，注意色与色的自然过渡。

2) 用叶筋笔蘸汁绿点染山上的树，点染要注意有浓有淡。再用叶筋笔蘸淡赭勾白塔边线。

3) 用白云笔蘸淡墨青(3分花青加6.5分水再加0.5分墨)侧锋染象鼻山的倒影，一笔一道地成直线染，不要填满。

4) 仍用白云笔画远山，颜色比染倒

图 38　染色

影的淡墨青稍淡。两笔一座山，像楷书的"八"字形，线条要稍有变化；趁湿，在山腰处蘸清水作半圆形涂抹，显示云的亮部，使山与白色的画纸自然过渡。

4．加染完成（图39）

1）用淡墨、深汁绿（8分汁绿加2分墨）分别适当地皴擦山的暗部，注意皴、擦时要有疏有密，不要将原来的底色全部盖掉；以墨绿（7分汁绿加3分墨）点苔点，加强山上树丛的立体感。

2）色干后，将画纸翻过来，对背景进行"背染"。先将画纸用清水喷湿，吸去多余水分，再用大提笔蘸淡墨青（比染远山的色度更淡）染水和天空，以增强画面的空间感。

3）画纸全部干透，用叶筋笔蘸淡墨画前左角的竹竿和竹枝，蘸浓墨撇竹叶。赭墨（3分赭加7分墨）画桃树枝干。用淡曙红（3分曙红加7分水）点树梢，像一簇簇盛开的桃花；稍干，用深曙红点，显示近处的桃花。石绿点叶。浓墨画鸭子，用笔如楷书的"乙"字；朱膘画嘴；浓墨干后，重墨补鸭子阴影。

4）题款、签名、盖章。画题《春江水暖》字稍大些；作画时间和签名字要小些。这是很重要的一着，写不好，前功尽弃！可先用一张纸，写好题款草稿，放在画的背面摹写。这样，全画就完成了。

图39　加染完成

图40　《春江帆影》

练习

勾勒、皴、擦、染、点是山水画的技法。请你对照临摹《春江帆影》(图40)这幅画，运用已学过的上述技法，完成这幅山水画的习作。

Lesson Nine　Landscapes

This lesson deals with the techniques and steps for painting landscapes.

Traditional Chinese landscape painting has a unique national style, and is very particular about brush work, ink and color. The painters draw inspirations from nature. Just as Shi Tao put it, "Drink in all the wonderful peaks while conceiving a landscape." They observe nature and sketch from it. By combining observations with knowledge and rearranging the landscape, they are able to come up with pictures that are more beautiful than they really are.

The model painting in the lesson takes a famous Chinese scenic spot — Elephant Trunk Hill in Guilin — as its subject matter. It is called *Spring Water Becomes Warm*, which originates from the poem by Su Dongpo, a great poet of the Song Dynasty:

Beyond the tiny cluster of bamboo,
There are a few sprays of peach blossoms;
When spring arrives to warm the river,
The ducks are the first to know it.

1. Tools and materials

A *yejin* brush, a medium-sized *lanzhu* brush, *baiyun* brush, a large *ti* brush, ink, *xuan* paper, six color-mixing trays, brush-washing jars and used *xuan* paper or tissue (for testing colors and blotting water). Pigments: cyanine, gamboge, malachite green, ochre, vermilion, bright red and white.

2. Steps in painting landscapes

It is not easy to paint landscapes. Beginners can learn from copying the model painting.

Copying and outlining the illustrations of Elephant Trunk Hill (Illustration 36)

1) Cover the model picture with a piece of *xuan* paper and use an HB pencil to trace the outlines of the hill and the other parts of the paining (Appendix V). The purpose is to get a general outline, and there is no need to bring out every detail on your draft.

2) Dip the *yejin* brush (or a medium-sized *lanzhu* brush for a larger painting) in thick ink and draw the Elephant Trunk Hill by using the *zhongfeng* and *cefeng* methods. Traditional Chinese painting attaches great importance to the use of ink and brush, which is the key to creating a good landscape.

Chapping (cun), striking (ca) and ink-coloring (Illustration 37)

1) Dip the *yejin* brush (or a medium-sized *lanzhu* brush in doing a larger painting) in thick ink (the ratio of ink and water is 1 to 1) and chap the dark sides of the hill with the *cun* method. First use light ink and then thick ink, and make sure that traces of the brush can be seen on the paper. Strike gently by assimilating sketching techniques, and avoid turning the painting into a black mess. The brush should be filled with as little ink as possible. If there is too much ink on the brush, press it on the used *xuan* paper to get rid of the unwanted ink.

2) When the ink dries up, wet the hill with clean water by spraying and blot the extra water with the tissue. Dip the medium-sized *lanzhu* brush in light ink (3 portions of ink and 7 portions of water) and color the dark sides of the hill that have been treated with the *cun* and *ca* methods, so as to enhance the three-dimensional effect. Then use the *yejin* brush with heavy ink to paint the trunks of trees on the hill, dot the leaves, and draw the white tower. Some trunks and leaves should be done in light ink to enhance the sense of distance and space.

Coloring (Illustration 38)

Coloring, which should be done from progressive density, serves to increase the three-dimensional effect and the sense of space. When the ink is dry, paint it increasingly darker where necessary. Keep the paper clean.

1) Wet the whole painting with clear water by spraying and blot the extra moisture. Dip the *baiyun* brush in ochre to color the bright side of the rocks, and then color their dark sides in jade green (6 portions of cyanine, 3.5 portions of gamboge and 0.5 portion of water). You may add a little light ink to change the color and make it look solid. Color the painting in a flexible way and pay attention to the natural transition between colors.

2) Use a *yejin* brush dipped in light green to stipple the trees on the hill. Light green should be alternated with dark green. Then draw the contour of the white tower light ochre with the *yejin* brush.

3) Dip the *baiyun* brush in blackish blue (3 portions of cyanine, 6.5 portions of water and 0.5 portion of ink) and color the inverted reflection of the hill in the water with the *cefeng* method. This should be done vertically stroke by stroke. Avoid filling it all.

4) Paint the mountains in the distance with the *baiyun* brush, in a color that is lighter than that of the inverted reflection. Paint each mountain peak with two strokes that look like the Chinese character 八. The lines should be slightly varied to give each peak a different shape. While the color is wet, touch up the middle sections of the peaks with clean water in arced strokes to bring out the clouds half way up the mountains and yield a natural transition between the mountains and the white paper.

Finishing coloring (Illustration 39)

1) Use light ink and dark green (8 portions of light green and 2 portions of ink) and the

cun and *ca* methods to touch up the dark parts of the hill with a good texture of denseness and sparseness. Avoid obliterating the color base. Stipple the moss in blackish green (7 portions of light green and 3 portions of ink) to enhance the three-dimensional feeling of the trees on the hill.

2) When the ink dries up, turn the paper over and wash-color its back. First spray the paper wet with clean water and blot away the extra, and then color where the water and the sky are located with a large *ti* brush in light blackish blue (lighter than the color of the distant mountains) to make the painting look more spacious.

3) Wait until the paper is completely dry and draw the bamboo poles and twigs in the left front corner in light ink with a *yejin* brush and the bamboo leaves in thick ink. Color the peach tree trunks and branches dark reddish brown color (3 portions of ochre and 7 portions of ink), and stipple the ends of the branches in light bright red (3 portions of bright red and 7 portions of water) to set off clusters of bright peach flowers. When the color is a little dry, stipple the flowers in the front with dark bright red and the leaves with malachite green. Paint the duck in thick ink like the Chinese character 乙 in regular script, and draw its beak in vermilion. After the thick ink is dry, add a shadow to the duck in heavy ink.

4) Write the colophon and stamp your seal. Write the title *Spring Water Becomes Warm* in bigger characters than you do the date and your signature. This is a very important finishing step which should be dealt with carefully; otherwise, your painting will be a failure in spite of all your efforts. Your may do a draft on a separate piece of paper, put it underneath the painting and trace the characters. By now, your painting is completed.

Exercises

Outlining, chapping, striking and stippling are techniques for painting landscapes. Copy from the model painting *Sailing Boats on Faraway Spring Water* (Illustration 40) with the skills you have learned in this lesson.

附录 1　楷书笔画书写顺序举例

规　则	字例	书写笔画顺序 1	2	3
先上后下	天 春	二 夫	天 春	
先左后右	神 教	礻 孝	神 教	
先外后内	风 向	几 勹	风 向	
先横后竖	井 丽	二 一	井 百	 丽
先撇后捺	人 禾	丿 丿	人 手	 禾
先横后撇	龙 右	一 一	ナ ナ	龙 右
先中间后两边	水 业	亅 丨	水 业	 业
先进门后关门	目 圆	冂 门	目 圆	目 圆

附录 2　临摹方法举例

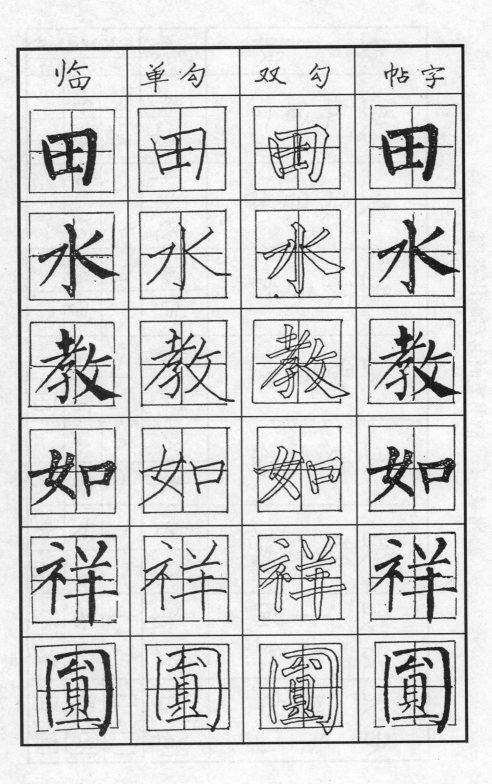

临	单勾	双勾	帖字
田	田	田	田
水	水	水	水
教	教	教	教
如	如	如	如
祥	祥	祥	祥
圍	圍	圍	圍

附录 3 楷书基本笔画运笔法字帖

楷书基本笔画点运笔练习

必	六	下	主
弟	以	注	法
室	光	深	海
玄	亦	清	源

楷书基本笔画横运笔练习

一	七	十	仁
三	上	千	甘
土	上	平	寺
万	正	五	言

楷书基本笔画挑和折运笔练习

此	以	目	口
氏	玄	四	五
傲	即	刀	百
持	塔	皆	且

楷书基本笔画竖运笔练习

仁	神	十	川
伐	初	千	聞
林	悟	引	部
福	陵	申	律

注：聞－闻

楷书基本笔画撇和捺运笔练习

大	右	丘	八
夫	发	乎	自
者	舍	出	名
成	月	彩	欲

楷书基本笔画钩运笔练习

水	子	伐	光
则	乎	風	先
奇	寺	紫	氣
氏	成	也	見

注：氣—气 見—见 風—风 則—则

附录 4　楷书基本笔画综合练习

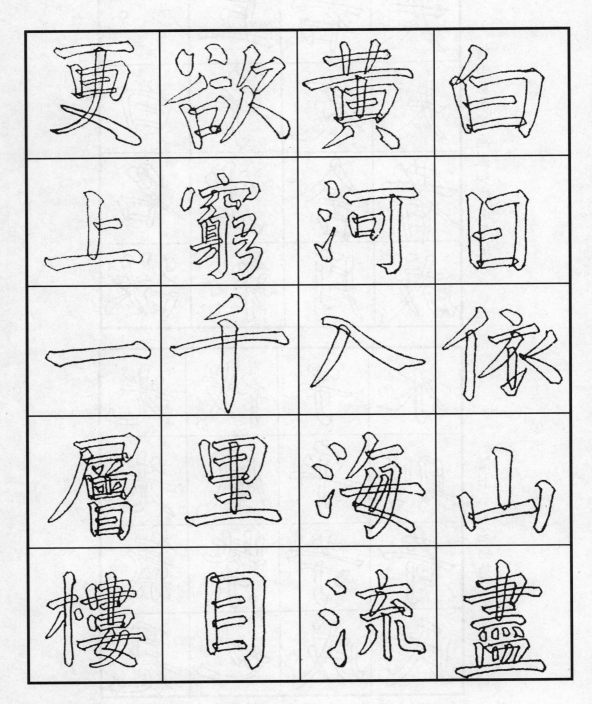

注：盡－尽　窮－穷　層－层　樓－楼

附录 5 山水画《春江水暖》

《春江水暖》

附录 6 各课课时安排

习字入门三法	1课时
楷书基本笔画运笔法	12课时
楷书基本笔画综合练习	2课时
中国画的基本知识	3课时
梅的画法	2课时
竹的画法	2课时
荷花的画法	2课时
小鸡的画法	2课时
山水的画法	3课时

剪纸入门

PAPER-CUTTING FOR BEGINNERS

剪纸入门

萧文茵　编写
罗晓英　翻译

Paper-Cutting for Beginners

Compiled by Xiao Wenyin
Translated by Luo Xiaoying

第一课　初学剪纸

一、关于剪纸

中国剪纸是一种装饰性、趣味性很强的艺术，是中国传统艺术的重要组成部分，具有悠久的历史和独特的风格。剪纸艺人只用一把剪刀或刻刀就能把一张纸剪刻成各种各样的形象，如山水、花鸟、走兽、人物等。熟练的剪纸艺人不需要在纸上画稿，也不需要任何样板，完全凭借记忆和高度的艺术想象力就能运剪如飞，在短短的几分钟内剪出流畅的线条和动人的形象。对于初学者来说，需要在纸上事先描画好图案，然后小心地依照线条进行剪刻。

二、剪纸工具

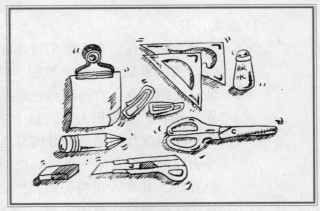

图 1　部分剪纸工具

剪刀　刀头细长，刀口咬合整齐，刀尖锋利，大小各一把，以便剪大幅图案及精细的部分。

刻刀　刀刃锋利，可准备宽、窄刀片各一把，以方便刻划大的部分及细小的部分。

垫板　胶合板、玻璃、腊盘等。垫板表面要光滑、厚实。垫板的面积大于刻纸的面积，但不能过大，太大会带来制作、携带的不方便。

另外，还要准备图画纸、色纸、铅笔、橡皮、格尺、回形针、糨糊、胶水、旧报纸等材料和工具。（图1：部分剪纸工具）

三、基本剪法及步骤

1．折叠剪纸

1）"囍"字

　　a．起稿实例操作：在图纸上设计好"喜喜"字的结构及笔画的粗细。"喜喜"字具有对称的特点，将纸折成四折，写半个"喜"字，剪完后打开，事半功倍。

　　b．装订实例操作：将设计好的画稿与色纸订在一起，要订得平整一些，上下对正，小稿用别针别好，大稿用大头针打十字花。

　　c. 刻制实例操作：先内后外，先刻掉字中镂空的小块面积，用刀尖沿着刻掉部分轻轻划开，刻掉部分便会自然跳出，然后，用剪刀沿着字的轮廓剪出来。

　　d. 粘裱实例操作：将"囍"字背面向上，放在桌上。拿另一张图画纸，刷上稀糨糊（或胶水），待纸张展开，没有多余的水分时，将图画纸翻过来，有糨糊的一面对着作品，贴在作品上，用手拂平后，马上翻过来，用旧报纸吸去多余的糨糊，反复几次。作品完成后，镶在镜框里。

步骤图如图2：

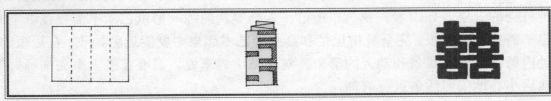

图2

2) 图案：花

　　a. 起稿实例操作：在图纸上设计好花的图案，构图要饱满，线条块面相结合，疏密要适当，装饰性强。将纸对折，画一半的稿即可。

　　b. 装订实例操作：将画稿与色纸叠在一起，叠平整些，上下对正，小稿用别针别好，大稿用大头针打十字花。

　　c. 刻制实例操作：刻划的时候要注意先刻内后刻外，先刻细部后刻粗。用小刀以顺时针方向一点一点地刻出小块面积，如有相连，不要硬拉，以免弄断。其次，用剪刀剪出图案的大体轮廓。

　　d. 粘裱实例操作：将图案背面向上，摊平。另拿一张图画纸，刷上稀糨糊（或胶水），待纸张展开，没有多余的水分时，将图画纸翻过来，有糨糊的一面对着作品，贴在作品上，用手拂平后，马上翻过来，用旧报纸吸去多余的糨糊，反复几次。作品完成后，镶在镜框里。

步骤图如图3：

图3

3) "寿"字

　　a. 起稿实例操作：由于这个字的上下左右具有对称、重复的特点，因此我们将色纸折叠成四角，在折叠的一角起稿。

b．刻制实例操作：剪完一角的稿之后，把它打开，"寿"字便展现在眼前。
步骤图如图4：

4）图案：团花   图 4

    a．起稿实例操作：团花的剪纸属于折叠剪纸，人们根据不同需要折成四角、五角、六角、八角……随便剪几刀，就会出现美丽的团花。根据下图的纹样，将纸折叠成八角，先剪出重叠后多出来的角，后在折叠的一角上画上花纹。

    b．刻制实例操作：根据花纹的图样，剪完稿的一角之后，把它打开，一幅美丽的团花就出现在眼前了。

步骤图如图5：

2．样板剪纸
1）图案：松鼠   图 5

    a．先复制剪纸的图案。复制的方法是：用一张薄薄的略显透明的纸铺在图案上，用削尖的铅笔沿着透过的轮廓线描下来，或者用复印机把图案复印下来。

    b．装订实例操作：用别针把复印下来的图案与色纸订在一起。

    c．刻制实例操作：根据图案的线条疏密、图形的轮廓进行裁剪。

    d．粘裱实例操作：将裁剪好的图案用胶水及糨糊粘在图画纸上或者镶在镜框里。

步骤图如图6：

图 6

2) 练习用的样版图案(图7)

图 7

Lesson One　The Basics of Paper-Cutting

1. Introduction to paper-cutting

Chinese paper-cutting is a highly alluring art for ornamental purposes. As an important part of Chinese folk art, it has a time-honored history and unique style. In the hands of an artisan, a piece of paper, with the help of a knife or a pair of scissors, can be turned into a wide variety of patterns — landscapes, flowers, birds, beasts, human figures etc. Skillful artists can create elegant lines and lovely images in a few minutes, based on memories and imagination. As for beginners, it is necessary to draw designs on the paper before making the cuts.

2. Tools for paper-cutting

Scissors:　two pairs of scissors, one big and the other small, sharp, slender.

Knife:　two sharp knives, one with a broad blade for cutting large designs, the other with a narrow blade for intricate cuttings.

Pad:　plywood, glass or plate, which should be smooth and wider than the paper to be cut but not too big.

Other materials include drawing paper, colored paper, pencil, rubber, ruler, clip, paste, glue and used newspaper. (Illustration 1: Some Tools for Paper-Cutting)

3. Basic methods and steps

Folding paper-cutting

1) Design of 喜喜, an auspicous Chinese character that means "double happiness" (Illustration 2)

   a. Sketching: Design the structure of the character and the size of the strokes. Fold the paper twice in half, draw one half of the character 喜, and unfold it after cutting the design out of the paper.

   b. Binding: Bind the draft paper and a piece of colored paper neatly with pins.

   c. Cutting: The cutting should proceed from the inside to the outside of the design. First carefully cut the small and hollowed part of the character with a knife, and then cut out the outline of the character with a pair of scissors.

   d. Mounting: Turn the character over on a table. Stick a piece of drawing paper covered with paste to the character. Smooth it and turn it over. Absorb the excessive paste with used newspaper; repeat it several times until the job is done. Place the work in a frame.

2) Design of a flower (Illustration 3)

   a. Sketching: Design a flower with a well-rounded structure that has good spacing between lines and surfaces. Fold the paper in half, and draw half of the flower.

   b. Binding: Bind the draft paper and a piece of colored paper neatly with pins.

   c. Cutting: Cut the design out of the paper, by proceeding from the inside to the outside. Cut the details out by moving a knife clockwise; do not pull the joining parts in case they break. Then cut out the contours.

   d. Mounting: Turn the pattern over on a table. Stick a piece of drawing paper covered with paste to the pattern. Smooth it and turn it over. Absorb the excessive paste with used newspaper repeatedly. Place the work in a frame.

3) Design of the character 寿, meaning "longevity" (Illustration 4)

   a. Sketching: Fold the colored paper in half twice, first horizontally and then vertically. Begin drawing the design on one quarter of the paper.

   b. Cutting: Cut the design out of the double-folded paper, and unfold it.

4) Round floral pattern (Illustration 5)

a. Sketching: This design can be cut out of a piece of paper that has been folded diagonally into a variety of regular polygons. Let us do it according to Illustration 5: fold the colored paper diagonally four times, and draw the pattern on one segment of the octagon.

b. Cutting: Cut the folded paper along the lines of the pattern, and then unfold it.

Model paper-cutting

1) Design of a squirrel (Illustration 6)

a. Copy the design: Put a piece of thin, transparent paper on one of the model designs and copy it by tracing the lines with a sharpened pencil. You may also xerox it.

b. Binding: Bind the copied design and a piece of colored paper with pins.

c. Cutting: Cut the paper along the lines of the pattern.

d. Mounting: Stick the finished design to a drawing paper or place it in a frame.

2) Models for exercises (Illustration 7)

第二课 立体剪纸

如今，剪纸有了新的发展，从过去的绘画、剪、刻的手法发展到采用绘画、剪刻、折叠、黏合的综合手法，原来平面化的图案转为有层次、近似浮雕的立体图案，有不少爱好者利用立体剪纸的这一特点，把它运用到实际生活当中去，譬如自制贺卡、灯罩、纸笔筒、面具等。

一、制作步骤

起稿 在图纸上设计好各个部分的图案。构思要精密，要考虑好制作的程序和制作的效果。

分别制作各个部分 先用小刀刻出小面积的图案，再用大刀裁剪大的轮廓。用刀背轻轻地刻划虚线部分，注意千万不能刻断，并按照虚线的走向把纸折叠起来。

重叠黏合 为了增加立体感，可将各个部分按照已经设计好的图案一一地粘贴在一起。

二、课堂制作

1. 亲手制作一张贺卡，送给老师、同学或亲友，是一件很有意思的事情。

操作方法：先按图样画好，用小刀刻出雪花。刻时要注意不要把虚线刻断。做双片雪花时应让标有相同字母的地方宽度也相同。再衬上一张卡纸，最后在空白处写上你的贺词，雪花卡片就做好了。（图8）

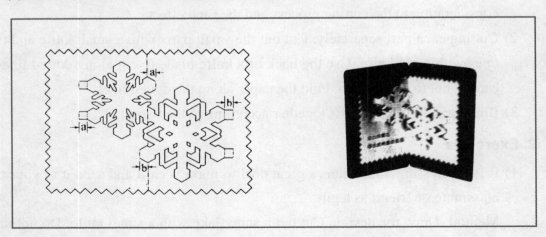

图 8

2．灯罩也是在圆柱、棱柱等基本形体的柱面、柱棱上进行切折加工而成的。根据下图制作一个漂亮的灯罩。（图9）

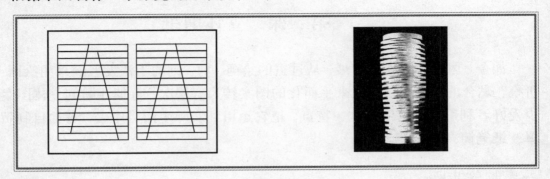

图 9

Lesson Two　Three-Dimensional Paper-Cutting

Paper-cutting artists have developed a variety of new techniques that integrate drawing, cutting, folding and mounting. As a result paper-cuts today are no longer limited to plain, one-dimensional designs. There have emerged a good assortment of three-dimensional works that can easily pass for fine examples of relief sculpture. Many paper-cutting fans have adopted these techniques, and they are making their own New Year and birthday cards, lampshades, pen containers, masks etc.

1. Procedure

1) Sketching: Draw the details of a design on a piece of drawing paper by giving full consideration to the cutting process and the final effect.

2) Cutting each part separately: Cut out the small parts with a small knife and the large ones with a big knife. Use the back of a knife blade to cut along dotted lines but be careful not to break them. Fold the paper along the dotted lines.

3) Binding: Glue all the parts together according to the design.

2. Exercises

1) It is interesting and means a great deal to make a card and send it to your teacher, classmate or friend as a gift.

Method: Draw the design. Cut out a snowflake with a small knife. Do not break the dotted lines. When you cut double snowflakes, be sure they are of the same size if they have the same letters. Attach a piece of card-board paper underneath it and write a message in the blank space. And the card is ready. (Illustration 8)

2) The lampshade is made from a cylinder or prism through paper cutting and folding. Make a beautiful lampshade according to the following design. (Illustration 9)

附录 剪纸作品欣赏

舞蹈

荷塘雨露

老鼠嫁女

猪八戒背媳妇

学中国功夫

BASIC CHINESE MARTIAL ARTS

学中国功夫

刘　刚　编写
印　妮　翻译
周　健　审校

Basic Chinese Martial Arts

Compiled by Liu Gang
Translated by Yin Ni
Revised by Zhou Jian

第一课　中国功夫概述

　　大家可能都看过李小龙或成龙主演的功夫片，他们的功夫出神入化，克敌制胜，所向披靡，令人神往。那么，什么是中国功夫呢？实际上，西方人所说的"中国功夫"，指的就是中国传统武术。

　　武术是以技击为主要内容，通过套路、搏击等运动形式，来增强体质、培养意志的民族传统体育，是中国几千年历史文化的一部分。在这一课里，我们要给大家介绍中国武术的起源、武术的分类、武术的基本手型和基本步型。

一、武术的起源

　　中华武术，源远流长。她是中华民族在长期生活与斗争实践中逐步积累和发展起来的一项宝贵遗产。她起源于我国远古祖先的生产劳动。在原始社会生产力极为低下的社会条件下，人们为了生存的需要，就必须依靠群体力量同自然界搏斗。在狩猎的生产活动中，人们不仅靠拳打、脚踢、躲闪等徒手动作与野兽搏斗，还拿起石头、木棒与野兽抗争，逐渐积累了劈、砍、刺的技能。这些是武术形成的物质基础。

二、武术的分类

　　武术的形式可分为拳术和器械两大类。拳术是徒手练习的套路运动，主要有长拳、太极拳、南拳、形意拳、八卦掌、通背拳、象形拳等。下边我们分别作简要的介绍。

　　长　拳　是以拳、掌、勾为其主要手型和弓步、马步、仆步、虚步、歇步为其基本步型，并由蹿蹦跳跃、闪展腾挪、起伏转折和跌扑滚翻等动作和技术组成的姿势舒展、动作灵活、快速有力、节奏鲜明的拳术。

　　太极拳　是一种柔和、缓慢、轻度的拳术。

　　南　拳　动作刚健有力，拳法快捷多样，气势凶猛逼人，流传于中国南方各地。

　　形意拳　以三体式为基本姿势，以劈、蹦、钻、炮、横五种手法为基本拳法，其动作整齐简练，发力沉着，朴实明快。

　　通背拳　是以摔、拍、穿、劈、钻五种手法为主要内容，通过圈揽勾劫、削摩拔扇等手法的运用而生化出许多动作的拳术。

　　八卦掌　是一种以摆扣步走转为主，包括推、托、带、领、穿、搬、截、拦等掌法变换内容的拳术。

　　象形拳　是模拟各种动物的特长和形态，以及表现某些古代人物的搏击形象和生活形象的拳术。

武术的器械，即所谓"十八般兵器"，在不同的历史时期和不同的武术流派中所指均不相同。器械的种类很多，如今主要指刀、枪、剑、棍、斧、钺、勾、叉、棒、锤、鞭等十八种武器，可分成四大类。

长器械　有棍、枪、大刀等。

短器械　有刀、剑、匕首等。

软器械　有三节棍、九节鞭、绳标、流星锤等。

双器械　有双刀、双剑、双钩、双枪等。

中国武术最重要的价值之一是它集健身、防身、修身养性、艺术观赏于一体，并不断地发展完善。

在许多大中学校，武术都被列为体育课程的教学内容，在业余体校设有很多武术课程，各地的武术协会还建立了很多辅导站，吸引了越来越多的武术爱好者。

如今很多外国人渴望来华习练武术，每年都有大量的海外武术迷来到中国的武术学校、武术辅导站和体育学院参观学习。

武术是人们增强体质、振奋精神的一种好手段。武术正逐渐走向世界，为世界人民所认识和喜爱。

图1　　　图2

三、武术的基本手型和基本步型

1．手型

拳　四指并拢握拳，拇指紧扣食指和中指的第二指节。（图1）

掌　四指并指伸直，拇指弯曲紧扣于虎口处。（图2）

勾　五指第一指节捏拢在一起，屈腕。（图3）

图3

2．手法练习

冲拳

预备姿势：两脚左右开立，与肩同宽，两拳抱于腰间，肘尖向后，拳心向上。

动作说明：收腹、挺胸、直腰，右拳从腰间向前猛力冲出，力达拳面，臂要伸直，高与肩平。（图4a，4b）

要求与要点：动作要协调，冲拳要有力。

图4a　　图4b

架拳

预备姿势：与冲拳同。

动作说明：右拳向下、向左、向上经头前向右上方划弧架起，拳眼向下，眼看左方。练习时，左右可交替。（图5a，5b）

要点与要求：松肩，肘微屈，前臂内旋。

图5a　　图5b

推掌

预备姿势：与冲拳同。

动作说明：右拳变掌，前臂内旋，并以掌根为力点向前猛力推击。推击时要转腰、顺肩，臂要伸直，高与肩平，同时左肘向后拉。（图6）

图6

亮掌

预备姿势：与冲拳同。

动作说明：右拳变掌，经体侧向右、向上划弧，至头部右前上方时，抖腕亮掌，臂成弧形。（图7）

图7

3．步型

弓步　左脚向前一大步，脚尖微内扣，左腿屈膝半蹲，膝与脚尖垂直。右腿挺膝伸直，脚尖内扣，两脚全脚着地。（图8）

要求与要点：前腿弓，后腿绷；挺胸，塌腰，沉髋；前后脚成一条线。

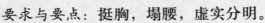

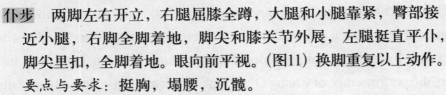

马步　两脚平行开立（约为本人脚长的三倍），脚尖正对前方，屈膝半蹲，膝不超过脚尖，大腿接近水平，全脚着地，身体重心落于两腿之间，两手抱拳于腰间。（图9）

要求与要点：挺胸，塌腰，脚跟外蹬。

图8

虚步　两脚前后开立，右脚外展45度，屈膝半蹲，左脚脚跟离地，脚面绷平，脚尖稍内扣，虚点地面，膝微屈，重心落于右腿上。两手叉腰。眼向前平视。（图10）换脚重复以上动作。

要求与要点：挺胸，塌腰，虚实分明。

图9

仆步　两脚左右开立，右腿屈膝全蹲，大腿和小腿靠紧，臀部接近小腿，右脚全脚着地，脚尖和膝关节外展，左腿挺直平仆，脚尖里扣，全脚着地。眼向前平视。（图11）换脚重复以上动作。

要点与要求：挺胸，塌腰，沉髋。

图10

歇步　两腿交叉靠拢全蹲，左脚全脚着地，脚尖外展，右脚前脚掌着地，膝部贴近左腿外侧，臀部坐于右腿接近脚跟处。（图12）换脚重复以上动作。

要求与要点：挺胸，塌腰，两腿靠拢并贴紧。

图11

掌握了基本手法与步法，就可以开始学习长拳了。

图12

Lesson One   Learning Chinese Kung Fu

You have probably seen some kung fu films starring Bruce Lee or Jackie Chan, who have captivated the viewers with their enchanting performances of superb and invincible martial arts. Well, what in the world is Chinese kung fu? The word "kung fu" that appears in English dictionaries actually refers to *wushu*, or the traditional Chinese martial arts.

Wushu, or martial arts, is a sport for physical conditioning and willpower training, with a history of several thousand years. In this lesson we will give you a brief introduction to its origin and main styles, and its basic skills and movements.

1. Origin

The Chinese martial arts has a long history. It is a rare legacy originated from the life and labor of our forefathers over the long years of practice and accumulation. To survive in a low-productivity environment,they had to rely on the strength of the collective. When hunting they either fought the animals barehanded by striking with fist, kicking and dodging, or used stones and sticks, gradually accumulating the skills of hacking, cutting and thrusting — the basics of the Chinese martial arts.

2. Categories

The Chinese *wushu* is divided mainly into two fields: free-style boxing and the maneuvering of weapons.

In *wushu* competitions today the boxing style comes under seven categories.

Chang Quan

Chang Quan is characterized with three major hand postures of fist, palm and hook and five stances of bow stance, riding stance, crouch stance, empty stance and resting stance. Accompanied by kicking, jumping, dodging, punching, striking, pounding, turning and tumbling, the performance of Chang Quan looks swift and agile, forceful and rhythmical.

Taiji Quan (Shadow-Boxing)

The movements of Taiji Quan are slow, unhurried and gentle.

Nan Quan (Southern-Style Boxing)

The southern-style boxing movements are forceful and energetic, with various striking ways used by those carrying arms. Explosive shouts accompany each movement. Nan Quan is popular in the southern part of China.

Xingyi Quan

This style is characterized with three basic postures and five basic hand movements.

Its movements are simple but forceful and rhythmic.

Tongbei Quan

Tongbei Quan is characterized with falling, patting, cutting through, cleaving and quick moving while bending the body. With other hand and foot movemens, Tongbei Quan may yield numerous sets of movemens.

Bagua Zhang (The Eight Trigrams Palm)

This boxing style combines a lot of turning, walking, pushing, leading, holding, pulling, blocking and other movements.

Xiangxing Quan (The Imitation Boxing)

This is a vivid, lively style with much leaping and rolling in imitation of various animals.

Different historical periods and *wushu* schools have different sets of "eighteen weapons." Today, the term mainly includes knife, spear, sword, club, hatchet, battle-axe, shovel, fork, bludgeon, hammer, whip etc.

These weapons used in *wushu* practice today fall into four groups:

Long weapons

Club, spear, broad knife etc.

Short weapons

Knife, sword, dagger etc.

Soft weapons

Three-section club, nine-section chain, rope dart, flying hammers (made up of two iron balls linked by a long iron chain) etc.

Twin weapons (for two hands)

Twin broad knives, twin swords, twin hooks, twin lances etc.

A major feature of *wushu* has been its constant development through the ages. It is a combination of physical exercises for self-protection and self-discipline with art.

Wushu is on the physical education curriculum of most schools and colleges, and *wushu* courses are offered in colleges of physical culture. There are *wushu* classes in many spare-time sports schools, and *wushu* associations in different localities have set up coaching stations, attracting more and more enthusiasts.

Today, many foreigners are coming to China to learn *wushu*. Every year, *wushu* clubs, schools, coaching stations, and sports colleges all over China are visited by a constant stream of *wushu* fans from overseas.

As a good exercise to stay in shape and good health, *wushu* is gaining popularity throughout the world.

学中国功夫

3. Basic hand and foot movements

1) Hand Postures

Fist (Illustration 1)

Keep the four fingers closely together and turn them into a fist. Press the thumb tightly on the second joint of the forefinger and the middle finger.

Palm (Illustration 2)

Keep the fingers together and straight with the thumb bent at the bottom of the forefinger.

Hook (Illustration 3)

Keep the tip⁻ of the thumb and fingers together, and bend the wrist.

2) Hand Techniques

Fist punching

Preparation posture: Feet apart as wide as the shoulders and up-facing fists on the hips.

Action illustration: Stretch out the right fist forcefully, while turning the forearm and the palm downward at shoulder level with the force reaching the fist. (Illustrations 4a & 4b)

Main points: Turn the waist and shoulder when extending the fists. Chest out and arms straight. The strike should be swift and forceful. Keep the fists as close to the ribs as possible and the fists should go straight forward.

Arm raising

Preparation posture: Same as that of the fist punching.

Action illustration: Swing the right fist downward, turn it to the left and then overhead with the fist hole facing slightly down, eyes looking left. You may alternate your right hand and left hand when practicing. (Illustrations 5a & 5b)

Main points: Shoulders relaxed, elbows slightly bent, and forearm turning inward.

Palm pushing

Preparation posture: Same as that of the fist punching.

Action illustration: Unfold the right fist to a palm while turning the forearm inward and stretching it forward at shoulder level. Keep the fingers pointing upward and turn the palm sideways. Pull the left elbow backward at the same time. (Illustration 6)

Palm exposing

Preparation posture: Same as that of the fist punching.

Action illustration: Open the right fist, swing the arm to the right and overhead, turn the wrist, with the palm facing upward. (Illustration 7)

3) Stance Position Movements

Bow stance

Bend the left leg with toes bent slightly inward, knees perpendicular with the toes; keep the right leg straight with the toes tucked in. Place feet firmly on the ground. (Illustration 8)

Main points: Keep the front leg bent, back leg straight, chest out, waist straight and two feet at a line.

Riding stance

Stand with feet parallel and apart (about three times the length of your foot), toes pointing forward, knees bent, in a half crouching position (knees not exceeding toes), thighs nearly parallel to the ground. Place your feet firmly on the ground, with the center of your body weight between your legs and your fists on hips. (Illustration 9)

Main points: Chest out, waist straight, and heels outward.

Empty stance

Bend the right leg in a half-squatting position, with the right foot turned outward about 45 degrees. Take a half step forward with the left foot, lift the heel, with toes lightly touching the ground, knee slightly bent, body weight on the right leg; hands on hips and look ahead. (Illustration 10) Repeat with the other leg.

Main points: Chest out, waist straight, with each leg performing a different function.

Crouch stance

Legs apart, bend the right knee in a squatting position, and keep the right thigh and lower leg close and buttocks close to the lower leg, with the right foot firmly on the ground, the right toes and knee pointing ahead. Keep the left leg straight, toes tucked in, foot on the ground, eyes looking ahead. (Illustration 11) Repeat with the other leg.

Main points: Chest out, waist straight, hip low.

Resting stance

Stand with legs apart, upper body turned to the left; put the left foot horizontally in front of the right one, bend the knees in a squatting position, with the left foot firmly on the ground. Lift the right heel, toes pointing ahead, buttocks as close to the right heel as possible. (Illustration 12) Repeat with the other leg.

Main points: Chest out, waist straight, two legs as close to each other as possibie.

You can start practicing Chang Quan after you have grasped these basic hand postures and stance position movements.

第二课　长拳（1）

长拳是在中国流传很广的传统拳术之一，其特点是姿势舒展，动作灵活，节奏鲜明，快速有力，非常适合青少年练习。长拳的基本姿势共有以下33种，我们分四课来学习。本课学习预备姿势及前八种姿势。

第一段
一、拗弓步冲拳
二、蹬腿冲拳
三、弓步冲拳
四、换跳步弓步冲拳
五、丁步冲拳
六、弓步劈拳
七、半马步推掌
八、弓步穿掌

第三段
十七、弓步上架冲拳
十八、擂拳弹踢
十九、马步冲拳
二十、歇步冲拳
二十一、仆步切掌
二十二、弓步挑掌
二十三、腾空飞脚
二十四、弓步推掌

第二段
九、马步架冲拳
十、弓步撩掌
十一、虚步下截拳
十二、垫步弓步连环冲拳
十三、弓步侧身掼拳
十四、震脚弓步双推掌
十五、击掌拍脚
十六、弓步顶肘

第四段
二十五、震脚侧身弓步双冲拳
二十六、马步压肘
二十七、弓步搂手冲拳
二十八、盖步缠手侧铲腿
二十九、并步上冲拳
三十、绞步下劈掌
三十一、弓步分掌
三十二、虚步架冲拳
三十三、收势

图1

图2

预备姿势　两脚并拢站立。眼看前方。（图1）两手握拳，屈肘抱于两腰侧，拳心朝上。头向左转，眼平视左前方。（图2）

要点　挺胸，两肩后张，两拳紧贴腰侧。

第　一　段

一、拗弓步冲拳

左脚向左上一步，脚尖向斜前方；右腿微屈，成半马步，左臂屈肘向上，向左格挡，拳眼向后，拳与肩同高；右拳仍抱于腰间，拳心向上，目视左拳。（图3）右腿蹬

直成左弓步。上体左转，左拳收至腰侧，拳心向上；右拳向前冲出，高与肩平，拳眼向上。目视右拳。（图4）

要点　成弓步时，右腿充分蹬直，脚跟不要离地。冲拳时，尽量转腰顺肩。

图3　　　图4

二、蹬腿冲拳

重心前移至左腿，右腿屈膝提起，脚尖勾起，脚跟用力向前蹬出，高与腰平。右拳收至腰侧，左拳向前冲出。目视前方。（图5）

要点　支撑腿可微屈，蹬腿要用爆发力，力达脚跟。

三、弓步冲拳

右脚向前落步成右弓步，左拳收至腰侧，右拳向前冲出，拳眼向上。目视前方。（图6）

要点　动作要协调，冲拳要有力。

图5 　　　图6

四、换跳步弓步冲拳

重心后移，右脚稍向后移动。右拳变掌，随臂内旋，以拇指侧向下划弧挂至右膝内侧；左拳变掌，伸向右臂下方，左掌背贴靠右肘外侧，掌指前方。目视右掌。（图7）

右腿自然上抬，上体稍向左扭转。右掌挂至左肩前，左掌伸向右腋下。目随右掌转视。（图8）

图7　　　图8

右脚全脚掌用力向下跺踏，同时左脚急速离地抬起。右手由左向上、向前捋盖而后变拳收至右腰侧；左掌伸直向下，经后向上、向前屈肘下按，掌心向下，高与肩平。上体右转。目视左掌。（图9）

左脚向前落步，右腿蹬直成左弓步。右拳向前冲出，高与肩平；左掌插于右腋下，掌背贴靠腋窝。目视右拳。（图10）

图9　　　图10

要点　换跳步动作要连贯、协调。震脚时右腿要稍屈，全脚掌着地。两肩放松，抡臂速度要快。

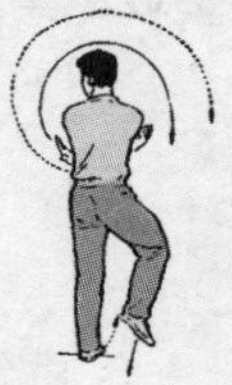

五、丁步冲拳

上体右转，重心移至右腿，左脚脚跟提起收于右脚内侧成丁步；右拳收至腰侧，左掌变拳向前冲出，拳眼向上。目视左拳。（图11）

图11

六、弓步劈拳

上体左转，左脚向前上半步，同时左拳变掌向下、向右、向上绕一小环向左前方伸出，掌心向上，略高于肩，右拳由下向后、向上、向前环绕劈出，高与耳平，拳眼向上；左掌接托右前臂；右腿同时上步，屈膝半蹲成右弓步。目视右拳。（图12）

图12

七、半马步推掌

左脚向前跨一步，重心移至两腿中间，左脚脚尖向前成半马步，上体右转，左掌向左侧推出，掌指向上。右拳变掌收至左肩前。（图13）

图13

要点 两掌同时做动作，左掌推出要有力。

八、弓步穿掌

右脚向前跨一步，成右弓步。左掌收至右腋下，掌心向下；右掌从左掌背上方向前穿出，略高于肩，掌心向上，目视右掌。（图14）

图14

Lesson Two   Chang Quan (I)

Chang Quan is one of the most popular traditional Chinese boxing styles. It is characterized by expansive and agile movements. The pace of Chang Quan is swift and energetic, which is especially suitable for young people to practice. The following 33 postures are its basic movements to be practiced in the next four lessons. Now let us begin with the preparation postures and first eight movements.

Chapter One

1. Punching in bow stance with the left leg bent

2. Kicking and punching

3. Punching in bow stance with the right leg bent

4. Punching in stamping step bow stance

5. Punching in T-stance

6. Striking in bow stance

7. Pushing palm in half riding stance

8. Extending palm in bow stance

Chapter Two

Chapter Three

Chapter Four

Preparation Posture

Stand with feet close together, eyes looking ahead. (Illustration 1) Place up-facing fists on the waist, turn the head to the left and look ahead. (Illustration 2)

Main Points

Keep chest out and place fists on hips.

Chapter One

1. Punching in bow stance with the left leg bent

Take a step forward with the left foot, with the toes forward in a slanting way. Bend the right knee in a half riding stance. Bend the left elbow while raising the fist at shoulder level, with knuckles facing upward. Place the right fist on the waist with palm facing up and eyes fixed on the left fist. (Illustration 3)

Bend the upper body slightly forward, with the left knee bent and the right leg straight in the bow stance, take the left fist back to the waist with the palm facing up, punch the right fist from the waist with its hole facing up at shoulder level and eyes following the right fist. (Illustration 4)

Main points: When standing in the bow stance, keep the right leg as straight as possible without lifting the heel from the ground. When punching, turn the waist and shoulder forcefully while extending the fist as far as possible.

2. Kicking and punching

Shift the body weight to the left leg, lift the right leg with the knee bent and toes pointing upward, kick forward forcefully at waist level; take the right fist back to the waist, and punch the left fist forward, eyes looking ahead. (Illustration 5)

Main points: Kick the leg forcefully, force reaching the heel, with the knee straight. The supporting leg may slightly bent.

3. Punching in bow stance with the right leg bent

Land on the right foot to form a right bow stance, take the left fist back to the waist and punch the right fist forward with the hole of the fist pointing up. Eyes look ahead. (Illustration 6)

Main points: Movements should be well coordinated; punching should be powerful.

4. Punching in stamping step bow stance

Shift the body weight backward, take the right foot back with toes touching the ground. Change the right fist into a palm and move it down left in an arc. Change the left fist into a palm and swing it to the right arm; keep the back of the left palm close to the outside of the right elbow. Eyes follow the right palm, and fingers point forward. (Illustration 7)

Lift the right leg while the upper body turns slight to the left, swing up the right palm to the front of the left shoulder and move the left palm to the right armpit. Eyes follow the right palm. (Illustration 8)

Stamp the right foot, then lift the left foot swiftly. Swing the right palm from the left to the right in an arc, change it to fist and bring it back to the waist. Swing the left palm downward from the rear in an arc that turns up and then forward at the shoulder level, with the palm facing down. Turn the upper body to the right. Eyes follow the left palm. (Illustration 9)

Land with the left foot forward and stretch the right leg to make a left bow stance. Punch the right fist to the shoulder level, while bringing the left palm to the right armpit, with the back of the palm kept close to the armpit. Eyes follow the right fist. (Illustration 10)

Main points: The movement of the stamping step should be energetic and well coordinated. Slightly bend the right knee while stamping. Relax the shoulders and swing the arm quickly.

5. Punching in T-stance

Turn the upper body to the right and shift the weight to the right foot. Lift the left heel with toes on the ground, put it inside of the right foot to take the T-stance. Bring the right fist back to the waist; change the left palm into a fist and punch forward with the hole of the fist pointing up. Eyes follow the left fist. (Illustration 11)

6. Striking in bow stance

Turn the upper body to the left, the left foot taking half a step forward, while the left fist becomes palm, swings first down to the right, then up left in a little hoop and, with the palm facing up, stretches forward a bit above shoulder level. The right fist swings from rear and raises over the head, then forward a bit above shoulder level with its hole pointing up and pounding the right arm on the center of the left palm. At the same time the right foot steps forward and the knee bends so that the body half squats to take a right bow stance. Eyes follow the right fist. (Illustration 12)

7. Pushing palm in half riding stance

The left foot steps forward and the toes point forward, with the body weight shifted to both legs in a half riding stance while the upper body turns right. Stretching the left palm forward with the fingers pointing up. Change the right fist into a palm and bring it back to the front of the left shoulder. (Illustration 13)

Main points: Move the hands together and stretch the left palm forcefully.

8. Extending palm in bow stance

The right foot takes a step forward in a right bow stance, and the left palm returns to the right armpit facing down. Stretch the right palm forward a bit higher than shoulder level facing up. Eyes follow the right palm. (Illustration 14)

第三课　长拳（2）
第 二 段

九、马步架冲拳

右脚尖里扣，同时上身随之左转，两腿屈膝成马步，右掌变拳收至右腰侧，拳心向上；同时，左臂微屈肘，左掌向前横架于头顶上方。上动不停，右拳从腰侧向平直冲出，拳心向下。目视右拳。（图15）

图15

要点　上下肢动作要协调一致，两肩稍后张，左臂成弧形，右拳与肩平。

十、弓步撩掌

左脚脚跟碾地，脚掌外转；右脚脚掌碾地，脚跟外转。同时右拳变掌，向左前下方撩出，掌心向上，稍高于膝；左掌下盖，附于右肘内侧。同时身体左转成左弓步，眼平视前方。（图16）

图16

十一、虚步下截拳

左腿蹬立起，重心移至右腿。右腿屈膝下蹲，左脚后移半步，以前脚掌虚点地成左虚步，同时左掌变拳向前下方截拳，拳心向下；右掌变拳，收至右腰侧，拳心向上。眼平视左前方。（图17）

图17

要点　移步、收掌的动作必须协调一致，形成虚步截拳后，两肩要松沉，要挺胸、直背、塌腰。

十二、垫步弓步连环冲拳

左脚向前跨半步，右脚向左脚处跟步踏地，同时，左脚再向前上半步，随即右脚向前跨出一步，成右弓步。左拳收于腰间；右拳向前冲出，拳心向下。目视右拳。（图18）上动不停，右拳立即收至右腰侧，拳心向下；左拳迅速冲出，拳心向下。目视前方。（图19）

图18

要点　动作应连贯协调，冲拳要有力，左肩前伸，右肩后牵，两脚掌全部着地，切勿拔跟。

图19

十三、弓步侧身掼拳

图20

两脚碾地，身体左转成左弓步。同时左拳变掌贴身向下，向左环绕至左斜上方，略高于头；右拳从腰间经上向左掌反臂扣击，右拳眼向下。身体略向左侧前倾。目视双拳。（图20）

要点 动作须连贯协调，右拳击掌时要用力。身体左前倾时，仍要保持挺胸、塌腰的姿势。

十四、震脚弓步双推掌

左脚掌内扣，右腿屈膝提起，右拳变掌，身体向右转，同时双掌向右前方盖压。（图21）上动不停，右脚在左脚内侧震脚；右膝略屈，左腿随之屈膝稍后抬。同时两掌收于两腰侧，掌心向上。（图22）上动不停，左脚向前落步成左弓步。同时两掌向前平直推出，掌指朝上，目视两掌。（图23）

图21
图22

图23

要点 震脚和按掌、进步和推掌应同时进行，协调一致。推掌之后，两肩松沉，两臂伸直，两腕尽量向上弯曲，掌心向前，掌指与眉齐。

十五、击掌拍脚

图24　　图25

左掌向上移至头上，右掌即向上拍击左掌心，左掌心同时迎击右掌背，两臂微屈。同时左腿直立，右脚后移，脚尖点地，作前踢准备。（图24）上动不停，右脚脚面绷平，迅速向前踢起，右掌迎击右脚面。同时左掌向后摆成侧上举，掌心向侧。目视右脚。（图25）

要点 右脚踢起时，脚面要绷平，击掌要协调、准确、响亮。

十六、弓步顶肘

右脚下落扣于左膝弯，身体微向左转，目视左方。同时两掌向左下方环绕至左腰侧，右掌变拳，拳面贴于左掌心。（图26）右脚向右前方跨出一步成右弓步，同时右肘向右前方顶出，肘与肩平。左掌仍附于右拳面上。头向右转，目视右前方。（图27）

图26

图27

要点 两掌要随腰的转动而摆动。顶肘要有力，要挺胸、直背。

Lesson Three   Chang Quan (II)
Chapter Two

9. Arm raising and punching in riding stance

The right foot turns inside, while the upper body turns left with knees bent in a riding stance, while the right palm becomes a fist and returns to the waist facing up. At the same time, raise the left palm over the head, bend the elbow slightly while the right fist punches to the right side facing down. Eyes follow the right fist. (Illustration 15)

Main points: The movements of the four limbs should be simultaneous and coordinated. The shoulders spread out slightly backward, the left arm bends into an arc, and the right fist should be at shoulder level.

10. Palm turning in bow stance

The left heel grinds the ground till the sole turns outside; and the right foot sole grinds the ground till the heel turns outside. At the same time, unfold the right fist into a palm and swing the arm from the right to the left side of the body in an arc with the palm facing up and slightly above knee level; the left palm covers the inner side of the right elbow. At the same time, turn the body left in a left bow stance. Eyes look forward. (Illustration 16)

11. Striking downward in empty stance

Lift the left foot, shift the body weight to the right leg. Keep the right leg bent in a half squatting position, and the left foot takes half a step backward. Lift the left heel, with the toes slightly touching the ground in an empty stance. At the same time, gather the left palm into a fist and slice it downward with its palm facing down. Change the right palm to a fist and bring it back to the waist with its palm facing up. Eyes look left forward. (Illustration 17)

Main points: The foot step must be in sync with palm movement. Relax the shoulders, and keep chest out and waist straight.

12. Fist punching in stamping step bow stance

The left foot takes half a step forward, the right foot takes a step close to the left foot, then the left foot takes another half step and the right foot takes one more step forward to form a right bow stance. Bring the left fist to the waist, punch the right fist facing down. Eyes look forward. (Illustration 18)

Bring the right fist back to the waist with its palm facing down, punch the left fist swiftly with its palm facing down. Eyes look ahead. (Illustration 19)

Main points: The movements should be coordinated; punch forcefully with your left shoulder forward and right shoulder backward as much as possible, while keeping the heel on the ground.

13. Fist pounding in bow stance

The feet grind the ground and the body turns left into a left bow stance. Change the left fist into a palm and swing it to the rear and raise it a bit higher than the head to the left; raise the right fist over the head and pound it on the center of the left palm with the hole of the right fist facing down. The body tilt to the left side and eyes look at the fists. (Illustration 20)

Main points: Make sure movements are simultaneous and coordinated. Pound forcefully, keep the chest out and the waist straight even when the body tilts to the left.

14. Double palm pushing and foot stamping in bow stance

Move the sole of the left foot till the toes point inward, lift the right leg and bend the knee. Change the right fist into a palm, turn the upper body right and swing the palms first right and then forward. (Illustration 21)

Stamp the right foot and put it close to the left foot; slightly bend the right knee, then bend the left leg back and bring the palms facing up to both sides of the waist. (Illustration 22)

While the upper body movements continue, move the left foot forward to form a left bow stance and stretch the palms forward and level, with the fingers pointing upward. Eyes look at the palms. (Illustration 23)

Main points: Foot stamping, the landing of the feet and the movement of the palms should all be done simultaneously and in sync. After stretching the palms, relax the shoulders, straighten the arms, keep the wrist bent and the palms pointing forward. Keep the fingers at eyebrow level.

15. Striking the palms and tapping the foot

Raise the left palm over the head and raise the right palm to tap the center of the left palm, with the arms slightly bent. Stretch the left leg, and move the right foot backward with its tip on the ground. Prepare to kick. (Illustration 24)

While the upper body movement continues, stand on the left leg and stretch the right foot and kick forward swiftly, with the right palm moving to tap the instep of the right leg. At the same time, swing the left palm facing sideways to the rear to balance the body. Eyes look at the right foot. (Illustration 25)

Main points: The right foot kicks with the ankle stretched flat, and the taps on the instep must take place quickly, resoundingly and in good timing.

16. Bending elbow in bow stance

Bend the right knee, place the right foot close to the back of the left knee, and turn the upper body left, eyes looking left. Move the coupled hands down left in a circular movement to the left side of the waist, where the right hand folds into a fist so that it is covered by the palm of the left hand. (Illustration 26)

The right foot makes a step up right and the knee bends into a bow stance, while the right elbow thrusts forward and right at shoulder level. All the while the right fist remains on the left palm. Turn the head right, eyes looking ahead. (Illustration 27)

Main points: The coupled palms must swing with the turn of the waist. The right elbow must thrust forcefully while keeping the chest out and the upper body straight.

第四课 长拳（3）

第 三 段

十七、弓步上架冲拳

左脚跟和右脚掌同时碾地使身体左后转，左腿屈膝，右腿伸直成左弓步。同时左掌向上横架于头顶，掌心向前上方；右拳随转体收经右腰侧，即向前平直冲出，拳心向下。目视右拳。（图28）

图28

十八、搂拳弹踢

左臂不动，右前臂内屈，右拳向内环绕屈肘反砸，拳心向上。同时右腿抬起向前弹踢，脚面绷平，右拳反砸后置于右膝内上方；左腿微屈。目视前方。（图29）

图29

十九、马步冲拳

右脚脚尖内扣向前落步，左脚脚掌碾地使脚跟里转，身体随之左转，两腿半蹲成马步。同时，左掌变拳，经右前方向下回收至左腰侧，拳心向上；右拳立即向右侧平直冲出，拳眼向上，高与肩平。眼看右拳。（图30）

要点 落步、转体和屈膝半蹲的动作必须与冲拳协调一致；形成马步后，两肩稍向后张。

图30

二十、歇步冲拳

上体左转，左脚向右脚后插步，两腿全蹲成歇步。同时右拳向上、向左划弧，于胸前屈肘收至右腰侧，拳心向上。左拳从左腰间向前冲出，拳心向下。头向左转，眼平视左前方。（图31）

图31

二十一、仆步切掌

右脚尖内扣，右腿蹬直；左腿屈膝提起，脚尖内扣。右拳变掌，掌心向上，从腰间经左臂内侧向前方穿出；左拳变掌，收至右腋下，掌心向下。目视右掌。（图32）

上动不停，右腿全蹲；左腿向左前方伸直平铺成仆步。左掌不动；右掌经上向下绕弧切下，小指侧贴地。眼看左前方。（图33）

图32

图33

二十二、弓步挑掌

重心前移，右腿蹬直，左腿屈膝半蹲，成左弓步。左掌随即向前上挑起，高与肩平，掌指向上；右掌摆向后成反勾手，勾尖向上。目视前方。（图34）

图34

二十三、腾空飞脚

右腿向前上步，膝部微屈，准备蹬地起跳。同时右勾手变掌，向前、向上摆起，左掌先上摆，然后向前拍击右掌背。（图35）

右脚蹬地跳起，左腿屈膝紧贴上身，脚尖向下。右腿相继上摆，脚面绷平。右手向下拍击右脚面，左掌向上向左侧平摆。目视前方。（图36）

图35

要点 蹬地时身体要向上纵，不要向前冲。左膝尽量上提，击响要在腾空阶段完成。初练时，拍击动作也可在左脚落地后完成。拍击要准确、响亮。

图36

二十四、弓步推掌

左脚落地；右脚于体前下落，右腿屈膝成右弓步。左掌变拳收至左腰侧，拳心向上；右掌收至右腰侧，随即向前平直推出成立掌，掌尖与眉齐。目视右掌。（图37）

图37

Lesson Four　Chang Quan (III)
Chapter Three

17. Arm raising and punching in bow stance

The left heel and the right foot grind against the ground and the body turns left, with the left leg bending and the right leg stretching to take a left bow stance. At the same time, raise the left palm over the head with the palm facing upward; bring the right fist to the right side of the waist and punch it level forward with its palm facing down. Fix the eyes on the right fist. (Illustration 28)

18. Swinging the fist and shooting the leg

Keep the left arm unmoved. Bend the right arm and pound the elbow with the palm facing up. The right foot kicks forward with the instep stretched tight and the left knee bent slightly. The right fist pounds downward and rests above the inside of the right knee. Eyes look ahead. (Illustration 29)

19. Punching in riding stance

Move the right foot forward with toes turned inward. The sole of the left foot grinds against the ground till its heel turns inside, the upper body turns left, and the knees bend in a riding stance. At the same time, fold the left palm into a fist, swing it forward in the right direction, bring it downward and rest it facing up at the left side of the waist; punch the right fist with its hole facing up at shoulder level. Eyes follow the right fist. (Illustration 30)

Main points: The movements should be simultaneous and coordinated. In the riding stance, keep the shoulders slightly backward.

20. Punching in resting stance

Turn the upper body left, plant the left foot horizontally behind the right foot, and bend both knees in a squatting position to assume a resting stance. At the same time, swing the right fist up left in an arc, then bring it back to the right hip with the palm facing up. The left fist punches forward with its palm facing down. Turn the head to the left, and look left ahead. (Illustration 31)

21. Palm thrusting in crouch stance

Stretch the right leg with toes turning inward; bend the left knee, and raise the left leg with toes turning inward. Turn the right fist into a palm, thrust it facing up and left diagonally past the inner side of left arm; unfold the left fist into a palm, and bring it facing downward to the right armpit. Eyes follow the right palm. (Illustration 32)

Bend the right knee to take a squatting posture and extend the left leg into a crouch stance. Keep the left palm unmoved. Swing the right palm down in an arc with the side of the little finger on the ground. Eyes look left ahead. (Illustration 33)

22. Palm lifting in bow stance

Shift the body weight forward, stretch the right leg and bend the left knee in a half squatting position to take a left bow stance; lift the left palm to shoulder level, then forward with fingers pointing upward. Swing the right hand backward and change it into a hook with its fingers pointing up. Eyes look ahead. (Illustration 34)

23. Flying foot in midair

Take a step forward with the right foot, bend the knee slightly to poise for a jump. At the same time change the hooked right hand into a palm, and swing it upward from the back of your body to the front while clapping the back of the right hand with the left palm over the head. (Illustration 35)

While air-borne, swing the right foot swiftly upward and tap the right instep with the right palm, bend the left knee close to the upper body with the toes pointing down. Swing the left hand left forward. Eyes look ahead. (Illustration 36)

Main points: When the foot stamps on the ground, jump up. Raise the left foot as high as possible. Tap the instep of the right foot in midair accurately and resoundingly.

24. Palm pushing in bow stance

Take a big step forward with the right foot and bend the right knee so as to form a right bow stance. Fold the left palm into a fist and take it to the left side of the waist with its palm facing up. Bring the right palm to the right side of the waist and strike it forward with the tip of the fingers pointing up at eyebrow level. Eyes follow the right palm. (Illustration 37)

学中国功夫

第五课 长拳（4）

第 四 段

二十五、震脚侧身弓步双冲拳

右掌收至腰侧变拳。右脚收至左脚内侧震踏，左脚向前跨出一步成左弓步。同时身体左后转并左倾，两拳向左上方冲出，两臂伸直，拳眼相对。目视左上方。（图38）

图38

二十六、马步压肘

右拳收至腰侧，右脚碾地，使身体右后转；左脚随即上步，两腿半蹲成马步。同时左臂屈肘由上向下压，拳心向上。目视左拳。（图39）

图39

要点 转体压肘要迅速。

二十七、弓步搂手冲拳

左拳变掌，掌心翻向下，向左前方平搂后变拳收至左腰侧。同时左脚尖外转，右膝蹬直成左弓步。右拳向前冲出，拳心向下。目视前方。（图40）

图40

二十八、盖步缠手侧铲腿

左拳变掌盖握于右腕上；右拳变掌内旋缠绕，随即抓握变拳，拳心向上，收至右腰侧。上身随之右转，同时右腿向前盖步。（图41）

图41

上动不停，左腿屈膝提起，向左侧方向伸直铲出，脚掌朝下，高与腰平。目视左侧。上体微右倾。（图42）

图42

要点 盖步缠手要协调，右掌变拳，手要迅速收回。铲腿要有力。

二十九、并步上冲拳

左腿落步，重心移至左腿；右腿向左腿靠拢，成并步直立。左掌经上伸至头右侧；右拳贴身向上冲出，右臂伸直，拳心向左。左掌顺落于右腋旁成立掌，掌心向右。眼睛随左手动作环视，后向左转头，注视左方。（图43）

图43

三十、绞步下劈掌

左腿向左侧跨出半步，脚尖外转，上体向左后拧转成两腿交叉，同时右拳变掌向下劈至左胯侧，掌背贴胯；左掌附于右上臂外侧。目视左下侧。（图44）

图44

三十一、弓步分掌

右腿向右跨出一步，屈膝半蹲；左腿挺膝伸直，成右弓步。右臂由下向前上分至掌高于肩，掌心向上；同时左臂向下，向后分至掌与腰平，掌心朝下。目视右掌。（图45）

图45

三十二、虚步架冲拳

以右脚掌、左脚跟为轴向左转体，同时右臂经下向左、向前撩至与肩平，掌心向上；左臂略屈收，左掌盖于右前臂上。目视右掌。（图46）

图46

上动不停，重心后移，右腿屈膝半蹲；左腿后移半步，左脚前掌点地，成左虚步。右掌变拳，向上架于头右上方。同时左掌迅速收至腰侧变拳，随即向左前方冲出，拳心向下。目视左前方。（图47）

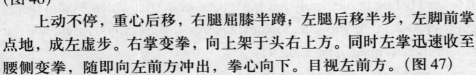

图47

三十三、收势

右脚尖稍外转，右腿蹬直立起。同时上身稍向右转，左脚随之向右脚靠拢并步。同时两拳收抱于两腰侧，拳心均朝上。（图48）眼向左侧平视。脸转向正前方。两拳变掌，直臂下垂，仍成立正姿势。（图49）

图48

图49

Lesson Five   Chang Quan (IV)
Chapter Four

25. Stamping foot and double fist punching in bow stance

Take the right palm to the side of the waist and fold it into a fist. Bring the right foot to the inner side of the left foot and stamp, take the left foot a step forward to make a left bow stance. At the same time, the upper body turns left behind. Punch with the fists above the head to the left side with arms stretching out and the two fist holes facing each other. Eyes look left upward. (Illustration 38)

学中国功夫

26. Withdrawing elbow in riding stance

Bring the right fist to the waist, grind the right foot against the ground and turn the body right behind. Then make a step forward with the left foot and bend the knees in a riding stance. At the same time, bend the left elbow and pound with the palm facing up. Eyes look at the left fist. (Illustration 39)

Main points: Turn the body and pound the elbow swiftly.

27. Taking back fist and punching in bow stance

Unfold the left fist into a down-facing palm, swing it forward to the left, then fold it into a fist and rest it by the side of the hip. At the same time, turn the toes of the left foot outward and stretch the right knee in a left bow stance. Punch the right fist forward with its palm facing down. Look straight ahead. (Illustration 40)

28. Side kick with twining hands

Change the left fist into a palm and cover it on the right wrist; change the right fist into a palm and revolve it inward before immediately turning it back into a fist with the palm facing upward and taking it back to the right hip side. Meanwhile, turn the upper body right and put the right foot in front of the left one.(Illustration 41)

Lift the left leg and bend the knee; kick left forcefully at the hip level, the sole facing down. Follow the left foot with your eyes. Bend the upper body to the right. (Illustration 42)

Main points: The movements of the twining hands should be coordinated. Change the right palm into a fist and bring it back swiftly. Kick forcefully.

29. Punching with feet together

Stand on the left foot and shift the gravity of the body to the left foot. Move the right leg close to the left leg so as to bring the feet together and stand erect. Raise the left palm in front of the right shoulder. Raise the right fist, stretch the arm upward with the palm facing left. Put the left palm beside the right armpit facing right. Eyes follow the left palm and then turn left. (Illustration 43)

30. Thrusting palm downward in cross stance

The left foot takes half a step left with its tip turning outward, and the upper body turns to the left behind to form a cross stance. At the same time unfold the right fist into a palm and thrust it left diagonally past the inner side of the left arm. The back of the right hand rests close to the left hip. Left palm stays beside the right upper arm. Look down left. (Illustration 44)

31. Extending palms in bow stance

The right foot takes a step forward with the knees bent, and the left leg stretch to take a right bow stance. Swing the right arm down and then raise it till the palm is above shoulder level and facing up. At the same time, swing the left arm down to the back till the palm facing down is at waist level. Eyes follow the right palm. (Illustration 45)

32. Arm raising and punching in empty stance

Turn the body left with the sole of the right foot and the left heel as the pivot, while swinging the right arm down left and then up to the shoulder level, with the palm facing up. Slightly bend the left arm and put the left palm on the right forearm. Follow the right palm with your eyes. (Illustration 46)

Shift the weight of the body backward, bend the right leg into a half squatting position. Then the left foot makes half a step backward with toes on the ground to assume a left empty stance. Gather the right palm into a fist, raise it over the head. At the same time, change the left palm into a fist and bring it beside the hip swiftly, and let the down-facing fist punch forward. Eyes look left ahead. (Illustration 47)

33. Finishing posture

Turn the tiptoes of the right foot outward slightly while the right leg straightens to assume a standing position. In the meantime, let the the upper body turn right slightly and move the left foot close to the right foot. Put the fists by the hips, and let the fists point up. Eyes look left. (Illustration 48)

Turn the face straight forward. Change fists into palms and let the arm hang naturally on either side of the body. (Illustration 49)

第六课　二十四式简化太极拳（1）

太极拳是中国的一种传统拳术，流派很多，流传很广。动作柔和缓慢，既能用于技击，又有增强体质和防治疾病的作用。太极拳的动作适合于绝大多数人练习。我们将要学习的是二十四式简化太极拳，属于杨式太极拳。我们分五课来学习，本课学习前五种姿势。

第一段
一、起势
二、左右野马分鬃
三、白鹤亮翅
四、左右搂膝拗步
五、手挥琵琶

第二段
六、左右倒卷肱
七、左揽雀尾
八、右揽雀尾
九、单鞭
十、云手

第三段
十一、单鞭
十二、高探马
十三、右蹬脚
十四、双峰贯耳
十五、转身左蹬脚

第四段
十六、左下势独立
十七、右下势独立
十八、左右穿梭
十九、海底针
二十、闪通臂

第五段
二十一、转身搬拦捶
二十二、如封似闭
二十三、十字手
二十四、收势

第　一　段

一、起势

图1

1. 身体自然直立，两脚开立，与肩同宽，脚尖向前，两臂自然下垂，两手放在大腿外侧，眼平看前方。（图1）
   要点　头颈正直，下颏微向后收，不要故意挺胸或收腹。精神要集中（起势由站立姿势开始，然后左脚向左分开，成开立步）。

2. 两手向前平举，高与肩平，与肩同宽，手心向下。上体保持正直，两腿屈膝下蹲，同时两掌轻轻下按，两肘下垂与两膝相对。眼平看前方。（图2）
   要点　两肩下沉，两肘松垂，手指自然微屈，重心落于两腿中间。屈膝松腰，臀部不可凸出。两臂下落要和身体下蹲的动作协调一致。

图2

二、左右野马分鬃

1. 上体微向右转，重心移至右腿上。同时，右手收在胸前平屈，手心向下；左手经体前向右下划弧放在右手下，手心向上，两手相对成抱球状。左腿随之收到右脚内侧，脚尖点地。眼看右手。（图3）

2. 上体左转，左脚向左前方迈出，右脚跟后蹬，右腿自然伸直，成左弓步；同时上体继续向左转，左右手慢慢分别向左上右下分开，左手高与眼平（手心斜向上），肘微屈；右手落在右胯旁，手心向下指尖向前。眼看左手。（图4）

3. 身体慢慢后坐，重心移至右腿上，左脚尖跷起微向外撇（大约45°～60°）。（图5）

4. 随即，左腿慢慢前弓，身体左转，重心再移至左腿上。同时左手翻转向下，收在胸前平屈，右手向左上划弧放在左手下，两手心相对成抱球状；右脚随之收到左脚内侧，脚尖点地；眼看左手。（图6）

5. 右腿向右前方迈出，左脚自然伸直，成右弓步；同时上体右转，左右手分别慢慢向左下右上分开，右手高与眼平（手心斜向上），肘微屈；左手放在左胯旁，手心向下，指尖向前。眼看右手（图7）（图8是图7的正面图）

6. 与3、4动作相同，只是左右相反。（图9）

7. 与5动作相同，只是左右相反。（图10）

   要点 上体不可前俯后仰，胸部必须宽松舒展。两臂分开要保持弧形，身体转动要以腰为轴，做弓步与分手的速度要均匀一致。做弓步时，迈出的脚先是脚后跟着地，然后脚掌慢慢踏实，脚尖朝前，膝盖不要超过脚尖；后腿自然伸直；前后脚夹角成45°～60°（需要时后脚脚跟可以后蹬调整）。野马分鬃式的弓步前后脚更要分在中轴线两侧，它们之间的横向距离（即以动作行进的中线为中轴，其两侧的垂直距离为横轴）宜保持在10～30厘米左右。

图3　　图4

图5　　图6

图7　　图8

图9　　图10

三、白鹤亮翅

上体微向左转，左手翻掌向下，左臂平屈胸前，右手向左上划弧，手心转向上，

学中国功夫

与左手成抱球状；眼看左手。然后，右脚跟进半步，上体后坐，身体重心移至右腿；身体先向右转，面向右前方，眼看右手；然后左脚稍向前移，脚尖点地，成左虚步，同时上体微向左转，面向前方，两手随转体慢慢地分别向右上左下分开，右手上提停于右额前，手心向左后方，左手落于左胯前，手心向下，指尖向前，眼平看前方。（图11a,11b）

图11a

要点　完成姿势胸部不要挺出，两臂上下都要保持半圆形，左膝要微屈，身体重心后移和右手上提、左手下按要协调一致。

四、左右搂膝拗步

1. 右手从体前下落，由下向后上方划弧至右肩部外侧，手与耳同高，手心斜向上；左手由左下向上、向右下方划弧至右胸前，手心斜向下；同时上体微向左再向右转；左脚收至右脚内侧，脚尖点地，眼看右手。（图12）

图11b　　图12

2. 上体左转，左脚向前（偏左）迈出成左弓步；同时右手屈回由耳侧向前推出，高与鼻尖平；左手向下由左膝前搂过落于左胯旁。指尖向前，眼看右手手指。（图13）

3. 右腿慢慢屈膝，上体后坐，重心移至右腿上，左脚尖翘起微向外撇，随即脚掌慢慢踏实，左腿前弓，身体左转，重心移至左腿上，右脚收到左脚内侧，脚尖点地；同时左手向外翻掌由左后向上划弧至左肩外侧，肘微屈，手与耳同高，手心斜向上；右手随转体向上、向左下划弧落于左肩前，手心向下；眼看左手。（图14）

图13　　图14

4. 与2动作相同，只是左右相反。（图15）

5. 与3动作相同，只是左右相反。（图16）

6. 与2动作相同。（图17）

图15　　图16

　　要点　前手推出后，身体不可前俯后仰，要松腰松胯。推掌时要沉肩垂肘、沉腕舒掌，同时要与松腰、弓腿上下协调一致，两脚跟的横向距离保持约30厘米左右。

图17　　图18

五、手挥琵琶

右脚跟进半步，身体后坐，身体重心转至右腿上，上体半面向右转，左脚稍提起向前移，变成左虚步，脚跟着地，脚尖翘起，膝部微屈，同时左手由左下向上挑举，高与鼻尖平，掌心向右，臂微屈；右手收回放在左臂肘部里侧，掌心向左，眼看左手食指。(图18)

要点　身体要平稳自然，沉肩垂肘，胸部放松。左手上起时不要直向上挑，要由左向上、向前，微带弧形。右脚跟进时，脚掌先着地，再全脚踏实。身体重心后移和左手上起、右手回收要一致。

Lesson Six   Twenty-Four Steps of the Simplified Taiji Quan (I)

Taiji Quan is a traditional style of Chinese boxing with many schools. It has spread far and wide in China. The movements of Taiji are gentle, slow, and unhurried. Useful in the art of attack and defense, and for treating illness and strengthening the constitution, it is suitable for most people. What we are going to practice is the twenty-four steps of the simplified Taiji Quan in Yang's style. We will do it in five lessons. Now, let us begin the first five movements.

Chapter One

1. The start
2. Parting the wild horse's mane
3. White crane spreading its wings
4. Brushing past right and left knees and twisting steps
5. Playing the lute

Chapter Two

6. Stepping back with whirling arms
7. Grasping the peacock's tail on the left
8. Grasping the peacock's tail on the right
9. Single whip
10. Waving hands like clouds

Chapter Three

11. Single whip
12. Patting the horse from on high

13. Kicking with right heel

14. Striking opponent's ears with both fists

15. Turning and kicking with left heel

Chapter Four

16. Crouching down and standing on left leg

17. Crouching down and standing on right leg

18. Shuttling back and forth

19. Needle at the sea bottom

20. Flash arms

Chapter Five

21. Turning body and punching

22. Closing up

23. Crossing hands

24. Finishing move

Chapter One

1. The start

1) Stand naturally erect, with feet shoulder-width apart, tiptoes forward, arms down and hands by the outer sides of the thighs. Eyes turn level to the front. (Illustration 1)
Main points: Keep the head and neck erect and the chin slightly drawn in. Do not thrust the chest out or pull in the belly intentionally, and concentrate. (The start begins with a standing position at attention, then you move your left foot left so that you stand with your feet slightly apart.)

2) Raise your hands slowly forward to shoulder level and width, palms down. Keep the upper part of your body upright, legs bent to a squat. Press the palms gently downward; keep elbows down and knees opposite each other. Eyes keep to the front. (Illustration 2)
Main points: Drop the shoulders; keep elbows relaxed and down and fingers slightly bent naturally. Keep the body weight between the legs. Bend the knees and relax the waist. Do not thrust the buttocks out. Dropping of the arms and squatting should be harmonious.

2. Parting the wild horse's mane

1) Turn the upper part of the body slightly right and shift the weight to the right leg. At the same time, draw the right arm to the chest and bend it horizontally, palm down. Move the left hand in a curve before the body to the right and downward and place it below the right hand, palm up. Keep the palms in a gesture as if to hold a ball. Withdraw the

left foot immediately to the inner side of the right foot, tiptoe on the ground. Eyes should be on the right hand. (Illustration 3)

2) Turn the upper part of the body slightly left and move the left foot forward to the left, right heel on the ground and right leg naturally straight, to form a left bow stance. Then continue to turn the upper part of the body left, move the hands slowly with the turning of the body, the left hand upward to the left until it reaches eye level and the right hand downward to the right. Left palm should be obliquely up, elbow slightly bent. The right hand should fall by the hip side, fingers forward, palm down. Eyes should be on the left hand. (Illustration 4)

3) Drop the upper part of the body slowly downward and backward and shift the body weight to the right leg, left tiptoe up and slightly outward (about 45 to 60 degrees). (Illustration 5)

4) Immediately afterwards, bend the left leg slowly, turn the body to the left and shift the body weight to the left leg. At the same time, turn the left hand downward, move the left arm in front of the chest and bend it horizontally; move the right hand in a curve upward to the left and place it under the left hand, palms facing each other in a position as if to hold a ball. Withdraw the right foot immediately to the inner side of the left foot, tiptoe on the ground. Eyes should be on the left hand. (Illustration 6)

5) Move the right leg forward to the right and bend the right knee to form a right bow stance while keeping the left leg naturally straight. At the same time, turn the body right, move the left hand downward to the left and the right hand upward to the right until it reaches eye level (palm obliquely up), and keep the elbows slightly bent. Finally, place the left hand at the left hip side, with its palm facing down and fingertips pointing forward. Eyes should be on the right hand. (Illustration 7) (Illustration 8 is a frontal view of Illustration 7)

6) The same as 3), 4), only left and right in the reverse. (Illustration 9)

7) The same as 5), only left and right in the reverse. (Illustration 10)

Main points: Do not bend the body forward or backward. Let the chest be relaxed and comfortable. Keep the arms in a circle when they are separated. Turn the body with the waist as the axis. Movements of the bow stance and the separation of the hands should be executed at an even speed. In moving a foot to form a bow stance, the heel should land first before the whole sole slowly gets a firm foothold with its tiptoe pointing forward and the kneecap not exceeding the tiptoe. Straighten the rear leg naturally. The angle between the feet should be about 45 to 60 degrees. (When needed, the position of the heel of the rear foot can be adjusted.) In making the bow stance for parting the wild

学中国功夫

horse's mane, the heels of the feet each should be located on either side of the central axis. The crosswise distance between them should be about 10 to 30 centimeters. (In other words, the center line of the movement is the vertical axis and perpendicular distance on both sides of the axis should be equal.)

3. White crane spreading its wings

Turn the upper part of the body slightly to the left, let the left palm face down, and bend the left arm horizontally in front of the chest. Move the right hand in an arc upward to the left, with the palm facing up, to join the left hand in a position as if to hold a ball. Eyes should be on the left hand. Then, move the right foot half a step forward, with the upper part of the body sitting back, and shift the body weight to the right leg. Turn the upper part of the body first to the right, and face right forward. Eyes should be on the right hand. Next, move the left foot slightly forward, tiptoe on the ground, to form a left empty stance. At the same time, turn the upper part of the body slightly to the left, and face forward. Move the right hand upward to the right until it reaches forehead level, with the palm to the left backward; move the left hand downward until it reaches the left hip, with the palm facing down, and fingers pointing forward. Eyes should look straight. (Illustrations 11a & 11b)

Main points: Do not thrust the chest out. Keep both arms in semi-circles. Bend the left knee slightly. The shifting of the body weight backward, the raising of the right hand and the pressing down of the left hand should agree with each other.

4. Brushing past right and left knees and twisting steps

1) Drop the right hand before the body and move it in a circle from below backward and upward to the outer side of the right shoulder. Raise the hand to ear level, palm obliquely up. At the same time, move the left hand upward from left below to the right chest, palm obliquely down. Turn the upper part of the body slightly first to the left and then to the right. Withdraw the left foot to the inner side of the right foot, tiptoe on the ground. Eyes should be on the right hand. (Illustration 12)

2) Turn the upper part of the body to the left, move the left foot forward (slightly to the left) to form a left bow stance. At the same time, withdraw the right hand and bend and push it forward from the ear at nose level. Move the left hand downward and pass the left knee to the left hip, fingers forward. Eyes should be on the right hand's fingers. (Illustration 13)

3) Bend the right leg slowly with the upper part of the body sitting back. Shift the body weight to the right leg, move the left tiptoe up and slightly outward, and then plant the

sole slowly and firmly on the ground. Bend the left leg forward, turn the body to the left, shift the body weight to the left leg, and move the right foot to the inner side of the left foot, tiptoe on the ground. At the same time, turn the left palm outward and move it upward from the left back in a circle to the outer side of the left shoulder, elbow slightly bent, hand to the ear level, palm obliquely up. In sync with the turning of the body, move the right hand upward and then down left in a circle until it is in front of the left shoulder, palm downward. Eyes should be on the left hand. (Illustration 14)

4) The same as 2), only left and right in the reverse. (Illustration 15)

5) The same as 3), only left and right in the reverse. (Illustration 16)

6) The same as 2). (Illustration 17)

Main points: In pushing out the forward hand, do not bend the body forward or backward; relax the waist and hips, drop the shoulders and elbows, and relax the wrists and palms. At the same time, they must agree harmoniously with the relaxation of the waist and the bending of the legs. The crosswise distance between the heels is about 30 centimeters.

5. Playing the lute

Move the right foot half a step forward, with the upper part of the body sitting back. Shift the body weight to the right leg. Turn the upper part of the body half to the right, raise the left foot slightly and move it forward a bit to form a left empty stance, with the heel on the ground and the tiptoe pointing up and the knee slightly bent. At the same time, lift the left hand upward from left downward to the level of the nose tip while keeping the palm facing right and the arm slightly bent. Withdraw the right hand and place it to the inner side of the left elbow while keeping the palm facing left. Eyes should be on the left forefinger. (Illustration 18)

Main points: Keep the body steady and stable, drop the shoulders and relax the chest. Raise the left hand from left upward and forward with a slight curve. In moving the right foot forward, the sole should land first, then the whole foot. There should be harmonious agreement when the body weight is shifted backward, the left hand raised and the right hand drawn back.

学中国功夫

第七课　二十四式简化太极拳（2）

第 二 段

六、左右倒卷肱

1. 上体右转，右手翻掌，手心向上，经腹前由下向后上方划弧平举，臂微曲，左手随后翻掌向上；随着向右转体，眼看右手。（图19）

图19　　图20

图21　　图22

图23　　图24

2. 右臂曲肘折向前，右手由耳侧向前推出，手心向前，左臂屈肘后撤，手心向前，撤至左肋外侧，同时左腿轻轻提起向后（偏左）退一步，脚掌先着地，然后全脚慢慢踏实，身体重心移至左腿上，成右虚步，右脚随转体以脚掌为轴扭正，眼看右手。上体微向左转，同时左手随转体向后上方划弧平举，手心向上，右手随即翻掌，掌心向上；随着向左转体，眼看左手。（图20）

3. 与2动作相同，只是左右相反。（图21）

4. 与2动作相同。（图22）

5. 与3动作相同。（图23）

   要点　前伸的手不要伸直，后侧手也不可直向后抽，随转体仍走弧线。前推时要转腰松胯，两手的速度要一致，避免僵硬；退步时，脚掌先着地，再慢慢全脚踏实，同时，前脚随转体以脚掌为轴扭正。退左脚略向左后斜，退右脚略向右后斜，避免使两脚落在一条直线上。后退时，眼神随转体动作先向左右看，然后再转看前手，最后退右脚时，脚尖外撇的角度略大些，便于接做下一个动作。

七、左揽雀尾

1. 上体微向右转，同时右手随转体先向后方划弧平举，手心向上，左手放松，手心向下，眼看左手。身体继续向右转，左手自然向下落，掌逐渐经腹前划弧至右肋前，手心向上；右臂曲肘，手心转向下，收至右胸前，两手相对成抱球状；同时身体重心落在右腿上，左腿收到右脚内侧，脚尖点地，眼看右手。（图24）

2. 上体微向左转，左脚向前方迈出，上体继续向左转体，右腿自然蹬直，左腿屈膝，成左弓步；同时左臂向左前方绷出（即左臂平曲成弓形，用前臂外侧和手

背向前方推出），高与肩平，手心向后，右手向右下捋放于右胯旁，手心向下，指尖向前；眼看左前臂。（图25）

要点　绷出时，两臂前后均保持弧形。分手、松腰、弓腿三者必须协调一致。

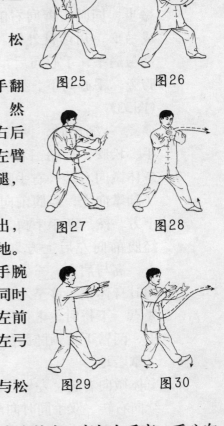

图25 　　　　图26

3．身体微向左转，左手随即前伸翻掌向下，右手翻掌向上，经腹前向上、向前伸至左前臂下方，然后两手下捋，即上体向右转，两手经腹前向右后上方划弧，直至右手手心向上，高与肩齐，左臂平屈胸前，手心向后，同时身体重心移至右腿，眼看左手。（图26，27）

要点　下捋时，上体不可前倾，臀部不要凸出，两臂下捋须随腰旋转，仍走弧线。左脚全掌着地。

图27　　　　图28

4．上体微向左转，右臂屈肘折回，右手附于左手腕里侧，相距约5厘米，上体继续向左传，双手同时向前慢慢挤出，左手心向后，右手心向前，左前臂要保持半圆，同时身体重心逐渐前移变成左弓步，眼看左手腕部。（图28）

要点　向前挤时，上体要正直。挤的动作要与松肩、弓腿相一致。

5．左手翻掌，手心向下，右手经左腕上方向前、向右伸出，高与左手齐，手心向下，两手左右分开，宽与肩同；然后右腿屈膝，上体慢慢后坐，身体重心移至右腿上，左脚尖翘起；同时两肘屈肘回收至腹前，手心均向前下方，眼平看前方。（图29，30）

图29　　　　图30

6．上式不停，身体重心慢慢前移，同时两手向前、向上按，掌心向前；左腿前弓成左弓步；眼平看前方。（图31）

要点　向前按时，两手须走曲线，手腕部高与肩平，两肘微屈。

图31　　　　图32

八、右揽雀尾

1．上体后坐并向右转，身体重心移至右腿，左脚尖里扣；右手向右平行划弧至右侧，然后由右下经腹前向左上划弧至左肋前，手心向上；左臂平屈胸前，左手掌向下与右手成抱球状；同时身体重心再移至左腿上，右脚收至左脚内侧，脚尖点地；眼看左手。（图32）

2. 上体微向右转，右脚向前方迈出，上体继续向右转体，左腿自然蹬直，右腿屈膝，成右弓步；同时右臂向右前方绷出（即右臂平曲成弓形，用前臂外侧和手背向前方推出），高与肩平，手心向后，左手向左下捋放于左胯旁，手心向下，指尖向前；眼看右前臂。（图33）

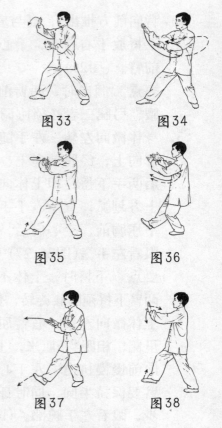

图33　　　　图34

图35　　　　图36

图37　　　　图38

要点　绷出时，两臂前后均保持弧形。分手、松腰、弓腿三者必须协调一致。

3. 身体微向右转，右手随即前伸翻掌向下，左手翻掌向上，经腹前向上、向前伸至右前臂下方，然后两手下捋，即上体向左转，两手经腹前向左后上方划弧，直至左手手心向上，高与肩齐，右臂平屈胸前，手心向后，同时身体重心移至左腿，眼看右手。（图34）

要点　下捋时，上体不可前倾，臀部不要凸出，两臂下捋须随腰旋转，仍走弧线。左脚全掌着地。

4. 上体微向右转，左臂屈肘折回，左手附于右手腕里侧，相距约5厘米，上体继续向右转，双手同时向前慢慢挤出，右手心向后，左手心向前，右前臂要保持半圆，同时身体重心逐渐前移变成右弓步，眼看右手腕部。（图35）

要点　向前挤时，上体要正直。挤的动作要与松肩、弓腿相一致。

5. 右手翻掌，手心向下，左手经右腕上方向前、向左伸出，高与右手齐，手心向下，两手左右分开，宽与肩同；然后左腿屈膝，上体慢慢后坐，身体重心移至左腿上，右脚尖翘起；同时两肘屈肘回收至腹前，手心均向前下方，眼平看前方。（图36）

6. 上式不停，身体重心慢慢前移，同时两手向前、向上按，掌心向前；右腿前弓成右弓步；眼平看前方。（图37，38）

要点　向前按时，两手须走曲线，手腕部高与肩平，两肘微屈。

九、单鞭

1. 上体后坐，重心逐渐移至左腿上，右脚尖里扣，同时上体左转，两手（左高右低）向左弧形运转，直至左臂平举，伸于身体左侧，右手经腹前运至左肋前。手心向上向后，眼看左手。身体重心再逐渐移至右腿上，上体右转，左腿向右脚靠拢，脚尖点地，右手向下经腹前向右上方划弧（手心由里转向外），至右侧

方变勾手，臂与肩平；左手向下经腹前向右上划弧停于右肩前，手心向里；眼看左手。（图39，40，41）

2. 上体微向左转，左脚向左侧方迈出，右脚跟后蹬成左弓步。在身体重心移至左腿的同时，左掌慢慢转向前推出，手心向前，手指与眼齐平，臂微屈，眼看左手。（图42）

   要点 上体保持正直，松腰。完成动作时，右臂肘部稍下垂，左肘与左膝上下相对，两肩下沉。左手向外翻掌前推时，要随转体边翻边缓慢推出，上下要协调一致。

图39　图40

图41　图42

十、云手

1. 身体重心移至右腿上，身体渐向右转，左脚尖里扣；左手经腹前向右上划弧至右肩前，手心斜向后，同时右手变掌，手心向后；眼看左手。（图43）

2. 上体慢慢左转，身体重心随之逐渐左移；左手由脸前向左侧运转，手心渐渐转向左方；右手由右下经腹前向左上划弧，至左肩前，手心斜向后；同时右脚靠近左脚，成小开立步（两脚距离约10～20厘米）；眼看左手。（图44）

3. 上体再向右转，同时左手经腹前向右上划弧至右肩前，手心斜向后；右手向右侧运转，手心翻转向右，随之左腿向左横跨一步；眼看左手。（图45）

4. 与1动作相同，只是左右相反（图46）

5. 与2动作相同，只是左右相反（图47）

6. 与3动作相同，只是左右相反（图48）

   要点 身体转动要以腰脊为轴，松腰、松胯转，要自然圆活，速度要缓慢均匀。上下肢移动时，身体重心要稳定，需要在一条直线上，右脚最后跟步时，脚尖微向里扣，便于接"单鞭"动作。

图43　图44

图45　图46

图47　图48

Lesson Seven   Twenty-Four Steps of the Simplified Taiji Quan (II)

Chapter Two

6. Stepping back with whirling arms

1) Turn the upper part of the body to the right; turn the right palm up and move it past the abdomen from below to the back upward in a circle and raise it horizontally, arm slightly bent. Turn the left palm upward immediately. With the body turning right, eyes look at the right hand. (Illustration 19)

2) Bend the right arm at the elbow before pushing the right hand forward from the ear side, palm facing forward. Bend the left elbow and draw it backward to the outer side of the left ribs, palm facing forward. At the same time, raise the left leg lightly and move it one step backward (slightly to the left). Plant the sole first and then the whole foot slowly but firmly on the ground. Shift the body weight to the left leg to form a right empty stance. Turn the right foot to the forward position with the sole as an axis as the body turns. Eyes should be on the right hand. Then turn the upper part of the body slightly to the left while moving the left hand up backward in an arc and raising it horizontally, with the palm facing up. Turn the right palm up immediately. With the body turning left, eyes look at the left hand. (Illustration 20)

3) The same as 2), only left and right in the reverse. (Illustration 21)

4) The same as 2). (Illustration 22)

5) The same as 3). (Illustration 23)

Main points: The pushing hand should not be straightened nor should the withdrawing hand be pulled back straight. They should move in an arc following the turning of the body. In pushing the hand forward, one should turn the waist, relax the hips, and move the hands at the same speed so as to avoid stiffness. In retreating, one should plant the sole first and then the whole foot slowly and firmly on the ground. At the same time, one should turn the fore foot to the forward position with the sole as an axis as the body turns. When the left foot retreats, move it a bit obliquely to the left. The same applies to the right foot. Avoid keeping both feet in a straight line. In retreating, the eyes should first look to the left and then to the right following the movement of the body, and then turn to the forehand. In the last movement of withdrawing the right foot, the angle of turning the tiptoe outward should be slightly larger for the convenience of continuing the next movement.

7. Grasping the peacock's tail on the left

1) Turn the upper part of the body slightly to the right, while moving the right hand up

backward in a curve with the turning of the body, and raising it horizontally, with the palm facing up. Relax the left hand, and let the palm face down. Eyes should be on the left hand. Continue to turn the body to the right, drop the left hand down naturally. Gradually turn the palm over and move it past the abdomen to the front of the right ribs in a curve, palm up. Bend the right elbow, turn the palm down and draw it back to the front of the right chest. Keep the hands in a position as if to hold a ball. At the same time, shift the body weight to the right leg and withdraw the left foot to the inner side of the right foot, tiptoe on the ground. Eyes should be focused on the right hand. (Illustration 24)

2) Turn the upper part of the body slightly to the left, move the left foot forward to the left, continue to turn the body to the left, straighten the right leg naturally and bend the left knee to form a left bow stance. At the same time, push forward the left forearm to the left (bend the left arm horizontally into the bow form and push it forward with the outer side of the forearm and the back of the hand) to shoulder height, palm backward. Drop the right hand down to the right hip, palm down and fingertips forward. Eyes should be on the left forearm. (Illustration 25)

Main points: In bending and pushing the left arm, both arms should be kept in an arc. Hand separation, waist relaxation and leg bending must agree with each other harmoniously.

3) Turn the body slightly to the left, stretch the left hand immediately and turn the palm down. Turn the right palm up, move it upward past the abdomen and stretch it forward to under the left forearm. Then stroke downward with both hands, that is, turn the upper part of the body to the right and move the hands backward past the abdomen to the right in a curve until the right palm reaches shoulder height upward and the left arm is bent horizontally in front of the chest, palm backward. At the same time, shift the body weight to the right leg. Eyes should be on the left hand. (Illustrations 26 & 27)

Main points: In stroking down with both hands, do not lean the body forward or thrust the buttocks out. The stroking should follow the turning of the waist in a curve. Plant the left sole on the ground.

4) Turn the upper part of the body slightly to the left, bend the right arm at the elbow and withdraw it till the right hand is about five centimeters near the the inner side of the left wrist. Continue to turn the upper part of the body to the left, and then push both hands forward with the left palm facing backward and the right palm facing forward. Keep the left forearm in a semicircle. At the same time, shift the body weight gradually forward to form a left bow stance. Eyes should be on the left wrist. (Illustration 28)

Main points: In pushing the hands forward, keep the upper part of the body upright. The pushing must agree with shoulder and leg bending.

5) Turn the left hand and let the palm face down. Move the right hand forward over the left wrist and stretch it forward to the right at the same level as the left hand, palm facing down. Move the hands apart to shoulder width. Then, bend the right knee, with the upper part of the body sitting slowly back, and shift the body weight to the right leg, left tiptoe pointing up. At the same time, bend both arms at the elbow and withdraw them to the front of the abdomen, palms facing ahead downward. Eyes look ahead. (Illustrations 29 & 30)

6) Shift the body weight slowly forward and, at the same time, press both hands forward and upward, palms forward. Bend the left leg to form a left bow stance. Eyes look forward. (Illustration 31)

Main points: In pressing the hands forward, move them in a curve with the wrists at shoulder height and both elbows slightly bent.

8. Grasping the peacock's tail on the right

1) Move the upper part of the body backward to a sitting position, turn it to the right and shift the body weight to the right leg, left tiptoe inward. Move the right hand horizontally to the right in a curve to the right side, and then move it from the right downward and past the abdomen in an arc to the left ribs, palm up. Bend the left arm horizontally in front of the chest, palm down, to join the right hand in a position as if to hold a ball. At the same time, shift the body weight to the left foot, and withdraw the right foot to the inner side of the left foot, tiptoe on the ground. Eyes look at the left hand. (Illustration 32)

2) Turn the upper part of the body to the right slightly and move the right foot forward to the right. Continue to turn the upper part of the body to the right; straighten the left leg naturally and bend the right leg to form a right bow stance. At the same time, push the right arm forward (bend the right arm horizontally into the bow form and push it forward with the outer side of the forearm and the back of the hand) to shoulder height, palm backward. Drop the left hand down to the left hip, palm down and fingertips forward. Eyes look at the right forearm. (Illustration 33)

Main points: In bending and pushing the right arm, both arms should be kept in a circular form. Hand separation, waist relaxation and leg bending must agree with each other harmoniously.

3) Turn the body slightly to the right, stretch the right hand immediately and turn the palm down. Turn the left palm up, move it upward past the abdomen to under the right forearm. Then, stroke down with both hands, that is, turn the upper part of the body to the left and move the hands past the abdomen to the left backward in an arc until the left palm reaches shoulder height and the right arm is bent horizontally in front of the chest, palm backward. At the same time, shift the body weight to the left leg. Fix eyes on the right

hand. (Illustration 34)

Main points: In stroking down, do not let the upper part of the body bend forward or thrust the buttocks out. The stroking should follow the turning of the waist in a curve. Plant the left sole on the ground.

4) Turn the upper part of the body slightly to the right; bend the left arm at the elbow and move the left hand till it comes to a distance of about five centimeters near the inner side of the right wrist. Continue to turn the upper part of the body to the right; slowly push both hands forward, with the right palm facing backward and the left palm facing forward. Keep the right forearm in a semicircle. At the same time, shift the body weight gradually forward to form a right bow stance. Eyes should be on the right wrist. (Illustration 35)

Main points: In pushing the hands forward, keep the upper part of the body upright. The pushing must agree with shoulder relaxation and leg bending.

5) Turn the right palm down. Move the left hand forward over the right wrist and stretch it to the left at the same level as the right hand, palm down. Move the hands apart to shoulder width. Then, bend the left knee, with the upper part of the body sitting slowly back, and shift the body weight to the left leg, right tiptoe up. At the same time, bend both arms at the elbow and draw them back to the front of the abdomen, palms forward down. Eyes look forward. (Illustration 36)

6) Shift the body weight slowly forward and, at the same time, press both hands forward and upward, palms forward. Bend the right leg to form a right bow stance. Eyes should look toward the front. (Illustrations 37 & 38)

Main points: In pressing the hands forward, move them in a curve with the wrists at shoulder height and both elbows slightly bent.

9. Single whip

1) Move the upper part of the body backward to a sitting position and shift the body weight gradually to the left leg, right tiptoe inward. At the same time, turn the upper part of the body to the left; move both hands (left hand higher) to the left in an arc until the left arm is raised horizontally to the left side of the body, and the right hand moves past the abdomen to the front of the left ribs, palm back upward. Eyes should be on the left hand. Then shift the body weight gradually to the right leg, turn the upper part of the body to the right and draw the left foot to the right foot, tiptoe on the ground. Move the right hand upward to the right in an arc (turn the palm inside out) and change it into a hook hand at the right side, arm at shoulder height. Move the left hand first downward, then upward past the abdomen in an arc and finally to the front of the right shoulder, palm inward. Eyes look at the left hand. (Illustrations 39, 40 & 41)

2) Turn the upper part of the body slightly to the left, move the left foot left forward and stamp the right heel backward to form a left bow stance. While shifting the body weight to the left leg, turn over the left palm slowly and push it forward, palm forward, fingers at eye level and arm slightly bent. Eyes should be on the left hand. (Illustration 42)

Main points: Keeping the upper part of the body upright and relax the waist. In finishing the move, lower the right elbow a bit, form a vertical line between the left elbow and the left knee, and keep both shoulders dropped. While turning the left palm over and pushing it forward, the movement should be executed slowly with the turning of the body. All transition movements should be harmonious.

10. Waving hands like clouds

1) Shift the body weight to the right leg, turn the body gradually to the right, left tiptoe inward, and move the left hand past the abdomen and upward in an arc to the front of the right shoulder, palm obliquely backward. At the same time, turn the right hand into a palm that faces backward. Eyes should be on the left hand. (Illustration 43)

2) Turn the upper part of the body slowly to the left, shift the body weight gradually to the left, move the left hand from the front of the face to the left side of the face while gradually turning the palm to the left. Move the right hand from the right below, past the abdomen and upward to the front of the left shoulder in an arc, palm obliquely backward. At the same time, draw the right foot close to the left foot to form a standing position with feet apart (a distance of about 10 to 20 centimeters). Eyes should be on the left hand. (Illustration 44)

3) Turn the upper part of the body again to the right while moving the left hand past the abdomen and upward in an arc to the front of the right shoulder, palm obliquely backward. Move the right hand to the right side and turn the palm over to the right before moving the left foot a step left. Eyes should be on the left hand. (Illustration 45)

4) The same as 1), only left and right in the reverse. (Illustration 46)

5) The same as 2), only left and right in the reverse. (Illustration 47)

6) The same as 3), only left and right in the reverse. (Illustration 48)

Main points: Keep the upper body erect, waist and hips relaxed. The entire movement is smooth and natural, and at constant speed. The movement requires the waist serving as an axis. While the arms and legs are moving, the weight of the body should be stable. When the right foot is moved close to the left foot, the tiptoe should be turned slightly inward so as to continue the next move called "single whip."

第八课 二十四式简化太极拳（3）

第 三 段

十一、单鞭

1. 上体向右转，右手随之向右转，至右侧方时变成勾手；左手经腹前向右上划弧至右肩前，手心向内；身体重心落在右腿上，左脚尖点地，眼看左手。（图49）

2. 上体微向左转，左脚向左侧方迈出，右脚跟后蹬成左弓步。在身体重心移至左腿的同时，左掌慢慢转向前推出，手心向前，手指与眼齐平，臂微屈，眼看左手。（图50）

   <mark>要点</mark>　上体保持正直，松腰。完成动作时，右臂肘部稍下垂，左肘与左膝上下相对，两肩下沉。左手向外翻掌前推时，要随转体边翻边推出，不要翻掌太快。上下要协调一致。

图49　　　　图50

图51　　　　图52

十二、高探马

右脚跟进半步，身体重心移至右腿上。右勾手变成掌，两手心翻转向上，两肘微屈，同时身体微向右转，左脚跟逐渐离地。眼看左手。微微左转，右掌经耳旁向前推出，手心向前，手指与眼同高；左手收至左侧腰前，手心向上，同时左脚微向前移，脚尖点地，成左虚步，眼看右手。（图51）

<mark>要点</mark>　上体自然伸直，双肩要下沉，右肘微下垂。跟步换重心时，上体不要起伏。

十三、右蹬脚

1. 左手手心向上，前伸至右手腕背面，两手相互交叉，随即两手分开自两侧向下划弧，手心斜向下；同时左脚提起向左侧方进步（脚尖略外撇）；身体重心前移，右腿自然伸直，成左弓步；眼看前方。（图52）

2. 两手由外圈向里圈划弧合抱于胸前，右手在外（手心均向后）；同时右脚向左脚靠拢，脚尖点

图53a　　　　图53b

地。眼平看右前方。（图53a, 53b）

3. 两臂左右分开平举，肘部微屈，手心均向外，同时右脚屈膝提起，右脚向右前方慢慢蹬出。（图54）

要点　身体稳定，不可前俯后仰。两手分开时，腕部与肩平。蹬脚时左腿微屈，右脚尖回勾，分手和蹬脚协调一致。右臂和右腿在一条垂直线上。

图54

十四、双峰贯耳

1. 右腿收回，膝盖提起，左手由后向下向前下落至体前，两手心均翻转向上，两手同时向下划弧分落于右膝两侧；眼看前方，右脚向右前方落下，身体重心渐渐前移，变成右弓步，面向右前方；同时两手下垂，慢慢变拳，分别从两侧向上向前划弧至脸前成钳形状，拳眼都斜向后，两拳中间距离约10～20厘米。眼看右拳。（图55）

要点　头颈正直，松腰，两拳松握，沉肩垂肘，两臂均保持弧形。

图55

十五、转身左蹬脚

1. 左腿屈膝后坐，身体重心移至左腿，上体左转，右脚尖里扣；同时两拳变掌，由上向左右划弧分开平举，手心向前；眼看左手。（图56）

图56

2. 身体重心再移至右腿，左脚收到右脚内侧，脚尖点地；同时两手由外圈向里圈划弧合抱于胸前，左手在外，手心均向后；眼平看左方。（图57）

3. 两臂左右划弧分开平举，肘部微屈，手心均向外；同时左腿屈膝提起，左脚向左前方慢慢蹬出；眼看左手。（图58）

要点　身体稳定，不可前俯后仰。两手分开时，腕部与肩平。蹬脚时右腿微屈，左脚尖回勾，分手和蹬脚协调一致。左臂和左腿在一条垂直线上。

图57

图58

Lesson Eight   Twenty-Four Steps of the Simplified Taiji Quan (III)
Chapter Three

11. Single whip

1) Turn the upper part of the body to the right while moving the right hand in the same direction and changing it into a hook hand on the right side. Move the left hand past the abdomen and curve it upward to the front of the right shoulder, palm facing inward. Shift the body weight to the right leg, left tiptoe on the ground. Eyes should be on the left hand. (Illustration 49)

2) Turn the upper part of the body slightly to the left, move the left foot left forward and stamp the right heel backward to form a left bow stance. While shifting the body weight to the left leg, turn over the left palm slowly and push it forward, palm forward, fingers at eye level and arm slightly bent. Eyes should be on the left hand. (Illustration 50) Main points: Keep the upper part of the body upright and relax the waist. In finishing the move, lower the right elbow a bit, let the left elbow form a vertical line with the left knee, and keep both shoulders dropped. While turning the left palm over and pushing it forward, the movement should be executed slowly with the turning of the body. All transition movements should be harmonious.

12. Patting the horse from on high

Move the right foot half a step forward, shift the body weight gradually to the right leg, change the right hook hand into a palm and turn palms up, elbows slightly bent. At the same time, turn the body slightly to the right and lift the left heel gradually off the ground. Eyes should look to the left hand. Then turn the upper part of the body slightly to the left. Push the right palm forward from the side of the ear, palm forward, fingers at eye level; withdraw the left hand to the front of the waist on the left side, palm up. At the same time move the left foot slightly forward, tiptoe on the ground, to form a left empty step. Eyes should be on the right hand. (Illustration 51) Main points: Keep the upper part of the body upright and drop both shoulders, with the right elbow slightly down. The body should not rise or fall when you move your feet and shift your body weight.

13. Kicking with right heel

1) Turn the left palm up and stretch it forward to above the back of the right wrist to form

a cross. Then part the hands from both sides downward in a circle, palm down obliquely. At the same time, raise the left foot and move it obliquely forward to the left (tiptoe outward). Shift the body weight forward, right leg straightening naturally to form a left bow stance. Eyes look forward. (Illustration 52)

2) Draw stretched arms back in a curve to the chest, the right hand outside the left one (palms inward). Move the right foot to the left, tiptoe on the ground. Eyes look forward to the right horizontally. (Illustrations 53a & 53b)

3) Stretch each arm to its side horizontally, palms outward and elbows slightly bent. At the same time, bend the right knee, lift the right foot and kick forward slowly to the right. (Illustration 54)

Main points: Keep the body steady; do not lean forward or backward. When parting the hands, keep the wrists and the shoulders at the same level. When kicking, bend the left leg slightly, right tiptoe backward, to exert force on the heel. Hand movements and kicking should agree with each other harmoniously. Keep the right arm and right leg on a vertical line.

14. Striking opponent's ears with both fists

1) Withdraw the right leg, bend the knee and raise it horizontally. Move the left hand from behind, downward and forward, and drop it in front of the body, both palms turned up. Move both hands simultaneously downward in arcs and bring them to each side of the right knee. With eyes looking foward, plant the right foot forward to the right and shift the body weight gradually forward to form a right bow stance, face forward to the right. At the same time, drop the hands, change them slowly into fists and move them upward from both sides in an arced way until they stike the posture of a pair of pliers, 10 to 20 centimeters apart at ear level, with their holes facing obliquely backward. Eyes should be fixed on the right fist. (Illustration 55)

Main points: In finishing the move, keep the neck erect, waist relaxed, hands loosely closed and both shoulders and elbows lowered. Keep both arms curved.

15. Turning and kicking with left heel

1) Bend the left leg at the knee so that the body sits backward, shift the body weight to the left leg and turn the upper part of the body to the left, right tiptoe inward. At the same time, change the fists into palms and move them from above to both sides in arcs and raise them horizontally, palms forward. Eyes should be on the left hand. (Illustration 56)

2) Shift the body weight again to the right leg and withdraw the left foot to the inner side of the right foot, tiptoe on the ground. At the same time, move the hands toward each other in curves from the outer circle to the inner circle until they are coupled in front of the chest, with the left hand outside and both palms inward. Eyes look to the left. (Illustration 57)

3) Move the arms in horizontal arcs to separate the hands, elbows slightly bent, both palms facing outward. At the same time, kick forward slowly to the left with the left foot. Eyes should be on the left hand. (Illustration 58)

Main points: Keep the body steady; do not lean forward or backward. In pushing the hands outward, keep the wrists and the shoulders at the same level. In kicking, bend the right leg slightly, left tiptoe backward, and exert the force to the heel. Hand pushing and leg kicking should agree with each other harmoniously. Keep the left arm and the left leg on a vertical line.

第九课　二十四式简化太极拳（4）

第 四 段

十六、左下势独立

1. 左腿收回平屈，上体右转，右拳变成勾手，左拳向上、向右划弧下落，立于右肩前，掌心斜向后；眼看右手。右腿慢慢屈膝下蹲，左腿由内向左侧（偏后）伸出，成左仆步；左手下落（掌心向外）向左下顺左腿内侧向前穿出；眼看左手。（图59a，59b）

   图59a　　　图59b

   图60　　　图61

   要点　右腿全蹲时，上体不可过于前倾。左腿伸直，左脚尖须向里扣，两脚脚掌全部着地。左脚尖与右脚跟踏在中轴线上。

2. 身体重心前移，左脚跟为轴，脚尖尽量向外撇，左脚前弓，右腿后蹬，右脚尖里扣，上体微向左转并向前起身；同时左臂继续向前伸出（立掌），掌心向右，右勾手下落，勾尖向后；眼看左手。（图60）

3. 右腿慢慢提起平屈，成左独立式；同时右勾手变掌，并由后下方顺右腿外侧向前弧形摆出，屈臂立于右腿上方，肘与膝相对，手心向左；左手落于左胯旁，手心向下，指尖向前；眼看右手。（图61）

   要点　上体要正直，独立的腿要微屈，右腿提起时脚尖自然下垂。

十七、右下势独立

1. 右脚下落于左脚前，脚掌着地，然后以左脚前掌为轴转动脚跟，身体随之左转，同时左手向后平举变成勾手，右掌随着转体向左侧划弧，立于左肩前，掌心斜向后；左腿慢慢屈膝下蹲，右腿由内向右侧（偏后）伸出，成右仆步；右手下落，掌心向外，向右下侧顺右腿内侧向前穿出；眼看右手。（图62）

   图62

2．与"左下势独立"2动作相同，只是左右相反。（图63）

3．与"左下势独立"3动作相同，只是左右相反。（图64）
  要点 右脚尖触地后必须稍微提起，然后屈膝下蹲，重心由左腿移到右腿，保持身体正直，左腿微屈，左腿提起时脚尖自然下垂。

图63　　　　图64

十八、左右穿梭

1．身体微向左转，左脚向前落地，脚尖外撇，右脚跟离地，两腿屈膝成半盘坐式；同时两手在左胸前成抱球状（左上右下）；然后右脚收到左脚的内侧，脚尖点地；眼看左前臂。（图65）

2．身体右转，右脚向右前方迈出，屈膝弓腿，成右弓步；同时右手由脸前向上举并翻掌停在右额前，手心斜向上；左手先向左下再经体前向前推出，高与鼻尖平，手心向前；眼看左手。（图66，67）

图65　　　　图66

3．身体重心略向后移，右脚尖稍向外撇，随即身体重心再移至右腿，左脚跟进，停于右脚内侧，脚尖点地；同时两手在右胸前成抱球状；眼看右前臂。（图68）

4．同2解，只是左右相反。（图69）
  要点 完成姿势面向斜前方，手推出后，上体不可前俯。手向上举时，防止引肩上耸。一手上举一手前推要与弓腿松腰上下协调一致。做弓步时，两脚跟的横向距离保持在30厘米左右。

图67　　　　图68

十九、海底针

右脚向前跟进半步，身体重心移至右腿，左脚稍向前移，脚尖点地，成左虚步；同时身体稍向右转，右手下落经体前向后、向上提抽至肩上耳旁，再随身体左转，由右耳旁斜向前下方插出，掌心向左，指尖斜向下，与此同时，左手向前上下划弧落于左胯旁，手心向下，指尖向前；眼看前下方。（图70，71）

要点 身体要先向右转，再向左转。上体不可太前倾。避免低头和臀部外凸。左腿要微屈。

图69　　　　图70

图71

二十、闪通臂

上体稍向右转，左脚向前迈出，屈膝弓腿成左弓步；同时右手由体前上提，屈臂上举，停于右额前上方，掌心翻转斜向上，拇指朝下；左手上起经胸前向前推出，高与鼻尖平，手心向前；眼看左手。（图72，73）

要点　完成姿势上体自然正直，松腰、松胯；左臂不要完全伸直，背部肌肉要伸展开。推掌、举掌和弓腿动作要协调一致。弓步时，两脚横向距离同"揽雀尾"式。

图72

图73

Lesson Nine　Twenty-Four Steps of the Simplified Taiji Quan (IV)

Chapter Four

16. Crouching down and standing on left leg

1) Withdraw the left leg and bend it horizontally. Turn the upper part of the body slightly to the right. Change the right fist into a hook hand, move the left fist upward to the right in a curve and stand it in front of the right shoulder, palm obliquely backward. Eyes should be on the right hand. Then bend the right leg slowly to a squatting position and stretch the left leg from inside to the left side (slighly backward) to form a left crouch stance. Move the left hand down (palm outward) to the left and then forward along the inner side of the left leg. Eyes should be on the left hand. (Illustrations 59a &59b)

Main points: When the right leg is in a full squatting position, do not lean the upper part of the body forward too much. Keep the left leg straight, left tiptoe inward. Both soles completely touch the ground. Place the left tiptoe and right heel on the central axis.

2) Shift the body weight forward and pivot on the left heel, tiptoe turning outward as much as possible. Bend the left leg forward and kick backward with the right leg, right tiptoe inward. The upper part of the body rises while turning slightly to the left. At the same time, continue to stretch the left arm forward (standing palm), palm facing right. Drop the right hook hand down, hook backward. Eyes should be on the left hand. (Illustration 60)

3) Raise the right leg slowly and bend it horizontally so as to stand on the left leg. At the same time, change the right hook hand into a palm and move it from back below and along the outer side of the right leg and swing it forward in an arc. Bend the arm and put it vertically above the right leg, elbow and knee on a vertical line, palm facing left. Drop the left hand down by the left hip, palm down and fingertips forward. Eyes should be on the right hand. (Illustration 61)

Main points: Keep the upper part of the body upright and bend the standing leg slightly. The tiptoe is naturally down when the right leg is raised up.

17. Crouching down and standing on right leg

1) Plant the right foot in front of the left foot, sole on the ground. Then, pivot the front sole of the left foot and turn the body to the left. At the same time, raise the left hand backward horizontally and change it into a hook hand; move the right palm in an arc to the left side with the turning of the body and place it vertically before the left shoulder, palm obliquely backward. Bend the left leg at the knee slowly to a squat. Stretch the right leg from inside to the right side (slightly backward) to form a right crouch stance. Move the right hand down to the right and then forward along the inner side of the right leg, palm outward. Eyes should be on the right hand. (Illustration 62)

2) The same as "Crouching down and standing on left leg" 2), only left and right in the reverse. (Illustration 63)

3) The same as "Crouching down and standing on left leg" 3), only left and right in the reverse. (Illustration 64)

Main points: Lift the right tiptoe slightly after it touches the ground, then bend the right leg in a squatting position, with the body weight shifted from the left leg to the right. Keep the body erect. Bend the left leg slightly and lift it, the left tiptoe pointing downward naturally.

18. Shuttling back and forth

1) Turn the body slightly to the left and plant the left foot forward, tiptoe outward and upward. The right heel leaves the ground. Bend both knees to form a half sitting position. At the same time, place the hands before the chest in a position as if to hold a ball (left hand above and right hand below). Withdraw the right foot to the inner side of the left foot, tiptoe on the ground. Eyes should be on the left forearm. (Illustration 65)

2) Turn the body to the right and move the right foot forward to the right, leg bent, to form a right bow stance. At the same time, raise the right hand upward from before the face, turn the palm and rest it in front of the right forehead, palm obliquely up. Move the left hand first downward on the left side and then past the front of the body and push it forward to the height of the nose tip, palm forward. Eyes should be on the left hand. (Illustrations 66 & 67)

3) Shift the body weight slightly backward, right tiptoe outward, and then shift the body weight to the right leg, with the left foot following behind and stopping on the inner side of the right foot, tiptoe on the ground. At the same time, move the hands in front of the right chest in a position as if to hold a ball (right hand above and left hand below). Eyes should be on the right forearm. (Illustration 68)

4) The same as 2), only left and right in the reverse. (Illustration 69)

Main points: In finishing the move, turn the face obliquely forward. After pushing the hand, do not let the upper part of the body lean forward. When raising the hands, be sure not to raise the shoulders. The hands lifting and pushing should agree harmoniously with legs bending and waist relaxing. In making the bow stance, the crosswise distance between the heels should be about 30 centimeters.

19. Needle at the sea bottom

Move the right foot half a step forward, shift the body weight to the right leg and move the left foot slightly forward, tiptoe on the ground, to form a left empty stance. At the same time, turn the body slightly to the right, move the right hand downward past the front of the body, then raise it backward and upward to the ear. Turn the body left and move the right hand forward and downward from the right ear side, palm facing left and the fingertip obliquely down. At the same time, move the left hand forward and in an arc and drop it by the left hip, palm down and fingertips forward. Eyes should look down forward. (Illustrations 70 & 71)

Main points: First turn the body to the right and then to the left. Do not let the upper part of the body lean forward too much. Avoid lowering the head and protruding the buttocks. Bend the left leg slightly.

20. Flash arms

Turn the upper part of the body slightly to the right, move the left foot forward and bend the leg at the knee to form a left bow stance. At the same time, move the right hand upward in front of the body, bend the arm, raise it and rest it above the right forehead; turn the palm obliquely up, thumb down. Move the left hand upward and push it forward in front of the chest to the height of the nose tip, palm forward. Eyes should be on the left hand. (Illustrations 72 & 73)

Main points: In completing the move, keep the upper part of the body naturally upright and relax the waist and hips. Do not straighten the left arm completely. Extend the back muscles. Palm pushing, palm lifting and leg bending should agree with each other harmoniously. In forming the bow stance, the crosswise distance between the heels should be the same as that of "Grasping the peacock's tail."

第十课 二十四式简化太极拳（5）

第 五 段

二十一、转身搬拦锤

1. 上体后坐，重心移至右腿上，左脚尖里扣，身体
   向右后转，然后重心再移至左腿上。同时，右手
   随着转体而向右向下（变拳）经腹前划弧至左肋
   旁。拳心向下；左掌上举于头前方，掌心斜向
   上。眼看前方。（图74，75）

2. 向右转体，右拳经胸前向前翻转撇出，拳心向
   上，左手落于左胯旁，同时右脚收回后再向前迈
   出，脚尖外撇。眼看右拳。（图76）

3. 重心移至右腿上，左脚向前迈一步。左手上起经左
   侧向前平行划弧拦出，掌心向前下方，同时右拳收
   到右腰旁，拳心向上，眼看左手。（图77，78）

4. 左腿前弓变成左弓步，同时右拳向前打出，拳眼
   向上，高与胸平，左手随附于右前臂里侧。眼看
   右拳。（图79）

   要点 右拳不要握得太紧。右拳回收时，前臂要
   慢慢回旋划弧，然后再外旋停于右腰旁，拳心向
   上。向前打拳时，右肩随拳略向前伸，沉肩垂肘，
   右臂微屈。

二十二、如封似闭

1. 左手由右腕下向前伸，右拳变掌，两手心向上慢
   慢回收；同时身体后坐，左脚尖跷起，重心移至
   右腿。眼看前方。（图80）

2. 两手在胸前翻掌，向前推出，腕与肩平，同时左腿前
   弓变左弓步。眼看前方。（图81，82）

   要点 身体后坐时，避免后仰，臀部不可凸出。
   两臂随身体回收时，肩、肘部略向外松开，不要
   直着抽回。两手宽度不要超过两肩。

图74　　　图75

图76　　　图77

图78　　　图79

图80　　　图81

图82　　　图83

二十三、十字手

1. 身体重心移至右腿上，左脚尖里扣，向右转体。右手随着转体动作向右平摆划弧，与左手成两臂侧平举，肘部下垂，同时右脚尖随着转体稍向外撇，成右弓步。眼看右手。（图83,84）

图84　　　图85

2. 身体重心慢慢移至左腿上，右脚尖里扣然后右脚向左收回与左脚成开立步，两脚距离与肩同宽；同时两手向下经腹前向上划弧交叉于胸前，右手在外，手心均向后，成十字手。眼看前方。（图85）

　　要点　两手分开和合抱时上体勿前仰，站起后，身体自然正直，头微上顶，下颌稍向后收。两臂环抱时须圆满舒适，沉肩垂肘。

图86　　　图87

二十四、收势

两手向外翻掌，手心向下，慢慢下落于两胯外侧，眼看前方。（图86,87,88）

　　要点　两手左右分开下落时，全身注意放松，同时气息徐徐向下沉（呼气略加长），呼吸平稳后，把左脚收至右脚，再走动休息。

图88

Lesson Ten　Twenty-Four Steps of the Simplified Taiji Quan（V）
Chapter Five

21. Turning body and punching

1) Move the upper part of the body down backward into a sitting position. Shift the body weight to the right leg, left tiptoe inward, turn the body backward to the right and then shift the body weight to the left leg. At the same time, move the right hand downward to the right while changing it into a fist and turning the body, past the abdomen to the left ribs in an arc, palm facing down. Raise the left palm upward to the front of the head, palm obliquely up. Eyes should look toward the front. (Illustrations 74 & 75)

2) Continue to turn the body to the right, move the right fist past the chest and forward, turn it over and throw it out, palm facing up. Drop the left hand by the left hip. At the same time, withdraw the right foot and move it forward again immediately, tiptoe

outward. Eyes should be on the right fist. (Illustration 76)

3) Shift the body weight to the right leg and move the left foot with a follow-up step. Move the left hand upward from the left side in an arc and push it out, palm facing down forward. At the same time, withdraw the right fist to the right waist side, palm facing up. Eyes should be on the left hand. (Illustrations 77 & 78)

4) Bend the left leg forward to form a left bow stance. At the same time, strike forward with the right fist, fist hole up to chest level, and the left palm against the inner side of the right forearm. Eyes should be on the right fist. (Illustration 79)

Main points: Do not fold the right hand too tightly. When withdrawing the right fist, spin the forearm inward slowly in an arc, then spin it outward and rest it by the waist side, palm facing up. When the fist strikes forward, extend the right shoulder, and bend the right arm slightly.

22. Closing up

1) Stretch the left palm forward from under the right wrist, change the right fist into a palm, turn both palms up and withdraw them slowly. At the same time, move the body backward into a sitting position, left tiptoe upward, and shift the body weight to the right leg. Eyes should look to the front. (Illustration 80)

2) Turn the palms and push them out in front of the chest, the wrists at shoulder level. At the same time, straighten the right leg and bend the left leg forward to form a left bow stance. Eyes should look to the front. (Illustrations 81 & 82)

Main points: When sitting back, avoid leaning backward and thrusting the buttocks. Withdraw elbows in a relaxed way with the shoulders and elbows slightly outward, instead of withdrawing them straight. The width between the hands should be within the shoulder cross width.

23. Crossing hands

1) Shift the body weight to the right leg, left tiptoe inward, and turn the body to the right. Move the right hand with the turning of the body to the right horizontally in an arc. Raise both arms sideways horizontally, palms outward, elbows slightly bent. At the same time, move the right tiptoe slightly outward with the turning of the body to form a right bow stance. Eyes should be on the right hand. (Illustrations 83 & 84)

2) Shift the body weight slowly to the left leg, right tiptoe inward; withdraw the right foot to the left immediately to form a standing posture, the distance between the feet being shoulder width. At the same time, move both hands downward, past the abdomen and upward in an arc to cross each other in front of the chest, right hand outside, and both

palms backward. Eyes should be looking forward. (Illustration 85)

Main points: Do not let the upper part of the body lean forward when the hands move apart and together. When standing, keep the body naturally upright, raise the head slightly and drop the chin a bit. In forming the cross hands, keep the arms smooth and comfortable and drop the shoulders and elbows.

24. Finishing move

Turn both palms downward, and drop both arms slowly to both sides of the body. Eyes should look to the front. (Illustrations 86, 87 & 88)

Main points: When parting the hands and dropping them, be sure that the whole body is relaxed. At the same time, the energy stream flows slowly down (exhaling becomes slightly longer). After breathing becomes steady, withdraw the left foot to the right foot and then take a short walk.

学做中国菜

COOKING CHINESE DISHES

学做中国菜

胡建刚　编写／翻译

Cooking Chinese Dishes

Compiled and Translated by Hu Jiangang

第一课　中国菜概述

中国菜世界闻名，它重视烹饪技术，菜式多样，讲究"色、香、味、形、养"，是历史悠久的中华饮食文化的重要组成部分。

一、四大菜系

中国菜在内容上可分为地方菜系、宫廷菜系、官府菜系、寺院菜系和少数民族菜系，而其中地方菜系是最主要的部分。地方菜系种类也较多，最著名的是苏菜（江苏菜）、川菜（四川菜）、粤菜（广东菜）、鲁菜（山东菜），因为他们体现了中国东西南北四个地方菜系的基本特点，也是中国菜的典型代表，所以我们一般称之为"中国四大菜系"。

苏菜主要分布在南京、上海、苏州、无锡等地，其菜肴以偏重甜味为重要特色。苏菜制作要求原料干净、新鲜，刀工细腻，菜式随季节变化明显，口感清爽，注重原汁原味。著名菜肴有蟹粉狮子头、金陵盐水鸭、炸响铃等。

川菜主要分布在中国的西南地区，如四川、云南、贵州等地。它以大量使用辣椒、花椒等麻辣调料著称，选料丰富，烹调方法根据材料的变化而变化，口味浓厚，口感强烈，所以有"味在四川"的说法。著名的菜肴有宫爆鸡丁、麻婆豆腐等。

粤菜主要分布在广东省，它包括广州菜、潮州菜和东江菜（客家菜）。广州菜的主要特点是选材独特、广泛：蛇、鼠、虫、龟等都可以拿来做菜，且配料丰富，花色多样。据统计，在广州，有正式名字的菜有5,000多种，点心有800多种，所以人们常常说"吃在广州"。潮州菜的特长在于烧制海鲜、煲汤和制作甜点。而客家菜则以软香、量大且口味偏咸为主要特色。粤菜的代表菜肴有东江酿豆腐、豉汁蒸排骨、蚝油鲜菇等。

鲁菜是中国北方的代表菜系。它既是先前中国皇家宫廷菜的主体，也是当今北京城里最主要的菜系之一，它既善于炮制海鲜，也善于煎、炖、拔丝，口味讲究"清、鲜、软、脆、纯"，著名菜肴有糖醋鲤鱼、腰果虾仁等。

二、常用烹调工具与切配用具

要想做出一道美味的中国菜，常用烹调工具与切配用具是必不可少的。如锅、碗、盘、汤勺、筷子、漏勺、锅铲、手勺、菜刀、砧板、蒸笼、调味罐等。（图1、图2）

图1 蒸笼和锅　　图2 勺子筷子等

三、常用调料（图3）

调料在中国菜的制作中占有十分重要的地位，所用调料不同，菜肴的口味也会不同。我们常用的调料有：油、豆瓣酱、酱油、腐乳、海鲜酱、番茄酱、豆豉、醋、蚝油、米酒。

此外还有盐、糖、味精、鸡精、辣椒、姜、葱、蒜等。

图3　调料

四、常用刀法

由于原料的形状会直接影响到每一道菜最后的外形和特点，所以做中国菜时，对刀法的要求就比较高。中国菜的刀工技术有上百种，其中常用的有：

1. 平刀法　刀和墩板基本保持平行，将原料切成片。具体刀法有推片法、直片法。

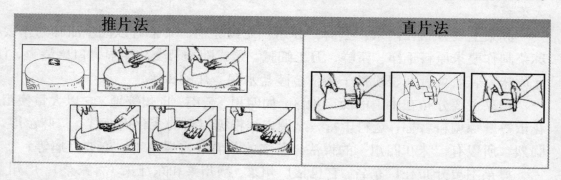

2. 剞(jī)刀法　刀作垂直或倾斜等不同方向的运动，在原料上切出或刻上各种花纹，分为直刀剞和斜刀推剞。

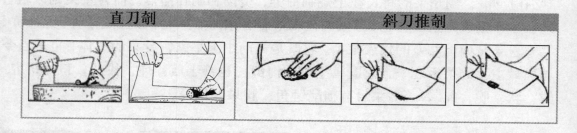

3. 斜刀法　刀和墩板呈斜角，刀倾斜将原料切成片，分为拉片法和推片法。

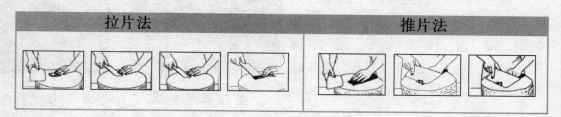

4. **直刀法**　刀和墩板基本保持垂直，将原料切开或切断，具体刀法有切、剁、砍。

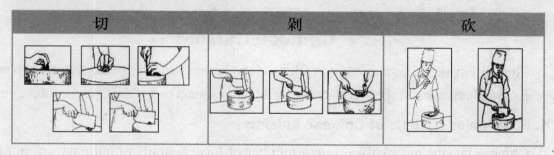

| 切 | 剁 | 砍 |

五、烹调方法

烹调方法丰富多样是中国菜的典型特点，我们常用的烹调方法有：

炒　旺火将锅中的油加热，将准备好的原料倒入锅中，并不断以锅铲翻动，使其受热均匀。

炸　旺火将油烧至高温，再放入原料，加热使其颜色逐渐改变。

煎　锅中放入少量油，加热后把原料平贴于锅内，依次使原料两侧颜色改变。

烹　原料放于锅中煎熟后，倒出多余的油，然后把准备好的酱汁和煎好的原料一起倒入锅中，稍炒即可。

熘　先把原料煎熟，再将准备好的芡汁倒在煎熟的原料上。

煮　先在锅中放入水，旺火将水烧至沸腾后，加入准备好的原料和调料，将锅较长时间地置于文火上，直到汤汁浓稠，食物变熟。

焖　将原料稍炒至变色后，马上放入清水和调料，加上锅盖，小火长时间地烧煮，直到汤汁熬干，食物烂熟。

炖　把原料和清水同时加入锅中，先用旺火把水烧至沸腾后，加入调料，再用文火长时间地烧煮至熟。

爆　先将原料煎熟后，倒出剩下的油，再将原料与调料一起放入锅里，稍炒即可。

勾芡　把淀粉加适量水搅拌均匀后淋在快要熟的食物上，使水淀粉吸收少量汤汁后包裹食物的外层，增色增味。

学做中国菜

Lesson One   General Introduction to Chinese Cuisine

Chinese cuisine is famous for its variety, elaborate cooking methods, and its emphasis on "color, fragrance, taste, shape and nutrition." It is one important part of the Chinese culinary culture.

1. Four major schools of Chinese cuisine

Chinese cuisine has evolved into a number of local schools of culinary art, but it also includes cooking styles that originated in the kitchens of the imperial courts, the mansions of high officials, temples, and minority peoples. The rich and varied local schools, however, are the mainstay of Chinese cuisine. The most well-known of them are the Su (Jiangsu), Chuan (Sichuan), Yue (Guangdong) and Lu (Shandong) schools, representing the culinary art of east, south, west and north China respectively. They are generally known as the "Four Major Styles of Chinese Cuisine."

The Su cuisine encompasses the cooking styles of Nanjing, Shanghai, Suzhou and Wuxi, which are characterized by a preference for sweet taste. In general, Jiangsu dishes emphasize the freshness of raw materials and the slicing and cutting skills. The materials used change with the seasons. Special attention is paid to retaining the raw materials' natural juice and flavor. Famous dishes include Lion Head prepared with minced pork and crab meat, Jinling Saltwater Duck and Deep-Fried Jingle Bells.

The Chuan cuisine is popular in the southwest provinces of Sichuan, Yunnan and Guizhou. It is specially known for its chefs' penchant for such flavoring condiments as dried Chinese prickly ash seeds and hot peppers. Predicated on extensive and meticulous choices of raw materials and a dazzling array of cooking methods, the Sichuan dishes are known for their unusual fresh and pungent flavors. This has prompted the saying, "The best flavors are found only in Sichuan." The famous dishes include Mapo Bean Curd and Diced Chicken with Dried Paprika.

The Yue cuisine features the culinary styles of Guangzhou and Chaozhou, and the Hakka dishes of Dongjiang. Guangzhou dishes are characterized by their special ingredients that range from the strange to the exotic, such as snakes, turtles and even insects. Another feature of Guangzhou dishes is their great variety. According to statistics, there are over 5,000 famous dishes and 800 refreshments, which have earned Guangzhou the reputation as the "Gourmets' paradise" in China and overseas. The Chaozhou style is marked for its uniquely prepared seafood, soups and desserts. The Hakkas of Dongjiang have developed their own dishes that are generous, ambrosially soft and fragrant, with a preference for saltiness. Among the best Yue dishes are Dongjiang Bean Curd, Steamed Spareribs with Soya-Bean Sauce and Mushroom with Oyster Sauce.

Enjoying a stellar reputation in north China, the Lu cuisine used to be the main stream of the nation's imperial kitchen fare. Today, it is one of the most popular culinary styles in Beijing. The Shandong school of cooking is known for its deep-frying, stewing and candying techniques and its elaborate preparation seafood, and its due emphasis on the cleanness, freshness, tenderness, crispness and purity of flavors. Its trademark dishes are Sweet and Sour Carp and Cashew Nuts with Shrimp Meat.

2. Kitchen utensils

The following utensils are needed to prepare delicious Chinese dishes: pan, bowl, plate, spoon, chopsticks, strainer, slice, ladle, knife, chopping block, food steamer, and condiment pots. (Illustrations 1 & 2)

3. Condiments (Illustration 3)

It is very important to decide what seasoning to choose when cooking Chinese dishes, because different tastes depend on different seasonings. The following are the common condiments used by Chinese chefs.

Oil, thick broad-bean sauce, soya sauce, fermented bean curd, seafood paste, ketchup, fermented soya beans, vinegar, oyster sauce, rice wine.

In addition, there are salt, sugar, monosodium glutamate, chicken extract, pepper, ginger, scallion, garlic etc.

4. Cutting techniques

Because different ways of cutting affect the texture and appearance of a dish, the mastery of the basic cutting techniques is vital to learning Chinese cuisine. Of more than one hundred cutting techniques, the most useful are as follows:

1) Flat-cutting   Flat-cuts are designed to create slices. Keep the knife almost parallel with the chopping block. For example, pushing-slicing and straight-slicing.

2) Scoring-cutting   Keep the knife vertical or slanting. Directional cuts are employed to carve patterns on the surface of ingredients. For example, straight-scoring and slanting-pushing scoring.

3) Slanting-cutting   Keep the knife slanting to create slices. For example, pulling-slicing and pushing-slicing.

4) Straight-cutting   Keep the knife almost vertical to the chopping block. Straight-cuts are

to create cubes, chunks and pastes. For example, slicing, chopping and hacking.

5. Cooking methods

Various cooking methods are characteristic of Chinese cuisine. Here we are to learn some basic methods:

Chao (Stir-fry)	Heat oil over a high heat and put the ingredients into a wok, then toss and turn repeatedly.
Zha (Deep-fry)	Heat a large amount of oil over a high heat, then put in the ingredients until what is being cooked appears golden on both sides.
Jian (Fry)	Heat a little oil and stick the ingredients to the wok. Both sides of the food should be fried until the color changes.
Peng	Fry the ingredients quickly in hot oil, pour away excess oil, and stir-fry them when sauce is added.
Liu (Quick-fry)	Fry the ingredients first, then spread the prepared starch sauce on them.
Zhu	Heat a large amount of water to boil over a high heat, then add all the ingredients and seasonings. Simmer over a gentle heat until the soup thickens.
Men (Simmer)	Stir-fry ingredients briefly until the color changes, then add water and seasonings; simmer over a low heat after boiling until the food has become almost dry and thoroughly cooked.
Dun (Stew)	Place the ingredients and water into a wok at the same time, bring the mixfure to the boil. After adding seasonings, turn down the fire to a gentle heat for a session of long, slow cooking.
Bao	Pour away excess oil after frying the ingredients, add seasonings and stir-fry until the dish is done.
Gouqian	Pour dissolved starch on the ingredients when the ingredients are nearly done. The starch will coat the food and make it more palatable.

第二课　学做家常菜

一、豉汁蒸排骨

主料　新鲜猪排骨　300克

作料　精盐3克　豆豉5克　酱油20克　淀粉20克　白糖5克　芝麻油、味精、大蒜、葱段各少许

制法　先将排骨洗干净，滤干以后加入盐、味精、豆豉、大蒜、酱油、白糖、芝麻油及淀粉，并搅拌调匀。然后将排骨均匀排放在平底盘中，放至中火上蒸大约十分钟后，把菜盘从锅中取出，再放上一些葱段即可。

二、宫保鸡丁（图4）

主料　鸡脯肉250克　油炸花生仁50克

作料　干辣椒7.5克　花椒粒15颗　酱油10克
淀粉40克　油125克　醋15克　精盐2.5克
白糖10克　花椒面、姜、葱段各少许

制法　干辣椒切成2厘米长的辣椒段备用。先用刀背拍打鸡肉，使其肉质疏松，然后切成鸡丁，并加入盐、水、淀粉，搅拌调匀；同时，把酱油、白糖、醋

图4　宫保鸡丁

和少许水一起放入配料碗中调配成备用调料。先将锅置于旺火上，放油加热后，投入干辣椒段、花椒粒，在其颜色被炸成红褐色时，下鸡丁翻炒，翻炒时使鸡丁互相散开；鸡丁将熟时，加入葱、姜、花椒面，翻炒片刻后，放入配料碗中的备用料汁和油炸花生仁，再一起炒一会儿，即可起锅装盘。

三、五香牛肉

主料　牛肉750克

作料　五香盐120克　姜5克　蒜苗5克　芝麻油25克　绍兴米酒30克　葱2段　茴香2粒　桂皮1片　盐、辣椒酱各少许

制法　先将牛肉抹上五香盐后放在盆里腌一天，然后取出，在净水中浸泡一会儿后，放入汽锅中，加水至牛肉完全浸入水中，同时也把葱、姜（用菜刀拍烂）、茴香和桂皮一并放进锅中，再放到大火上煮。在水开了之后，倒入

绍兴米酒和盐，并盖紧锅盖，移至小火上慢慢地焖，直到牛肉完全焖熟为止。取出冷却后，把牛肉切成一片一片放入盘中，撒上些蒜苗末、芝麻油和辣椒酱，菜就做好了。

四、麻婆豆腐

主料　鲜豆腐250克　牛肉75克

作料　清汤100克　油75克　青蒜15克　豆瓣25克　水淀粉10克　豆豉10克　生姜10克　花椒面、葱段、绍兴米酒、盐、味精各少许

制法　将鲜豆腐切成1.5厘米左右的方丁，放进沸水锅中过水两次（水中加少许盐），以除去豆腐的涩味；青蒜洗干净，切成小段；同时把牛肉、豆瓣、豆豉也都剁碎成粉末状。把锅里的油用旺火烧热后，放入牛肉末，随后加进盐、豆瓣末、豆豉末、姜、葱。等其炒出香味、颜色变红后，即倒入适量的清汤和绍兴米酒，调成鲜美的调味汁。然后在锅中放入豆腐，用小火稍煮一会儿就改成中火，并加入青蒜、味精，最后勾芡收汁。待汤汁浓稠后，盛入盘中，撒上花椒面即成。

Lesson Two　Learn to Cook Everyday Dishes

1. Steamed spareribs with soya-bean sauce

Main ingredients fresh spareribs 300g

Seasonings salt 3g   fermented soya beans 5g   soya sauce 20g   starch 20g   white sugar 5g a little garlic, chopped scallions, sesame oil and monosodium glutamate

Process Wash spareribs and drain, mix it with salt, monosodium glutamate, fermented soya beans, soya sauce, white sugar, sesame oil, garlic and starch. Then place spareribs in a plate, take it to steam for about 10 minutes over a gentle heat. Finally remove it and spread some chopped scallions on the spareribs before serving.

2. Diced chicken with dried pepper (Illustration 4)

Main ingredients chicken 250g fried peanuts 50g

Seasonings dried pepper 7.5g dried Chinese prickly ash seeds 15 pieces soya sauce 10g starch 40g   oil 125g   vinegar 15g   refined salt 2.5g white sugar 10g   a little   Chinese prickly ash powder, a few slices of ginger, scallion

Process Cut dried pepper into sections, 2cm long. Tenderize the chicken with the broad edge of cleaver to loosen the texture, and cut it into cubes. Mix cubes of chicken with refined salt and water before coating with dissolved starch. Mix soya sauce, white sugar, vinegar and water in a bowl. After heating oil over a high fire, fry chopped pepper with Chinese prickly ash seeds in the wok until brown, add chicken cubes and stir-fry. Then put in ginger slices, scallion and Chinese prickly ash powder. When chicken cubes get red, add seasoning mixture and fried peanuts. Toss them quickly for a while before putting the dish in a plate to serve.

3. Five-spiced beef

Main ingredients beef 750g

Seasonings spiced-salt 120g   ginger 5g garlic pedicel 5g sesame oil 25g Shaoxing rice wine 30g   green scallion 2 sections   fennel seed 2 pieces   cassia bark 1 piece a little refined salt and chilli sauce.

Process Marinate the beef with spiced-salt in a bowl for one day. Remove and soak in clear water for a moment. Put the beef in a boiler over a high fire, pour in fresh water until the beef is thoroughly submerged, add green scallion, ginger (patted soft with kitchen knife), fennel seeds and cassia bark. When water boils, put in the Shaoxing rice wine and refined salt, cover the boiler tightly and move it to a slow fire to simmer the beef gently until done. Then take out the beef and cool. Cut the beef into slices and put them in a plate, spread pieces of garlic pedicel on the meat, add sesame oil and a little chilli sauce. It is ready to serve.

4. Mapo bean curd

Main ingredients tender bean curd 250g   beef 75g

Seasonings clear soup 100g   oil 75g   garlic shoots 15g   fermented broad beans 25g dissolved starch 10g   fermented soya beans 10g   minced ginger 10g   a little Chinese prickly ash powder, chopped scallion, Shaoxing rice wine, refined salt, monosodium glutamate

Process Cut the tender bean curd into 1.5cm cubes, scald in boiling water twice (a little salt in boiling water). Cut the clean garlic shoots into small pieces. At the same time, cut up beef, and fermented broad beans and soya beans.

Heat oil on a high heat, stir-fry the beef until it becomes crisp, then add fermented broad beans and soya beans, salt, minced ginger and scallion. When it is cooked and turns fragrant, pour in clear soup and Shaoxing rice wine and put in bean curd. After boiling over a small heat for a short while, turn up the fire to a medium heat, and add dissolved starch, the garlic shoots, monosodium glutamate. When the soup thickens, put the dish in a plate, and spread Chinese prickly ash powder over the bean curd.

第三课　学做中国面点

一、三鲜水饺

主料　面粉1000克　　瘦猪肉600克　　虾仁200克　　鸡脯肉200克　　韭菜500克
　　　水发鱿鱼100克

作料　精盐5克　绍兴米酒5克　花生油15克　姜10克（以上原料可做100个左右的
　　　饺子）

制法

1. **和面**　把面粉倒入盆中，在中间扒一面窝，然后将水倒进面窝内，慢慢搅拌，
   把面粉调和均匀，最后做成一个面团。

2. **揉面**　为增强面团的黏性，面团做成后需要揉面。揉面又分两种，当面团较
   大时，就用双手的掌根压住面团，用力向外推揉，并加以多次卷叠、挤压；如
   果面团较小，则可用一只手抓住面团的一头，另一只手的掌跟将面团压扁并向
   外侧推挤，然后再卷叠、挤压，重复多次即可。

3. **搓条**　将揉好的面团从盆中取出，在案板上用刀切成若干块，并把块状的面
   团搓成长条状。

4. **擀皮**　把长条状的面团再切成若干大小适中
   的小方块,用手掌将其按扁，然后用左手的大
   拇指、中指和食指捏住面团的边缘，逆时针
   转动，右手拿擀面杖压住面饼的三分之一
   处，随着左手的转动，边转边擀。饺子皮要
   求四周薄、中间厚、皮子圆。(图5)
   （一般市场也有擀好的饺子皮卖。）

1　　　　　　　　2

图5　擀皮

5. **制馅**　将新鲜的韭菜洗干净之后，切成细末；把瘦猪肉、鸡脯肉和鱿鱼分别剁
   成肉泥，放入配料碗中，同时加进盐、油、姜、米酒等调料，并加入少量的水，
   然后朝同一个方向不停地搅拌，直到肉泥起粘性，没有水分渗出为止。最后把
   韭菜末和肉泥混和、调匀。

6. **包饺子**　包饺子就是用饺子皮把饺子馅包起来，饺子馅量的多少要根据饺子皮
   的大小来决定，而且饺子馅要放在饺子皮的中间。初学者以馅少量为好。包饺
   子的基本方法有两种：(图6)

   1) 挤捏法：先用左手托住饺子皮，右手上馅，然后对准边缘，把饺子皮儿合
      上，双手食指弯曲在下，拇指并拢在上，用力挤捏饺子皮边，粘牢。

2) 推捏法：左手托住饺子皮，右手上馅，对准边缘把皮合上后，右手的食指放在面皮边的外侧，大拇指放在饺子皮的内侧，拇指一推食指一捏，一直向前捻动，从而形成连续完整的花边。

1   2

图6　包饺子的方法

7. 煮饺子　锅中加入适量的水，水的多少应以能使下入锅中的饺子不会紧挨或粘连为准。水烧开后，单个、依次将包好的饺子放下锅，同时用手勺在锅内沿同一方向轻轻搅动，以免饺子粘连，然后将锅盖盖上。在锅内汤水重新沸腾后，把锅盖拿开，用手勺在锅内均匀搅动，使浮起的饺子能均匀受热。然后，往锅内加入少量冷水，使锅内开水的高温沸腾变得平缓，避免饺子皮因汤水沸腾剧烈而破裂，这就是"点水"。重复"点水"三到四次后，饺子一般就熟了，用漏勺将饺子捞出，盛入盘中即可。（图7）
醋、蒜、香油等是中国人吃饺子时的主要调味品。

图7　饺子

二、葱油饼

主料　精面粉300克

作料　色拉油30克　葱花40克　苏打粉10克
　　　糖8克　盐12克　热开水100克　水50克

图8　葱油饼

制法　先将盐溶解于水中，然后将面粉倒入盆里，并加入热开水，同时把溶解的盐水、苏打粉、糖也倒入盆中，一起搅拌。待面粉搅拌成团后，移到桌面上进行揉搓，并将面团揉成表面光滑的圆形。这时在面团上撒上葱花，沾上色拉油，盖上保鲜膜。放置约三十分钟后，用擀面杖由中间向外把面团擀成圆形，放入锅中煎烤。将其两面都煎至金黄色即熟，然后切成数块放入盘中。（图8）

Lesson Three   How to Make Dumplings and
Green Scallion Pancake

1.Three delicacies dumplings

Main ingredients wheat flour 1,000g lean pork 600g shrimp meat 200g chicken 200g squid 100g leek 500g

Seasonings refined salt 5g Shaoxing rice wine 5g peanut oil 15g ginger 10g (for 100 dumplings)

Process

1) Flour-mixing: Put flour into a basin, make it concave in the center and add some water. Stir the flour evenly to make a dough.

2) Kneading the dough: To make the dough sticky, knead it. If the dough is very big, press it down with your palms, knead the edge and roll it for several times; if the dough is small, hold one end of it with one hand, press and knead it with the other palm several times.

3) Rolling dough into strips: After kneading, remove the dough from the basin and cut it into pieces on kneading board. Roll each piece into strip.

4) Rolling out the dumpling wrappers: Cut strips into cubes. After pressing the cube flat, hold the edge of it with the thumb and other fingers of the left hand and move it counter-clockwise while roll about one third of it flat with a rolling pole held in the right hand. Wrappers should be round with thin edges and thicker center. (Illustration 5) (Wrappers can be bought at the market too.)

5) Making stuffing: Mince fresh leek after washing it and drain it. Cut up lean pork, chicken, squid separately, put them into a bowl together, stir them continuously in one direction after adding salt, oil, ginger, Shaoxing rice wine and a little water, until the stuffing is very sticky and no water is seen. Finally add the leek and mix them well.

6) Making dumplings: When making dumplings, the amount of stuffing should be in proportion to the wrapper. Moreover, stuffing should be in the center of the wrapper. Starting with a little stuffing might be more manageable for those just learning how to make dumplings. There are two ways of making dumplings: (Illustration 6)

a. Pressing and pinching: Hold one wrapper with your left palm and put the stuffing on it with your right hand. When both forefingers winding under the wrapper and both thumbs side by side over it, press and pinch the edge of the wrapper.

b. Pushing and pinching: Hold a wrapper with your left palm and put stuffing on it with your right hand. Close the wrapper with your right forefinger on the outside and right thumb inside it. Each time your thumb pushes the wrapper, pinch it with the forefinger. Repeat the act continuously until the whole edge is completed to wrap up the stuffing in the wrapper.

7) Cooking dumplings: Pour into the wok enough water for the dumplings not to stick together. When the water over a high fire is boiling, put dumplings in one after another and stir them with a ladle to separate them. Then cover the wok with a lid. When the water is boiling again we should remove that lid, stir the dumplings and pour in some cold water to avoid mashing wrappers. This is called *dianshui*. After three or four times of *dianshui*, we can ladle out the dumplings with a strainer, and place them in a plate for serving. (Illustration 7: Dumplings)

Vinegar, garlic and sesame oil are major seasonings when having dumplings.

2. Green scallion pancake

Main ingredient wheat flour 300g

Seasonings salad oil 30g   chopped green scallion 40g   baking soda 10g   sugar 8g   salt 12g   boiled water 100g   water 50g

Process Put salt into a bowl of water to dissolve. Pour flour into a basin and add boiled water. Then stir it after adding dissolved salt, sugar and soda. After making the flour into a dough, put it on a board to knead until it becmes smooth. Spread the chopped green scallion and salad oil on the dough and then cover it with plastic wrap. Thirty minutes later, roll out the dough, and fry it in the wok. Remove the cake to the plate when both sides of it are golden. The pancake is often cut into many separate pieces for serving. (Illustration 8: Green Scallion Pancake)

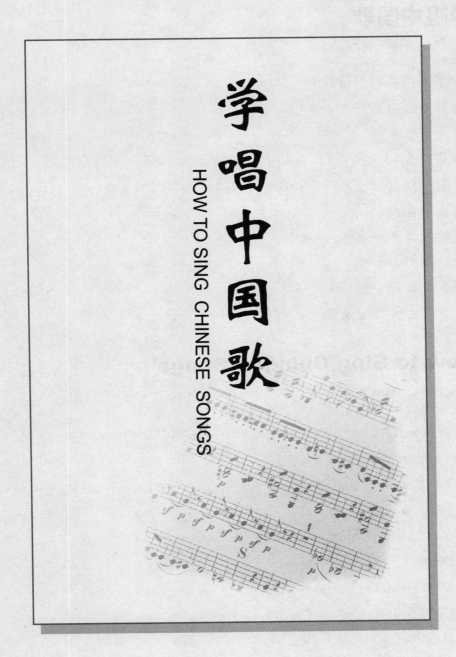

学唱中国歌

HOW TO SING CHINESE SONGS

学唱中国歌

文 雁 选编

How to Sing Chinese Songs

Compiled by Wen Yan

歌曲介绍　《中华人民共和国国歌》

　　这首歌曲创作于 1935 年，正值抗日战争爆发前期，原名《义勇军进行曲》，1949 年中华人民共和国成立后定为国歌。歌词作者是著名诗人、剧作家田汉，为之谱曲的是著名作曲家聂耳。

　　国歌的旋律和节奏很有特点，除了进行曲的快速外，还多处应用了三连音的节奏，给人以庄严、激昂、奋进和自豪的感觉。

Introducing "The National Anthem of the PRC"

　　"The National Anthem of the People's Republic of China" was composed in 1935, just before the War of Resistance Against Japan broke out. Originally named "March of the Volunteers", it was chosen as the national anthem of the People's Republic of China in 1949. Written by the famous poet and playwright Tian Han and set to music by the famous composer Nie Er, the song is characterized by a quick tempo, resembling an army marching at a fast clip. Triplets are used in many places in the music, which inspires in the audience a sense of solemnity, indignation and pride.

Zài Nà Yáoyuǎn de Dìfāng

在那遥远的地方

In a Remote Place

青海民歌

王洛宾 编曲

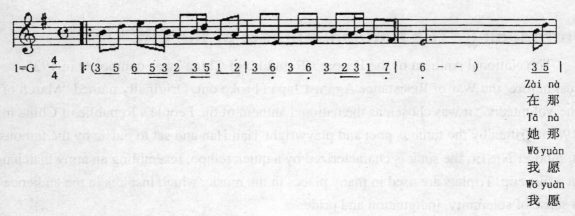

1=G 4/4

```
‖:(3  5  6  53 2  35 1  2 │ 3  6  3  6  3  23 1  7 │ 6 - - )           3 5 │
                                                           Zài nà
                                                           在 那
                                                           Tā nà
                                                           她 那
                                                           Wǒ yuàn
                                                           我 愿
                                                           Wǒ yuàn
                                                           我 愿
```

```
6  55 3  5  6.      5 4 │ 3 5  5 43 3  -  │ 3. 5 6  53 2  32 1. 2 │
yáoyuǎndedì fāng,        yǒuwèi hǎo gū niang,   rénmenzǒuguò tā de zhàng fáng
遥 远的地  方,             有位 好姑 娘,          人 们走过  她的 帐  房
fěnhóngdexiǎo liǎn,      hǎoxiànghóngtàiyáng,   tā  nàměilì dòng réndeyǎn jing
粉 红的笑 脸,              好像 红太 阳,          她 那美丽 动人的眼 睛
pāo qìlecái chǎn,       gēn tā qù mù yáng,     měitiānkànzhetǎdòngrénde yǎnjing
抛 弃了财 产,              跟 她去牧 羊,          每 天看着她动人的眼 睛
zuò yìzhīxiǎo yáng,    gēnzài tāshēn páng,    wǒ yuàntānázhexìxì de pí biān
做 一只小 羊,              跟 在她身 旁,          我 愿她拿着细细的皮 鞭
```

```
3. 5 1 2  3  217 │ 6 - - │ 3. 5 1 2  3  2 1 7 │ 6 - - ‖
dōu yàohuítóuliú liàndezhāngwàng.      bú duànqīngqīngdǎ zài wǒshēn shang.
都 要回头留 恋地张望。                   不 断轻轻打 在我身 上。
hǎo xiàngwǎnshangmíngmèideyuè liàng.
好  像晚上明 媚的月 亮。
hé  nàměilì de jīnbiānyī shang.
和 那美丽的 金边衣 裳。
bú duànqīngqīngdǎ zàiwǒshēnshang.
不 断轻轻轻打 在我身上。
```

歌曲介绍 《在那遥远的地方》

这是一首青海民歌，是由"西部歌王"王洛宾收集编写、又被人民广为传唱的歌曲。在辽阔的草原上，年轻人在那里放牧牛羊，自由自在地歌唱他们的爱情。在这首歌里，小伙子赞美他心爱的姑娘像太阳和月亮一样美丽；为了能和自己的心上人在一起，他愿意放弃一切，甚至希望自己变成一只小羊，永远守在姑娘身边。

Introducing "In a Remote Place"

This folk song, which originated in Qinghai Province and is very popular among the Chinese, was collected and rewritten by Wang Luobin, a composer lauded as "King of Songs in the West Region" in China. On the vast grassland of that region, young people freely sing of their love when herding sheep and cattle. In this song, a young man praises his beloved girl for being as beautiful as the sun and the moon. He is willing to give up everything so long as he can live with her. He even wishes to become a sheep to keep her company forever.

Kāngdìng Qínggē

康 定 情 歌

The Love Song of Kangding

四川民歌

Pǎo mǎ liū liū de shān shang, yì duǒ liū liū de
跑 马 溜 溜 的 山 上， 一 朵 溜 溜 的

Lǐ jiā liū liū de dà jiě, rén cái liū liū de
李 家 溜 溜 的 大 姐， 人 才 溜 溜 的

Yī lái liū liū de kàn shàng, rén cái liū liū de
一 来 溜 溜 的 看 上， 人 才 溜 溜 的

Shì jiān liū liū de nǔ zǐ, rèn nǐ liū liū de
世 间 溜 溜 的 女 子， 任 你 溜 溜 的

yún yāo, duān duān liū liū de zhào zài
云 哟， 端 端 溜 溜 的 照 在

hǎo yāo, zhāng jiā liū liū de dà gē
好 哟， 张 家 溜 溜 的 大 哥

hǎo yāo, èr lái liū liū de kàn shàng
好 哟， 二 来 溜 溜 的 看 上

ài yāo, shì jiān liū liū de nán zǐ
爱 哟， 世 间 溜 溜 的 男 子

Kāng dìng liū liū de chéng yāo, yuè liang
康 定 溜 溜 的 城 哟， 月 亮

kàn shàng liū liū de tā yāo, yuè liang
看 上 溜 溜 的 她 哟， 月 亮

huì dāng liū liū de jiā yāo, yuè liang
会 当 溜 溜 的 家 哟， 月 亮

rèn nǐ liū liū de qiú yāo, yuè liang
任 你 溜 溜 的 求 哟， 月 亮

wān	wān,	Kāng dìng liū liūde chéng yao!
弯	弯,	康 定 溜溜的 城 哟!
wān	wān,	kàn shàng liū liūde tā yao!
弯	弯,	看 上 溜溜的 她 哟!
wān	wān,	huì dāng liū liūde jiā yao!
弯	弯,	会 当 溜溜的 家 哟!
wān	wān,	rèn nǐ liū liūde qiú yao!
弯	弯,	任 你 溜溜的 求 哟!

歌曲介绍 《康定情歌》

这是一首四川民歌。在康定地区，青年人喜欢在月光下面对着古老的城墙、城外的高山和骏马唱起这首歌，来赞美他们的心上人，歌唱他们之间自由、真诚和热烈的爱情。歌词中的"溜溜的"、"端端"没有具体的含义，它们可以使歌曲更加优美动听。

Introducing "The Love Song of Kangding"

This is a folk song from Sichuan Province. When night falls and the moon sheds its silver light over the ancient city wall, the mountains beyond the city and the grazing steeds, young folks in the Kangding area of that province love to sing this song for their beloved ones and the true and passionate love between them. The words *liuliude* and *duanduan* in the song have no concrete meaning, only to make the lyrics sound more beautiful.

Mòlìhuā

茉 莉 花

Song of Jasmine

江苏民歌

歌曲介绍 《茉莉花》

在中国，茉莉是种很常见的植物。它的花朵娇小洁白，有一股持久的清香，所以女孩子们喜欢把它戴在头上。这是一首江苏民歌，歌词细腻地表达了一位姑娘既爱花又惜花的矛盾心情。在姑娘心里，茉莉花是最美丽的。花香怡人，她忍不住想把它摘下来，却又担心这样会伤害了茉莉花。她想：要是明年茉莉花不再发芽、开花了，那怎么办？

Introducing "Song of Jasmine"

Jasmine is a common plant in China. It has small white flowers with a lasting, subtle scent, and girls love to use it as a head ornament. The *Song of Jasmine* is a folk song from Jiangsu Province. Its lyrics exquisitely captures the mixed feelings of a girl, who cherishes the jasmine as the most beautiful flower in the world. The scent of the jasmine is so inviting that she has the urge to pick it, but at the same time she is worried that in doing so she would hurt the flower. What if the jasmine fails to sprout and bloom next year?

Fūqi Shuāngshuāng bǎ Jiā Huán

夫妻双双把家还

A Couple Going Home

黄梅戏《天仙配》选曲

歌曲介绍 《夫妻双双把家还》

　　这首歌曲是由黄梅戏《天仙配》选段改编的。《天仙配》讲述了七仙女（玉皇大帝的七女儿）和穷书生董永之间忠贞不渝的爱情故事，深受中国人民的喜爱。这首歌是夫妻二人在回家路上合唱的，旋律特别优美动听。他们心情愉悦，共同憧憬未来，期待甜美自由的新生活。

Introducing "A Couple Going Home"

　　This song is adapted from a famous episode from *Celestial Marriage,* on the repertoire of the *Huangmei* opera. A great favorite with the Chinese people, *Celestial Marriage* tells of the unswerving love between the Seventh Fairy (the seventh daughter of the Jade Emperor of Heaven) and the poor scholar Dong Yong. As the couple sing this song on their way home, its hauntingly beautiful melody exactly captures their pleasant mood and their great expectations of a promising future and a sweet and free new life.

Tóngzhuō de Nǐ

同桌的你

My Deskmate

高晓松　词曲

1=D　6/8

| 5 5 5 | 5 3 4 | 5. 　 7. | 6 6 6 | 6 4 6 |

Míngtiān nǐ shì fǒu huì xiǎng qǐ, zuó tiān nǐ xiě de rì
明天 你 是 否 会 想 起, 昨 天 你 写 的 日

Lǎo shī men dōu yǐ xiǎng bù qǐ, cāi bù chū wèn tí de
老师 们 都 已 想 不 起, 猜 不 出 问题 的

Nǐ cóng qián zǒng shì hěn xiǎo xīn, wèn wǒ jiè bàn kuài xiàng
你 从 前 总 是 很 小 心, 问 我 借 半 块 橡

Nà shí hou tiān zǒng shì hěn lán, rì zi zǒng guò de tài
那 时 候 天 总 是 很 蓝, 日 子 总 过 得 太

Cóng qián de rì zi dōu guò qù, wǒ yě jiāng yǒu wǒ de
从 前 的 日 子 都 过 去, 我 也 将 有 我 的

| 5. 　 5. | 5 5 5 | 5 7 6 | 5. 　 4 4 4 |

jì, míng tiān nǐ shì fǒu hái diàn jì,
记, 明 天 你 是 否 还 惦 记,

nǐ, wǒ yě shì ǒu rán fān xiàng piàn,
你, 我 也 是 偶 然 翻 相 片,

pí, nǐ yě céng wú yì zhōng shuō qǐ,
皮, 你 也 曾 无 意 中 说 起,

màn, nǐ zǒng shuō bì yè yáo yáo wú qī,
慢, 你 总 说 毕 业 遥 遥 无 期,

qī, wǒ yě huì gěi tā kàn xiàng piàn,
妻, 我 也 会 给 她 看 相 片,

								:	<u>$\dot{1}$ $\dot{1}$</u>	$\dot{1}$	$\dot{1}$		<u>5 6</u>	

<u>4 4</u> 4 <u>4 3</u> 2 | <u>1</u>· 1· ‖: <u>$\dot{1}$ $\dot{1}$</u> $\dot{1}$ $\dot{1}$ <u>5 6</u> |

céng jīng zuì ài kū de nǐ 。 Shéi qǔ le duō chóu shàn
曾 经 最 爱 哭 的 你 。 谁 娶 了 多 愁 善

cái xiǎng qǐ tóng zhuō de nǐ 。 Shéi qǔ le duō chóu shàn
才 想 起 同 桌 的 你 。 谁 娶 了 多 愁 善

xǐ huan hé wǒ zài yì qǐ 。 Shéi qǔ le duō chóu shàn
喜 欢 和 我 在 一 起 。 谁 娶 了 多 愁 善

zhuǎn yǎn jiù gè bēn dōng xī 。
转 眼 就 各 奔 东 西 。

gěi tā tán tóng zhuō de nǐ 。
给 她 谈 同 桌 的 你 。

$\dot{1}$ $\dot{1}$ <u>3</u>· | <u>$\dot{2}$ $\dot{2}$</u> $\dot{2}$ <u>$\dot{2}$ $\dot{1}$</u> 7 | 6· 6· |

gǎn de nǐ ， shéi kàn le nǐ de rì jì ，
感 的 你 ， 谁 看 了 你 的 日 记 ，

gǎn de nǐ ， shéi ān wèi ài kū de nǐ ，
感 的 你 ， 谁 安 慰 爱 哭 的 你 ，

gǎn de nǐ ， shéi ān wèi ài kū de nǐ ，
感 的 你 ， 谁 安 慰 爱 哭 的 你 ，

<u>7 7</u> 7 <u>7 7</u> $\dot{1}$ | 2· 5· | <u>7 7</u> $\dot{1}$ <u>2 $\dot{1}$</u> 7 |

shéi bǎ nǐ de cháng fà pán qǐ ， shéi gěi nǐ zuò de jià
谁 把 你 的 长 发 盘 起 ， 谁 给 你 做 的 嫁

shéi kàn le wǒ gěi nǐ xiě de xìn ， shéi bǎ tā diū zài fēng
谁 看 了 我 给 你 写 的 信 ， 谁 把 它 丢 在 风

shéi bǎ nǐ de cháng fà pán qǐ ， shéi gěi nǐ zuò de jià
谁 把 你 的 长 发 盘 起 ， 谁 给 你 做 的 嫁

歌曲介绍 《同桌的你》

　　这首歌曲曾经在中国的大学校园里十分流行。它用回忆的方式，描绘出年轻男女在交往中所产生的非常微妙的感情。这种感情是同学之间的友谊和好感，也有着初恋般的羞涩和喜悦。当作者回忆起这段情感，心里充满了忧伤和思念。那种纯洁和美丽，是永远也不会回来了。

Introducing "My Deskmate"

For a time this song was very popular on the Chinese campus for its nostalgic recollection of the subtle feelings between young men and women in college — the true feelings of friendship and trust, and the shyness and delight of first love. Past memories have filled the singer's heart with sadness and yearning, for gone for ever are the purity and innocence of these feelings.

Lóng de Chuánrén

龙 的 传 人

Descendants of the Dragon

侯德健　词曲

1=♭B　4/4

‖: 6　7 1　2　3 2　| i　 1 7　6 -　| 6　7 1　2　3 2　| i　1 2　3　|

Yáo yuǎn de dōng fāng yǒu yì tiáo jiāng,　tā de míng zi jiù jiào Chángjiāng.
遥 远 的 东 方 有 一 条 江,　它 的 名 字 就 叫 长 江。

Gǔ lǎo de dōng fāng yǒu yì tiáo lóng,　tā de míng zi jiù jiào Zhōng guó.
古 老 的 东 方 有 一 条 龙,　它 的 名 字 就 叫 中 国。

Bǎi nián qián níng jìng de yí ge yè,　jù biàn qián xī de shēn yè li.
百 年 前 宁 静 的 一 个 夜,　巨 变 前 夕 的 深 夜 里。

6　7 1　2　3 2　| i　 1 7　6 -　| 7　7　7　1 7　6　6 5　6 -　|

Yáo yuǎn de dōng fāng yǒu yì tiáo hé,　tā de míng zi jiù jiào Huáng hé.
遥 远 的 东 方 有 一 条 河,　它 的 名 字 就 叫 黄 河。

Gǔ lǎo de dōng fāng yǒu yì qún rén,　tā men quán dōu shì lóng de chuán rén.
古 老 的 东 方 有 一 群 人,　他 们 全 都 是 龙 的 传 人。

Qiāng pào shēng qiāo suì le níng jìng yè,　sì miàn chǔ gē shì gū xī de jiàn.
枪 炮 声 敲 碎 了 宁 静 夜,　四 面 楚 歌 是 姑 息 的 剑。

3　3　3　2 1　| 2　 2 3　2 -　| i　i　i　2 1　| 7　7 1　7 -　|

Suī bù céng kàn jiàn Cháng jiāng měi,　mèng li cháng shén yóu Cháng jiāng shuǐ;
虽 不 曾 看 见 长 江 美,　梦 里 常 神 游 长 江 水;

Jù lóng jiǎo dǐ xia wǒ chéng zhǎng,　chéng zhǎng yǐ hòu shì lóng de chuán rén;
巨 龙 脚 底 下 我 成 长,　成 长 以 后 是 龙 的 传 人;

Duō shao nián pào shēng réng lóng lóng,　duō shao nián yòu shì duō shao nián?
多 少 年 炮 声 仍 隆 隆,　多 少 年 又 是 多 少 年?

suī bù céng tīng jiàn Huáng hé zhuàng,   péng pài xiōng yǒng zài mèng li 。
虽 不 曾 听 见 黄 河 壮,   澎 湃 汹 涌 在 梦 里。

hēi yǎn jing hēi tóu fa huáng pí fū,   yǒng yǒng yuǎn yuǎn shì lóng de chuán rén 。
黑 眼 睛 黑 头 发 黄 皮 肤,   永 永 远 远 是 龙 的 传 人。

Jù lóng jù lóng nǐ cā liàng yǎn,   yǒng yǒng yuǎn yuǎn de cā liàng yǎn 。
巨 龙 巨 龙 你 擦 亮 眼,   永 永 远 远 地 擦 亮 眼。

歌曲介绍 《龙的传人》

在中国人的想象中，龙既能上天又能入水，它是神奇的、伟大的，是中国的象征。中国人都认为自己是龙的孩子。这首歌曲写于1978年，曾是首风靡一时的台湾校园歌曲。歌曲全文饱含着深厚的民族情感，表达了华夏子孙向往祖国统一的共同心声。"黑眼睛黑头发黄皮肤，永永远远是龙的传人"是这首歌的核心，能引起每一个中华子孙的强烈共鸣。

Introducing "Descendants of the Dragon"

In Chinese imagination, the dragon, which can fly in the sky and swim in the water, is magical and great. It is the symbol of China. The Chinese regard themselves as the childen of the dragon. Written in 1978, this Taiwan campus song was all the rage among the Chinese. Its lyrics, full of deep national emotion, give apt expression to the common aspiration of the Chinese for national reunification. "With black eyes, black hair and yellow skin, we are all descendants of the dragon" is the theme of this song, which strikes a strong chord in the mind of every Chinese descendant.

歌曲介绍 《我的中国心》

在过去的岁月里，华夏子孙饱受了祖国四分五裂的痛苦。但是，只要是中国人，无论他在哪儿生活，无论他穿的是西装洋服，还是中国传统服装，他都有一颗不变的中国心，有着一份深厚的中国情。这首来自香港的歌曲唱出了全世界华人的共同心声，所以，在有华人的地方，你都能听到这首歌。

Introducing "My Heart Still Belongs to China"

The Chinese people had their fill of the agonies of their homeland torn by war and turmoil. However, whoever they are, wherever they live, and whether they wear Western suits or traditional clothes, they all have a heart filled with profound love for their motherland if only they are Chinese. This song from Hong Kong expresses the common wish of all the Chinese in the world. You may hear this song where there are Chinese.

Tóng Yì Shǒu Gē

同 一 首 歌

The Same Song

陈 哲 词
孟卫东 曲

歌曲介绍　《同一首歌》

　　我们每一个人都必须独自经历各种困难和痛苦，一生中总免不了许多分离。但人间真爱让我们学会互相关心、理解和帮助。同舟共济，让我们更深地领悟生命的绚丽可贵，让我们更加珍惜相聚的分分秒秒。同样的感受给了我们同样的渴望，同样的欢乐给了我们同一首歌。

Introducing "The Same Song"

Nobody can avoid experiences of frustration, separation and affliction in their lives. But the true love between people teaches us to care and understand each other, stick together in times of adversity, appreciate the magnificence and value of life, and cherish the companionship of beloved ones. The same experiences give us the same aspiration, and the same happiness enables us to understand the same song of love.

Duìmiàn de Nǚhái Kàn Guòlái

对面的女孩看过来

Look Thither, the Girls Opposite

阿牛 词曲

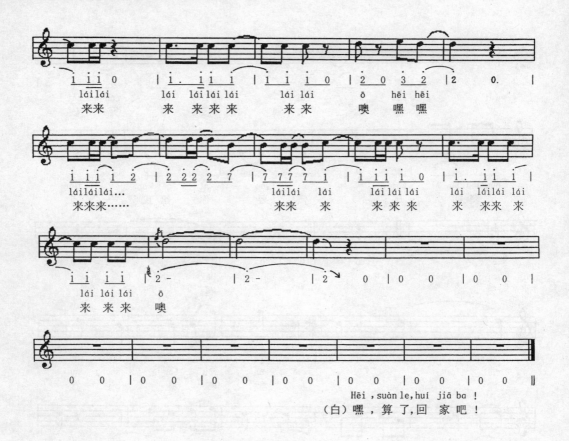

来来 | 来 来来来 | 来来 | 噢 嘿嘿 | 来来来…… | 来来 来 | 来来来 | 来 来来来 | 来 来来 噢 | （白）嘿，算了，回 家 吧！

歌曲介绍 《对面的女孩看过来》

　　情窦初开的男孩子渴望爱情，他感到一个人是寂寞的。于是，他走上大街，用各种各样的鬼脸和动作想吸引对面女孩子的注意，可惜他失败了。他发现原来每个女孩子都不简单，他一点儿也不知道她们在想什么。这是一首近年来深受年轻人喜爱的流行歌曲，旋律活泼流畅，歌词简单生动，具有很强的情节性和表演性。

Introducing "Look Thither, the Girls Opposite"

A lonely boy at the first awakening of love, is wandering on the street. By making faces and funny gesticulations, he tries to attract the attention of the girls across the street, but he fails. To his dismay, he discovers that no girl is as simple as he thought, and he has no way of reading their minds. This is a popular song among young people in recent years. It has quick rhythm and a simple but lively melody, and its vivid plot gives people the itch to act it out.

中国导游

TOURIST HIGHLIGHTS IN CHINA

中国导游

周　健　编写／翻译

Tourist Highlights in China

Compiled and Translated by Zhou Jian

中国导游

中国是一块令人神往的土地。她有壮丽的河山、悠久的历史、灿烂的文化和多姿多彩的民族风情。

中国疆域辽阔，有众多的名胜古迹，旅游资源十分丰富。预计到2020年，中国将成为世界第一大旅游目的地。

要想游遍中国，恐怕需要几年的时间。如果想在较短的时间内，尽可能地看看中国历史文化、自然风光、社会习俗和民族风情的话，我们可以沿着下面这条"S"形的路线看看中国的一部分精华。这条路线是北京→西安→成都→重庆→南京→苏州→上海→杭州→黄山→厦门→广州→桂林→昆明。

Tourist Highlights in China

China is a land of mystery and charm. Its glorious history, spectacular landscape, splendid culture and intriguing national customs offer a panorama of color and excitement for visitors.

China is a vast land with numerous scenic spots and historical sites. China is rich in tourism resources. It is estimated that, by 2020, China will be the world's most popular destination for tourists.

It would probably take you years to see all of China. But if you want to explore this country's history, culture, natural beauty, social and national customs in a short period, the following S-shaped tour would be a good choice, for it highlights some of the best parts of China, including Beijing, Xi'an, Chengdu, Chongqing, Nanjing, Suzhou, Shanghai, Hangzhou, Huangshan, Xiamen, Guangzhou, Guilin and Kunming.

第一课 首都北京

　　第一站是北京。北京是中华人民共和国的首都，也曾是元、明、清等朝代的都城。北京作为首都已有800年的历史，因此，北京拥有许多皇家宫殿、园林、陵墓和众多的名胜古迹、文化遗址。北京是中国最著名的旅游城市，来中国不可不看北京。

　　北京最负盛名的旅游点有长城、故宫、颐和园、天安门、天坛、十三陵、北海公园等。

　　全长6,350公里的万里长城是世界建筑史的奇迹，是中国的骄傲与象征。如果想看长城，最好去北京市区西北的八达岭或北面的慕田峪。（图1：万里长城）

　　看过电影《末代皇帝》的人一定会对故宫留下深刻的印象。故宫又被称为"紫禁城"，建成于1420年，明、清两代一共24位皇帝曾在这里居住过。它是中国保存得最为完好的古建筑群。故宫以太和殿、中和殿和保和殿为中心，共有9,999间房子，规模宏大，富丽堂皇。

图1　万里长城

　　坐落在北京市区西北10公里的颐和园，是中国最大的皇家园林之一，也是北京风景最美的地方。颐和园规模宏大，布局可分为政治活动区、生活居住区和风景游览区。全园面积的四分之三为昆明湖，北岸有一条728米长的长廊，（图2：颐和园长廊）是世界上最长的画廊。万寿山上有许多庙宇楼阁，如佛香阁、排云殿、智慧海等。昆明湖四周的铜牛、十七孔桥、玉带桥、石舫、苏州街、谐趣园等都是著名的建筑。

图2　颐和园长廊

　　天安门广场位于北京城的正中央，可供50万人举行集会，是世界上最大的广场之一。天安门城楼是中国的象征，1949年10月1日毛泽东在城楼上宣告了中华人民共和国的诞生。每天早晨在广场举行庄严的升国旗仪式。天安门也是故宫正门的入口。天安门的东西两侧分别为劳动人民文化宫和中山公园，天安门前的长安街笔直宽敞，两边分布着许多重要的建筑物，这条街被誉为"中国第一街"。广场东边是中国历史博物馆和中国革命博物馆；西边是人民大会堂和正在建设中的国家大剧院；南边有人民英雄纪念碑，毛主席纪念堂和前门。

　　天坛是明代建筑的完美形式，已经成为北京的象征。（图3：天坛）天坛是明、清两代皇帝们祭天祈年的地方。天坛的主要建筑是祈年殿、皇穹宇和圜丘。祈年殿是一座三重檐的圆形大殿，高38米，直径30米，宏伟壮观，奇妙的是大殿屋顶全由28根木柱相连支撑，竟然完全没有使用铁钉或水泥。当中四根柱子代表一年四季，中层12根柱子象征一年12个月，外层12根柱子表示一天的12个时辰。三层共28根柱子象征全天28星宿。天坛的许多建筑都有象征意义，例如天坛公园的北边是半圆形的，南边是方形的，象征着中国古代"天圆地方"的理论。

图 3　天坛

　　十三陵在京北昌平区，在这块40平方公里的地区埋葬着明朝的13位皇帝。由陵园入口到长陵的"神道"长7公里，道旁有24个巨大的石兽和12个石人，像是欢迎游客的仪仗队。定陵的地下宫殿是1956年发掘的，这里埋葬着万历皇帝和他的两个妃子。陈列室里展出了地宫出土的许多珍贵文物。

　　北海公园在故宫的西北边，是最精致的皇家园林。由于地处市中心，它成了北京人最喜爱的休憩去处。琼岛是全园的中心，山顶上屹立着高高的白塔，它建于17世纪。公园的北边有九龙壁和五龙亭。北海的南边是中南海，是中国最高领导人居住和办公的地方。

　　北京的好去处当然不只是这些，像市内东北角的雍和宫，是一座色彩鲜艳、具有独特建筑风格的喇嘛教寺院；西郊的香山公园，也是著名的皇家园林，附近的碧云寺、孙中山纪念馆、卧佛寺和香山红叶都是北京的胜景。此外，琉璃厂、圆明园遗址、景山公园、北京动物园、孔庙、国子监、大观园、中华世纪坛、卢沟桥、潭柘寺、戒台寺、周口店北京猿人遗址、十渡、龙庆峡、上方山云水洞等等都是值得推荐的去处。

Lesson One　The Capital City of Beijing

Beijing, the capital of the People's Republic of China, is the first leg of our itinerary. For 800 years it was the nation's capital during the Yuan, Ming and Qing dynasties. That explains the numerous imperial palaces, gardens, mausoleums, scenic spots, historic and cultural sites in Beijing, and vindicates its reputation as the most famous tourist city of China. No visit to China is complete without a stop at Beijing.

The city's best known tourist destinations include the Great Wall, Forbidden City, Summer Palace, Tian'anmen Square, Temple of Heaven, Ming Tombs, and Beihai Park.

The 6,350-kilometer-long Great Wall is reputed as a great wonder in the world architectural history. (Illustration 1: The Great Wall) It is the pride and symbol of China. If you want to have a good view of it, you'd better go to Badaling in the northwest of Beijing, or Mutianyu in north Beijing.

People may gain a lasting impression about the Imperial Palace if they watch the film, *The Last Emperor*. Completed in 1420, the Imperial Palace, also known as the Forbidden City, served as the residence of 24 Ming and Qing emperors. It is among the best preserved complexes of ancient buildings in China. The palace consists of Taihe (Supreme Harmony) Hall, Zhonghe (Middle Harmony) Hall and Baohe (Protecting Harmony) Hall as the center, and has a total of 9,999 rooms. The buildings of the Forbidden City are splendid and magnificent.

Ten kilometers northwest of Beijing stands the Summer Palace, one of China's largest imperial gardens. As one of the finest sights in Beijing, this magnificent garden used to be divided into three sections for court reception, living quarters and sightseeing respectively. Three quarters of the park are occupied by Kunming Lake, and along the north shore of the lake is the 728-meter-long corridor, the longest of its kind in the world. (Illustration 2: The Long Corridor of the Summer Palace) It is painted and decorated with mythical scenes. On the Longevity Hill are a cluster of temples and pavilions including Pavilion of Buddha's Fragrance, Precious Clouds Pavilion, and Buddhist Sea of Wisdom Temple. There are many famous sights around the lake: the Bronze Ox, the 17-Arch Bridge, the Jade Belt Bridge, the Marble Boat, the Suzhou Street, the Garden of Harmonious Interest, and so on.

Tian'anmen Square is the heart of Beijing. Big enough to hold half a million people, this public square is one of the largest in the world. Tian'anmen, or Heavenly Peace Gate, is a national symbol. It was from the rostrum atop this gate that Mao Zedong proclaimed the founding of the People's Republic of China on October 1, 1949. The national flag raising ceremony is held there at sunrise every day. Tian'anmen also provides the main entrance to the Imperial Palace. The Tian'anmen Gate is flanked by the Working People's Cultural Palace to the east and Zhongshan (Sun Yat-sen) Park to the west. The gate towers over the wide and straight Chang'an Avenue, which, lined with many important buildings on both sides, is billed as "No.1 Avenue of China." East of the square are the Museum of Chinese History, and the Museum of Chinese Revolution, and west, the Great Hall of the People and the National Theatre that is under construction. To the south are the Monument to the People's Heroes, Chairman Mao Zedong's Memorial Hall, and Qianmen Gate.

The Temple of Heaven represented the pinnacle of Ming-dynasty architecture. Today, it is a symbol of Beijing. (Illustration 3: The Temple of Heaven) It was here that the Ming and Qing emperors performed the major rite of the year to pray for good harvest. Main buildings here include the Hall of Praying for Good Harvest, the Imperial Vault of Heaven, and the Round Altar. The Hall of Praying for Good Harvest is a magnificent piece mounted on a three-tiered marble terrace. Amazingly, for a building 38 meters high and 30 meters in diameter, the wooden pillars ingeniously support the ceiling without nails or cement. The four pillars at the center represent the seasons, the 12 pillars that form the next ring denote the months of the year, and the 12 outer ones symbolize the hours of the day, each representing two hours. All these pillars represent the 28 constellations in ancient Chinese astronomy. Many buildings in the Temple of Heaven Park have symbolic meanings. For example, the north end is semi-circular and the south end is square, deriving from the ancient Chinese belief that the heaven is round and the earth is square.

The Ming Tombs are located in Changping District north of Beijing. Altogether 13 Ming emperors were buried in this 40-square-kilometer area, where 24 stone animals and 12 stone figures line a seven-kilometer "holy way" like a guard of honor. The Underground Palace of Dingling Mausoleum was opened in 1956. Buried here were Emperor Wanli and his two empresses. On display in the exhibition rooms are invaluable objects excavated from the Underground Palace.

To the northwest of the Forbidden City is the Beihai Park, an imperial garden of classic elegance. Because of its central location, Beihai Park is favored by Beijingers. The Jade Isle in the center of the park is topped by a white pagoda built in the 17th century. The main attractions on the north side of the park is the Nine-Dragon Screen and Five-Dragon Pavilion. To the south of the Beihai Park is Zhongnanhai, the seat of the Chinese government and the residence of top leaders.

More tourist attractions can be found in Beijing, of course. For example, the Lama Temple in the northeast of the city is the most colorful lamasery with unique architecture; the Fragrant Hill Park in the western suburbs is another imperial garden. There are also the Biyun Temple, Dr. Sun Yat-sen's Memorial Hall, the Temple of the Sleeping Buddha, and Red Leaves on Autumn Hill near the Fragrant Hill Park. Other tourist attractions include Liulichang, Ruins of Yuanmingyuan, Jingshan Park, Beijing Zoo, Confucian Temple, Imperial College, Grand View Garden, China Millennial Monument, Marco Polo Bridge, Tanzhe Temple, Jietai Temple, Site of Peking Man in Zhoukoudian, Shidu, Longqing Gorge and Cloud-Water Cave on Mount Shangfang.

第二课 古都西安

　　第二站是西安。西安在北京的西南方，从北京到西安要坐十几个小时的火车或一个半小时的飞机。西安是陕西省的省会，是古代丝绸之路的起点，古称长安。长安曾经是世界上最大的都市，堪与罗马、君士坦丁堡争雄。西安是我国七大古都之一（另外六个是北京、洛阳、南京、开封、安阳和杭州），2,000多年来，先后曾有13个王朝（包括最强盛的汉朝和唐朝)在此建都。西安及其附近有数不胜数的名胜古迹，西安可以说是一座大型的中国历史博物馆。

　　西安最负盛名的旅游点是被誉为世界第八奇迹的秦始皇兵马俑博物馆。西安市内的陕西省博物馆（碑林）、钟楼、大雁塔、城墙，市郊的半坡博物馆，骊山的华清池等都是著名的旅游胜地。

　　秦始皇兵马俑博物馆位于西安以东的骊山。秦始皇从13岁即位起就开始为自己建陵，一共花了36年才建成。1974年农民们在打井时，无意中发现了兵马俑。这可能是20世纪最为重要的考古发现。（图4：兵马俑）

图4　兵马俑

　　兵马俑坑在秦始皇陵墓东侧，已试掘三个坑。其中"一号坑"最大，东西长230米，南北宽62米，里面有6,000件兵马俑，它们都和真人真马一样高大，士兵或正立或跪姿射箭，每人的盔甲和面部表情都不相同。在坑里还发现青铜兵器10,000多件，其中被埋没两千余年的长剑依旧寒光闪闪。"二号坑"、"三号坑"也相继发掘出陶、俑、陶马1,000多件。1980年在秦陵西侧仅20米处挖掘出的一对铜车马，制作精美，栩栩如生，令人惊叹。考古学家相信，目前所发掘的兵马俑可能仅仅是秦陵四周整个地下大军中的一小部分，全部陵区的发掘可能需要几十年的时间。

　　碑林位于陕西省博物馆内，是全世界最大的"石书"图书馆。原址为孔庙，碑林是北宋元佑五年为保存唐开成年间镌刻的《十三经》而建立的。现有六个陈列室、六个游廊和一个碑亭，共展出刻字碑石2,300块，集中了从汉到清各代书法名家的手笔。真、草、隶、篆等字体都有，是一座宏伟的书法艺术宝库。博物馆里藏有大量来自丝绸之路的文物，还有战国时期的虎符等。

　　钟楼位于西安市中心，高36米，可以从钟楼北侧经地下通道沿阶梯登临而上。钟楼上有一口巨大的铁钟，过去每天击钟报时。登楼远眺，全市风光尽收眼底。

大雁塔屹立在城南大慈恩寺内，已成为西安的象征。（图5：大雁塔）寺庙始建于公元648年，是唐高宗即位前为追念母亲的慈恩而建。大雁塔建于652年，唐代名僧玄奘从印度取回大批佛经，大雁塔就是为玄奘译经而修建的。他在此主持翻译工作，译成1,335卷中文佛经。大雁塔高64米，为7层砖木结构，外观呈方形锥体，高大雄伟，古朴庄严。

图5　大雁塔

西安是中国完整保留了古城墙的城市之一。现存城墙为明朝开国皇帝朱元璋所建，建于原唐代首都长安城旧城基之上。城墙周长14公里，每边有一个城门，城门上建有三重城楼，四个城角建有角楼。城墙12米高，顶部有12米～14米宽。

半坡位于西安城东10公里处，是一处母系氏族原始村落遗址，距今已有6,000余年。遗址分为居住区、制陶区和墓葬区。展出的生产器具和生活用品有10,000余件。彩陶制作十分精美，上面绘有几何图案和动物形象，有的还刻有一些符号，据说是早期的文字。

华清池在西安以东30公里外的骊山脚下。大约3,000年前，人们就已经发现了这里的天然温泉。历代帝王们均在此修建宫苑。唐玄宗和杨贵妃经常来这里洗浴。在中国现代历史上，著名的"西安事变"就发生在此地。骊山温泉现被引入60个公共浴池内，可供400余人同时沐浴。

西安附近的茂陵、昭陵、乾陵、兴教寺、法门寺、唐城、西岳华山等都是值得推荐的去处。

西安是中国西北最重要的城市，也是古代丝绸之路的起点。丝绸之路自西安（古都城长安）起，经甘肃省河西走廊的武威、张掖、酒泉，到达敦煌后分为南北两路分别经阳关和玉门关进入新疆。北路经过吐鲁番、库车、喀什等地；南路经过若羌、和田等地。两路在今土库曼斯坦的马雷汇合后向西延伸至地中海。丝绸之路是古代中国连接西亚和欧洲最重要的交通道路，丝绸之路上历史文物和名胜古迹众多。例如敦煌莫高窟就是古代佛教雕塑和绘画艺术的宝库。除了丝绸之路，在西安的四周还有许多名胜古迹，例如东边的九朝古都洛阳、嵩山；北边的古长城遗迹、贺兰山小口子；西边的兰州、青海湖；南边的汉中和八百里秦川等等，都能引发思古之幽情。中国的西北有着独特的地貌和丰富的历史文物，随着中国西部的大开发，到西北去旅游观光的人越来越多。

离开历史文化名城西安，沿陇海铁路和宝成铁路西南行，就来到了被誉为"天府之国"的四川。

Lesson Two　Xi'an, the Ancient Capital

The second leg of our itinerary is Xi'an, known in ancient time as Chang'an. It takes about 12 hours by train or one and a half hours by plane to get there from Beijing in a southwestern tack. Xi'an is the capital of Shaanxi Province and the starting point of the ancient Silk Road. For a time, the city rivaled Rome and Constantinople as the largest city in the world. Over a period of 2,000 years Xi'an had seen the rise and fall of 13 Chinese dynasties, including the two strongest, the Han and Tang. It was one of the seven ancient capitals in the country, along with Beijing, Luoyang, Nanjing, Kaifeng, Anyang and Hangzhou. There are countless scenic spots and historic sites around the city, whose wealth of cultural heritage makes it a veritable museum of Chinese history.

The most famous tourist attraction in Xi'an is the Museum of Terracotta Warriors of the Qinshihuang Mausoleum, widely considered to be the Eighth Wonder of the World. The Shaanxi Provincial Museum, the Bell Tower, the Greater Wild Goose Pagoda, the City Walls, the Banpo Neolithic Village and the Huaqing Pool at Lishan Mountain are all famous tourist attractions.

The Museum of Terracotta Warriors is located at Lishan, east of Xi'an. Qinshihuang started to build his tomb at Lishan at the age of 13 when he ascended the throne. The gigantic project took 36 years to complete. In 1974, farmers digging a well uncovered what turned out to be perhaps the greatest archaeological discovery of the 20th century. (Illustration 4: Terracotta Warriors)

Of the three vaults excavated so far, No.1 Vault is the largest, containing some 6,000 terracotta figures on a floor 230 meters in length from east to west and 62 meters in breadth from north to south. These life-size pottery warriors, standing or kneeling to shoot arrows, each wears a different armor and expression. Over 10,000 brone weapons have been discovered there, including bronze swords that remain razor-sharp after being buried over 2,000 years. Over 1,000 pottery warriors and horses have been found in vaults No. 2 and No. 3. Almost as impressive is a pair of bronze chariots and horses unearthed in 1980, just 20 meters west of the Qinshihuang Mausoleum. Archaeologists believe that the army of terracotta warriors discovered so far is only part of an even larger terracotta army still buried around Qinshihuang's tomb. Complete excavation of the entire complex and the tomb itself may take decades.

Billed as the world's largest library of stone inscriptions, the Forest of Steles in the Shaanxi Provincial Museum was established in the former Confucian Temple in 1070 to preserve the "Kaicheng Stone Classics." There are six exhibition rooms, six galleries and a stele pavilion in this compound, where about 2,300 steles and tablets of past dynasties since the Han are stored. It is also a treasure house of Chinese calligraphy, with a superb collection of works by famous calligraphers from the Han Dynasty to the Qing Dynasty. The museum houses a fine collection of artefacts from the Silk Road, including a tiger-shaped tally dating back to the Warring States Period.

The 36-meter-high Bell Tower is a huge building in the center of Xi'an. A stairway that begins at the other end of an underpass on the north side leads up to the top floor of the tower, where a large iron bell used to mark the time each day. The tower offers a panoramic view of the city.

The Greater Wild Goose Pagoda in the Temple of Great Maternal Grace in south Xi'an is a symbol of the city. (Illustration 5: The Greater Wild Goose Pagoda) Emperor Gaozong of the Tang Dynasty built the temple in AD 648, when he was still a crown prince, and dedicated it to his deceased mother. The pagoda was built in AD 652 to house the Buddhist scriptures brought from India by the travelling monk Xuanzang, who then translated them into 1,335 Chinese volumes. The seven-storey wood-and-brick building rises to an imposing height of 64 meters.

Xi'an is one of the cities in China where the ancient city walls remain intact. The walls were built on the foundation of the walls of the Tang Forbidden City during the reign of Zhu Yuanzhang, the founding emperor of the Ming Dynasty. They form a rectangle with a circumference of 14 kilometers. On each side of the wall is a gateway with a tower of three terraces atop them. At each of the four corners is a watchtower. The wall is 12 meters high, with a width of 12 to 14 meters at the top.

Located 10 kilometers east of Xi'an, the Banpo Neolithic Village is the site of a residential area, a pottery-making area and a burial ground belonging to a matriarchal clan 6,000 years ago. More than 10,000 productive tools and daily-use utensils are on display. Much of the pottery is painted with geometric patterns or animal figures. Some of the vessels are carved with symbols, said to be the primitive forms of writing.

The Huaqing Pool at the foot of Lishan Mountain is 30 kilometres east of Xi'an. Hot springs were discovered there some 3,000 years ago, and emperors of later dynasties built palaces around the Huaqing Pool. Emperor Xuanzong of the Tang Dynasty and his concubine Lady Yang often came here to bathe. It is also where the famous Xi'an Incident took place in modern Chinese history. Today, water from the hot springs is diverted to 60 bathing pools which can accommodate 400 people at a time.

Other recommended tourist attractions in Xi'an include Maoling Mausoleum, Zhaoling Mausoleum, Qianling Mausoleum, Xingjiao Temple, Famen Temple, Tang City and Huashan

Mountain.

Xi'an, the most important city of northwest China, was the starting point of the ancient Silk Road, which went along the Hexi Corridor of Gansu Province and reached Dunhuang by way of Wuwei, Zhangye and Jiuquan, and then was divided into two routes from Dunhuang. The northern route passed Yumen Pass of Gansu, Turpan, Kuqa and reached Kashi in Xinjiang; and the southern route passed Yangguan Pass of Gansu, Ruoqiang, and reached Hotan in south Xinjiang. The two routes joined at Mary of Turkmenistan and extended to the coast of the Mediterranean Sea. The Silk Road was the most important link between China and West Asia and the European countries. Along this ancient road are numerous scenic attractions and places of historical interest. For example, the Mogao Grottoes at Dunhuang is a treasure house of ancient Buddhist art of sculpture and painting. Besides the Silk Road, the region around Xi'an abounds in scenic spots and historic sites, such as the ancient capital city of Luoyang and the Songshan Mountain to the east, the remains of the ancient Great Wall and Xiaokouzi scenic spot in Helan Mountain to the north, the city of Lanzhou and Qinghai Lake to the west, the city of Hanzhong and the vast Central shaanxi Plain to the south. All these places strike a deep chord in the hearts of the nostalgic. With the progress of the great initiative to develop the western region, more and more tourists will come to visit the unique landscape and rich historical relics in northwest China.

We now leave the historical and cultural city of Xi'an and go southwest along the Lanzhou-Lianyungang and Baoji-Chengdu railways for the third leg of our itinerary in the "Nature's Storehouse," which refers to Sichuan Province.

第三课 成都和重庆

第三站是成都。成都是四川省的省会，是其政治、经济、文化中心。重要的游览胜地有杜甫草堂、武侯祠、文殊院、王建墓、青羊宫、都江堰、峨眉山、九寨沟等等。

杜甫草堂位于成都西郊浣花溪畔，是唐代大诗人杜甫居住过的地方。杜甫47岁时由于贫困和战乱，从陕西流亡到成都，靠友人帮助在此地修建了茅屋。他在草堂居住了将近四年，写下了240多首诗篇，反映了人民的痛苦生活和自己进步的观点。杜甫被后代誉为"诗圣"，是中国人民最崇敬的诗人之一。

武侯祠位于成都市西南角，是纪念三国时蜀汉丞相诸葛亮的祠堂。在中国人的心目中，诸葛亮是忠诚与智慧的化身。该祠始建于西晋末年，到了明朝时又将蜀汉皇帝刘备庙与武侯祠合二为一，是一个君臣合庙，但人们一直称它为武侯祠。

文殊院是成都最大、保存最完好的佛教寺院，唐宋时名叫相信寺，清朝改名为文殊院。许多建筑物上都刻有优美的浮雕，寺院里存有400多尊佛像。文物中以唐玄奘法师的头盖骨最为珍贵。络绎不绝的香客和游客每天都把寺院挤得水泄不通。

青羊宫在成都市通惠门外，因历年在此举办花会而闻名，1959年改建为文化公园。青羊宫是成都地区最古老、最宏大的道教寺院。道教尊奉《道德经》的作者老子为祖。相传有一天老子邀朋友来这里看他，朋友到来后发现只有一个男童牵着两只羊。后来这位朋友才悟出男童就是老子本人，现院内有青铜铸的山羊两只。

青城山是一座道教名山，在成都以西65公里处。山高1,600米，山上有众多道教寺观，风景优美，自古就有"青城天下幽"的美誉。山下的建福宫现有道士100余人。

都江堰在成都西南60公里处，距青城山16公里。公元前256年秦国蜀郡郡守李冰父子为了解决岷江的旱涝问题，主持修建了这一宏伟、巧妙的水利工程，整个工程分为鱼嘴、飞沙堰和宝瓶口三个部分。这项2,200多年前的水利工程至今仍发挥着巨大的作用。

峨眉山在成都西南160公里处，可以乘火车或者汽车前往。峨眉山是中国四大佛教名山之一，素有"峨眉天下秀"之誉。主要寺庙及景点有报国寺、万年寺、雷音寺、清音阁、洪椿坪、洗象池、金顶等。山上多古木、奇花、珍禽、异兽、秀峰、溪涧、云海，自然景观十分秀丽，在海拔3,099米的金顶有时还可以看到著名的"佛光"，即阳光透过水汽形成的圆形彩虹，光环中能反射人影。万年寺水池中的琴蛙，洗象池一带的猴群，都为游人所乐道。

乐山大佛位于大渡河和岷江的交汇处，佛像高71米，由整座石崖雕刻而成，是世界上最大的佛像。大佛的耳朵有7米长，脚背有8.5米宽，它的大脚指头上可供几人围坐野餐。这项惊人的工程是由一位名叫海通的和尚在713年开始进行的，用了90年

的时间才完成。大佛身后是凌云寺，俗称大佛寺。（图6：乐山大佛）

图6　乐山大佛

九寨沟在四川北部南坪县，因景区中有九个藏族村寨而得名。九寨沟距成都约300公里，可以乘飞机或汽车前往。九寨沟是20世纪70年代发现的，近年来游客剧增。九寨沟是中国第一个自然风景保护区，也是大熊猫保护区。游览区面积约50平方公里，有六个景区，共有大大小小高山湖泊（当地人称海子）100多个。湖水清澈如镜，湖与湖之间形成多级瀑布。其中100多米宽、30米高的诺日朗瀑布极为壮观。人们步行在由瀑布、湖水、雪山、森林、白云、蓝天所构成的童话仙境中，感到超尘脱俗，流连忘返。九寨沟以南60公里处的黄龙国家公园，以奇异的水景而闻名。在长7.5公里、宽一公里的沟谷中散布着五彩斑斓（有蓝色、黄色、白色、绿色、褐色等）的梯田状水池和瀑布。每年农历6月16日在黄龙寺举行的盛大的庙会吸引了大批藏、回、羌等少数民族。（图7：九寨沟）

图7　九寨沟

第四站是重庆。重庆是中国西南最大的工商业城市，1997年被确立为中央直辖市，脱离了四川省。在京、津、沪、渝四个直辖市中，最年轻的重庆面积最大（8.2万平方公里）、人口最多（3,000万）。重庆是中国风格最独特的城市之一，三面环江，依山建城，市内几乎见不到自行车，最常用的交通工具是汽车、缆车和轮船。长江与嘉陵江在此会合。这里冬春多雾，因此山城重庆还有"雾都"之称。重庆附近的名胜有缙云山、大足石刻和长江三峡等。

缙云山座落于重庆市西北约60公里的北碚区。山势峻秀，遍山茂林修竹，文物古迹多，是游览避暑胜地，有"川东小峨眉"之称。

大足石刻在重庆西北160公里处，在中国石窟艺术中，大足堪与敦煌莫高窟、洛阳龙门和大同云岗并列。佛教、道教与儒教的石刻和雕像大大小小数以千计，散布在全县 40 余处。比较集中的地方在北山。

长江三峡是中国最著名的风景名胜之一。长江全长 6,300 公里，是中国最长的河流，也是世界第三大河。从重庆的奉节到湖北的宜昌之间有著名的长江三峡。自西向东分别是雄伟险峻的瞿塘峡、曲折秀丽的巫峡和滩多水急的西陵峡。全长 204 公里，峡谷最宽处 300 多米，最窄处不到 100 米，两边的悬崖绝壁，犹如刀劈一般。山高水急，飞流急湍，十分壮观。在瞿塘峡和巫峡连接处，游客还可以换乘小船去游览大宁河的"小三峡"。著名的巫山十二峰中，北岸的望霞峰纤丽奇俏，峰后有一石柱宛如少女，故此又称为神女峰。游船还要经过屈原的故乡秭归，现在中国人过端午节吃粽子的风俗，就是为了纪念战国时期这位著名的爱国诗人。乘游轮从重庆到武汉是一条水上游览热线，三峡不仅自然景观壮丽，而且名胜古迹众多。轮船在途中时常停泊，以便游客上岸参观游览。如果喜欢坐船的话，可以从重庆一直坐到南京、上海，大约需要一周的时间。中国正在三峡地区修建世界上最大的水利工程，坝顶海拔高程为 185 米，整个工程预计将于 2009 年完成。（图 8：长江三峡）

图 8　长江三峡

Lesson Three　Chengdu and Chongqing

Chengdu, on the third leg of our tour, is the capital and administrative, economic and cultural center of Sichuan Province. Its major tourist attractions include the Thatched Cottage of Du Fu, Temple of Marquis of Wu, Manjusri Monastery, Tomb of Wang Jian, Qingyang Taoist Temple, Dujiang Weirs, Emei Mountain and Jiuzhaigou Scenic Area.

The Thatched Cottage of Du Fu stands by the Flower-Washing Brook in the western suburbs of Chengdu. It was the former residence of the famous Tang-dynasty poet. At the age of 47, stricken by poverty and war and turmoil, he moved from Shaanxi to Chengdu, and settled down in this thatched hut built with the help of his friends. During the four years his stay there, he composed more than 240 poems reflecting the misery of the people and his enlightened views about it. Lauded by posterity as a "poet-sage," Du Fu is one of the greatest poets held in high esteem by the Chinese people.

The Temple of Marquis of Wu at the southwest corner of Chengdu was built to commemorate Zhuge Liang, Prime Minister of the Kingdom of Shu in the Three Kingdoms Period and an embodiment of loyalty and wisdom in China. This temple was built in the

中国导游

Western Jin Dynasty, and in the Ming Dynasty, a temple dedicated to Emperor Liu Bei of the Kingdom of Shu was added, but people still refer to it as the Temple of the Marquis of Wu.

The Manjusri Monastery is the largest and best-preserved Buddhist temple in Chengdu. Originally known as Xiangxin Temple, it was given its present name in the Qing Dynasty. Many buildings in the complex are decorated with exquisite relief carvings. There are more than 400 Buddhist figures in the temple, but its most precious historic relic is the skull of Monk Xuanzang of the Tang Dynasty. Bustling crowds of worshippers and visitors come in an endless stream every day.

The Qingyang Taoist Temple, situated beyond the Tonghui Gate of Chengdu, is known for its annual flower show. Converted into a cultural park in 1959, it is the oldest and most expansive Taoist temple in and around Chengdu. The story goes that Laozi, the enigmatic founder of Taoism and reputed author of *Daodejing* , asked a friend to meet him at the site. When the friend arrived he saw only a boy leading two goats by the rope. In a fabulous leap of thought, he realized that the boy was Laozi himself. Today, the goats are represented in bronze in the temple.

The 1,600-meter-high Qingcheng Mountain is a Taoist sanctuary some 65 kilometers west of Chengdu. There are many Taoist temples on its slopes. Acclaimed as the "most secluded place on earth," the mountain is well-known for its picturesque scenery. About 100 Taoist monks reside in the Jianfu Temple at the foot of the mountain.

Dujiang Weirs, an ancient irrigation project some 60 kilometers southwest of Chengdu and 16 kilometers to Qingcheng Mountain, was built in 256 BC by local people under the guidance of Li Bing, governor of the prefecture of Shu, and his son to tame the turbulent Minjiang River and divert its floods for irrigation purposes. The project, consisting of the Fish Mouth, Flying Sand Dam and Mouth of the Precious Bottle, is still playing a major water conservancy role today despite its long history of 2,200 years.

Emei Mountain, one of the four famous Buddhist mountains in China, is 160 kilometers southwest of Chengdu. One may get there by bus or train. As the saying goes,"The elegance of Emei is unmatched under heaven." The main temples and scenic spots are Baoguo Temple, Wannian Temple, Leiyin Temple, Qingyin Chamber, Hongchunping, Xixiang Pond and Golden Summit. Old trees, rare flowers, birds and animals, elegant peaks, brooks and sea of clouds compose a beautiful view of Emei. At its 3,099-meter-high summit, one may see the famous "Buddha's aureole" sometimes, which turns out to be a round rainbow produced by the refraction of water particles, in which reflections of people can be seen. The resounding croaking of the "zither-playing" frogs at Wannian Temple and the flocks of monkeys at Xixiang Pond are delightful attractions for visitors.

The 71-meter-tall Monumental Leshan Buddha qualifies as the globe's largest statue of the Buddha, carved as it was into the rock face of an entire cliff overlooking the confluence of the Dadu River and Minjiang River. The Buddha's ears are 7 meters long; his insteps are 8.5 meters broad, and his big toe is large enough to hold several people having a picnic. This breathtaking project was begun in the year AD 713 by a Buddhist monk called Haitong; it was completed 90 years later. Behind the giant Buddha is Lingyun Temple, which is commonly called Giant Buddha Temple. (Illustration 6: The Monumertal Leshan Buddha)

In Nanping County of northern Sichuan is Jiuzhaigou Nature Reserve. Nine Tibetan villages are located there; hence the name. It is about 300 kilometers from Chengdu, and you may go there by plane or bus. Jiuzhaigou was discovered in the 1970s, and is now full of visitors. It is the first nature reserve in China, and also a panda conservation zone. The total area of the nature reserve is about 50 square kilometers, which is divided into 6 scenic areas. The place is strewn with over 100 lakes (*haizi* in local language) of various sizes and shapes, as well as many waterfalls among these crystalline lakes. Nuorilang Waterfall, about 100 meters wide and with a 30-meter drop, is a spectacular natural phenomenon. Walking in this fairyland of waterfalls, lakes, snowy mountains, forests, white clouds and blue skies, people can easily feel as if they are transported from earthly matters. Huanglong Nature Reserve, 60 kilometers south from Jiuzhaigou, is famous for its colorful waters. This valley, studded with terraced, colored ponds (blue, yellow, white, green and brown) and waterfalls, is about 7.5 kilometers long by 1 kilometer wide. An annual temple fair held at Huanglong Temple around the middle of the sixth lunar month attracts droves of traders of Tibetan, Hui and Qiang ethnic backgrounds. (Illustration 7: Jiuzhaigou Scenic Area)

The fourth leg of our itinerary is Chongqing, the largest industrial and commercial city in southwest China. Chongqing was separated from Sichuan Province and became a municipality directly under the Central Government in 1997. Among the four municipalities of Beijing, Shanghai, Tianjin and Chongqing, this youngest member has the largest area of 82,000 square kilometers and the biggest population of 30 million. Chongqing is one of China's most unusual cities in that it is perched on steep mountains and skirted on three sides by water at the confluence of the Yangtze and Jialing rivers. Another unique aspect is the absence of bicycles. The common means of transportation are bus, cable-cars and boats. The mountain city Chongqing is also called "fog city" because of the thick fogs in winter and spring. The famous scenic spots near Chongqing are Jinyun Mountain, Dazu Stone Carving and the Three Gorges of the Yangtze River.

Jinyun Mountain is located in Beibei, about 60 kilometers northwest of Chongqing. Covered with dense forests and bamboo groves, it is a famous summer resort. With beautiful scenery and historic sites, it is also called the "Lesser Emei Mountain of East Sichuan".

Dazu, 160 kilometers northwest of Chongqing, runs parallel with Mogao in Dunhuang, Longmen in Luoyang and Yungang in Datong as China's four major Buddhist grottoes. Thousands of large and small cliff carvings and statues with Buddhist, Taoist and Confucian influences, are scattered in some 40 places in Dazu County, with the largest groups at North Hill.

The Three Gorges of the Yangtze River is regarded as one of the greatest scenic attractions of China. The 6,300-kilometer-long Yangtze is China's longest river and the third longest in the world. Between Fengjie in Sichuan and Yichang in Hubei lie three great gorges. From west to east, they are the Qutang Gorge, the Wuxia Gorge and the Xiling Gorge, stretching along 204 kilometres between rocky mountains that are almost perpendicular to the river, as if hewn by an axe. Most boats stop at the joints of the Qutang and Wuxia gorges, so that passengers can embark on smaller boats for tours of the "Little Three Gorges" of the Daning River. Of the twelve famous peaks at Wushan, the Wangxia Peak on the northern bank of the Yangtze looks uniquely handsome and lovely. Behind the summit of the peak stands a stone column that looks like a young maiden — graceful and self-assured. Hence the name: Goddess Peak. Down the river, after the ship passes the Wuxia Gorge, is Zigui, the native place of Qu Yuan, the ancient patriotic poet of the state of Chu during the Warring States Period. The Chinese custom of eating *zongzi* at the Dragon Boat Festival is dedicated to his memory. A cruise from Chongqing to Wuhan is a favorite with tourists, as many scenic spots and historic sites can be found along the Three Gorges. If you prefer, you may take a boat and sail directly from Chongqing to Nanjing or Shanghai, which takes about a week's time. China is building the word's largest hydraulic project in the Three Gorges area on the Yangtze River, with its dam as high as 185 meters above sea level. The entire project will be completed in 2009.
(Illustration 8: The Three Gorges of the Yangtze River)

第四课 南京、苏州、上海

第五站是南京。南京是江苏省省会，中国最富有吸引力的城市之一。南京是七大古都之一，历史上曾有10个朝代在此定都。山川形势险要，名胜古迹众多。南京夏季天气炎热，与重庆、武汉一起并称为"长江三大火炉"。南京的名胜主要有明城墙、中山陵、明孝陵、灵谷寺、玄武湖、夫子庙等等。

南京城墙是明朝遗迹，周长超过48公里，是世界上最长的城墙。它建于1366年至1386年间，约三分之二的城墙保存至今。城墙平均高度为12米，顶部宽7米，共有13个城门。现存有和平门、中华门等。中华门极为坚固，瓮城有四重之多，瓮城下的券洞共有27个，可以藏兵3,000人。

中山陵是中国革命先行者孙中山先生的陵墓。孙中山先生是国民党和共产党双方都尊崇的现代中国之父。1925年他在北京逝世。1926年按照孙先生遗愿在南京兴建陵墓，1929年春落成，同年6月，孙中山遗体由北京碧云寺移此安葬。陵园由广场、牌坊、墓道、陵门、祭堂、墓室等组成。从陵墓进口处石牌坊开始，上达墓室共有392级石阶。祭堂内有孙中山白色大理石全身坐像。墓室中央长方形石棺上有孙中山先生大理石长眠卧像，其下，葬着先生遗体。（图9：中山陵）

图9　中山陵

明孝陵是明代第一位皇帝朱元璋的陵墓，位于紫金山的南坡，中山陵的西边。陵墓前有一条长长的神道，两边屹立着一对对石狮、大象、骆驼、马、麒麟以及文官武将的雕塑。明孝陵是明代陵墓中规模最大的一个，但大部分建筑早已毁于战火。

灵谷寺位于钟山南坡（紫金山又名钟山），是钟山风景最佳处。主体建筑是无梁殿，后边有松风阁和灵谷塔。塔高66米，9层8面，登临塔顶可以眺望钟山胜景。

玄武湖是南京最大的湖，面积约5平方公里。游人可以在湖边漫步，也可以乘船到湖心五岛游玩，各岛之间有长堤和桥梁相连。由于位于市内，人们常常来此躲避南京市中心的喧嚣。

夫子庙即孔夫子庙，位于城南秦淮河畔，原是人们尊孔祭孔的地方。现在的夫子庙，一部分是修复的清末建筑，一部分是全新的仿古建筑。这里是大众文化娱乐购物的中心，到了周末，人山人海，热闹非常。人们在这里观赏民俗风情表演，品尝各种风味小吃。

　　从南京经上海到杭州，这条线路及周围地区一般被称为沪宁杭地区，地处长江三角洲，以太湖为中心，是中国有名的鱼米丝茶之乡。这里不仅经济发达，也是人文、风景名胜荟萃之地。沿途的镇江、扬州、常州、无锡、苏州、嘉兴等城市也都是著名的旅游城市。中国人常说"上有天堂，下有苏杭"。如果时间允许，不妨多看看这里的城市和乡村。

　　第六站是苏州，苏州是一座历史古城，始建于2,500年前的春秋末期，是当时吴国的国都。苏州是中国著名的丝绸生产中心和江南水乡园林城市。清末时城内有桥梁390座，园林270余处。现苏州古典园林尚存69处。其中最著名的有沧浪亭、狮子林、拙政园和留园，并称为苏州四大名园，分别代表了宋、元、明、清的建筑风格。与北京气魄宏大的皇家园林不同，苏州园林多系私人宅第，占地很小，却更多地表现了个人趣味，山、水、建筑、花木巧妙地结合成一幅幅山水风景画。（图10：苏州园林一景）

　　沧浪亭位于苏州市南，溪流和山林使它比较富有野趣。这是苏州最古老的园林，保持了宋代的建筑风格。其特色是园外山色与园内山景自然结合，是园林"借景"中的杰作。

图 10　苏州园林一景

　　狮子林建于元代至正二年。园内假山重叠，似形态各异的狮子，故得名。沿着深幽的洞壑和曲径漫步，给人留下美好的印象。碑亭里存有乾隆皇帝的手迹。

　　拙政园占地60余亩，是苏州最大的名园。拙政园建于明代，总体布局以水池为中心，亭台楼榭，临池而建。一窗一景，景随步移，极富诗情画意。

　　留园是清代名园，以精巧的分合布局见长，700米长的曲径回廊，连接着主要景点。种种雕花窗有数十种之多，留园也是擅长借景的园林杰作。太湖石"冠云峰"高近9米，是江南湖石之冠。拙政园、留园和北京颐和园、承德避暑山庄并称中国四大名园。

　　网师园是苏州最小的园林，仅有拙政园的十分之一，但却非常值得一游，因为它集中了各园的长处。中央为花园，东西两侧为住宅和书房。其中的明代建筑"殿移"连同明代家具、宫灯一起复制后，取名"明轩"，1981年被永久陈列在纽约大都会博物馆中。网师园的全景微缩景观则从1982年起陈列在巴黎蓬皮杜中心。

　　虎丘在苏州市西北阊门外，古称"吴中第一名胜"。据传春秋时吴王夫差的父亲阖闾葬于此，葬后三天，有一只白虎站立在上面，故名虎丘山。名胜有剑池、宝塔、千人石等。剑池方形，深2丈，据说埋有3,000柄名剑作为阖闾的殉葬品，故名剑池。"虎丘剑池"四个石刻大字为唐代书法家颜真卿所写。

寒山寺在阊门外枫桥镇上。寺得名于唐代诗僧寒山。唐代诗人张继那首《枫桥夜泊》（月落乌啼霜满天，江枫渔火对愁眠。姑苏城外寒山寺，夜半钟声到客船。）使寒山寺闻名中外，尤其对日本游客具有很大的吸引力。

上海是第七站。这个中国最有名的城市大概是老一辈外国人最熟悉的了。旧上海被称为"东方的巴黎"、"冒险家的乐园"。1949年后，上海成为中央直辖市。1990年中国宣布建立上海浦东新区和沿长江开放带，上海苏醒了。近年来上海经济迅速发展，城市面貌日新月异。上海变化速度之快，连当地人也感到陌生了。上海的旅游热点有外滩、豫园和城隍庙、玉佛寺、东方明珠电视塔、浦东新区、上海博物馆、鲁迅纪念馆等。

外滩是上海的象征，黄浦江畔那些类似纽约市中心20世纪30年代风格的新古典主义建筑还能使人们回想起旧上海的繁华。如今整个外滩又恢复了金融区的风貌。与外滩相连接的南京路以及淮海路是上海最繁华的商业区。站在外滩眺望黄浦江对岸的浦东新区，可以强烈感受到上海现代化的进程是如此迅速。

豫园和城隍庙相毗邻，位于上海市南市区。豫园占地20,000多平方米，是著名的江南古典园林。始建于明嘉靖年间，是四川布政司潘允端的私人花园。明末园荒景废，清代重建，有明清两代建筑风格。豫园由五条龙墙将全园分隔为7个景区、40处景观。附近城隍庙一带，极为热闹，四周密布着100多家土特产品商店和餐馆，游人如织，水泄不通。这里有极富特色的小吃和旅游纪念品商店，值得驻足。

图11　玉佛

玉佛寺是上海少数几个佛寺之一，每天吸引着大批游客，尤其是海外华人观光客。1882年，普陀山慧根和尚从印度返国途经缅甸时，请回玉佛五尊，途经上海时留下白玉雕释迦牟尼坐像和卧像各一尊，并建玉佛寺，后废。1911～1918年在安远路重建。玉佛由整块白玉精雕而成，高1.9米，重1吨，镶嵌着各种宝石。白玉佛长0.96米，侧卧在红木榻上。（图11：玉佛）

东方明珠广播电视塔位于上海黄浦江畔、浦东陆家嘴，1994年建成，塔高468米，为亚洲第一、世界第三高塔。东方明珠塔由塔座、下球体、上球体、太空舱等大小不等11个钢球组成，上球体直径为45米，是鸟瞰上海的最佳处。东方明珠塔极为壮观，是上海的标志性建筑和旅游热点之一。

浦东新区位于黄浦江以东、长江口西南，面积约为523平方公里，与外滩隔江相望。浦东自1990年全面开发开放以后，发展极为迅速。由东方明珠塔、杨浦大桥、南浦大桥、世纪大道、陆家嘴金融贸易区、中央公园、外高桥保税区、华夏文化旅游区等构成了现代化都市的壮丽景观。

上海博物馆始建于1952年。1996年，位于上海人民广场的上海博物馆新馆建成开放，建筑面积为38,000平方米，馆藏有种种珍贵文物12万余件，其中商周时代的青铜器、各个时期的陶瓷、书画、钱币、甲骨、符印、工艺品等最为丰富，中外闻名。

中国现代史上有许多名人曾在上海居住、工作过，因此上海的名人故居和纪念地比较多，其中著名的有孙中山故居、宋庆龄故居、鲁迅故居、鲁迅纪念馆、鲁迅墓、周（恩来）公馆、中共"一大"会址纪念馆等。此外上海值得推荐的去处还有南京路、人民广场、龙华寺、大世界游乐中心、上海动物园、上海展览中心等等。

Lesson Four　　Nanjing, Suzhou and Shanghai

Our fifth stop, Nanjing, the capital of Jiangsu Province, is one of China's most attractive cities. Nanjing was one of the seven ancient capitals of China, having served as the capital of 10 dynasties. Famous for its host of historic sites and strategic location, Nanjing, one of the "Three Furnaces on the Yangtze River" along with Chongqing and Wuhan, is hot and humid in summer. The main scenic spots and historic sites include the Ming City Wall, Sun Yat-sen Mausoleum, Mingxiaoling Mausoleum, Linggu Temple, Xuanwu Lake Park and Temple of Confucius.

Built between 1366 and 1386, averaging 12 meters high and 7 meters wide at the top, the Nanjing City Wall is a legacy of the Ming Dynasty. At 48 kilometers, it is the longest city wall ever built in the world. About two-thirds of the wall and some of its 13 gates, such as Heping Gate and Zhonghua Gate, have remained to this day. The Zhonghua Gate, has four enceintes of gates, making it almost impregnable and large enough to house a garrison of 3, 000 soldiers in its 27 vaults.

Dr. Sun Yat-sen was a pioneer of the Chinese revolution and regarded as the father of modern China by both the Chinese Communist Party and the Kuomintang. After he died in Beijing in 1925, the construction of his mausoleum was started according to his will in 1926 in Nanjing and completed in the spring of 1929. His remains were then moved there from the Biyun Temple in Beijing in June 1929. The mausoleum encompasses a square, an archway, stairways, a gate, a memorial hall and a tomb chamber. The tomb itself lies at the top of an enormous stone stairway of 392 steps. Inside the memorial hall is a seated statue of Dr. Sun Yat-sen. In the tomb chamber, a marble statue of Dr. Sun Yat-sen in sleep is placed on the sarcophagus that contains his remains.(Illustration 9: Sun Yat-sen Mausoleum)

The Mingxiaoling Mausoleum is the tomb of Zhu Yuanzhang, the first Ming-dynasty emperor. It lies on the southern slope of Zijin Mountain and west of Dr. Sun's tomb, and entrance to it is by a long path lined with stone statues of lions, elephants, camels, horses, unicorns, military men and civil officials. The mausoleum is the largest of all Ming tombs, but unfortunately, most of its surface buildings were destroyed in wars.

Linggu Temple at the southern slope of Zijin Mountain (also known as Zhongshan Mountain) offers the best views of the mountain and its surroundings. Its main building is the Beamless Hall, behind which are the Pine Wind Pavilion and the Linggu Pagoda, a nine-storey octagonal building of 66 meters. You can have a panoramic view of Zijin Mountain from the top of the pagoda.

Covering an area of five square kilometers, the Xuanwu Lake is the largest of its kind in Nanjing. Visitors can stroll along the causeways or take a boat to its central forested island and other four isles. The park's central location makes it a convenient place to escape the hustle of Nanjing.

The Temple of Confucius stands on the bank of the Qinhuai River. It is where people worshipped the great philosopher Confucius. What you see today are restored structures from the late Qing Dynasty and new buildings erected in recent years. Today, as Nanjing's main entertainment and shopping center, it is alway crowded at weekends and during public holidays, as people arrive to enjoy folklore shows and different kinds of traditional foods and local snacks.

The route from Nanjing to Hangzhou via Shanghai and the area along this route are called Hu-Ning-Hang District. Lying around the Taihu Lake and in the Yangtze River Delta, it has long been known as a land of fish, rice, silk and tea. It has a prosperous economy and many places of historic and cultural interest. The cities along this route, such as Zhenjiang, Yangzhou, Changzhou, Wuxi, Suzhou and Jiaxing, are all popular tourist destinations. As the Chinese saying goes, "In heaven there is paradise; on earth, Suzhou and Hangzhou." If your time allows, why don't you pay a visit to the cities and countryside in this part of the country.

Our sixth stop is Suzhou, a historical city established 2,500 years ago as the capital of the State of Wu in the Spring and Autumn Period. Today, it is a famed silk producing center and a celebrated retreat of fabulous gardens. It had 390 bridges and 270 gardens during the late Qing Dynasty. Of the 69 classical gardens that remain, the "Four Famous Suzhou Gardens" — Surging Wave Garden, Lion Grove Garden, Humble Administrator's Garden and the Garden to Linger In are typical examples of the architectural styles of the Song, Yuan, Ming and Qing dynasties respectively. Unlike the massive imperial gardens in Beijing, the classical gardens of Suzhou are mostly small private propery, yet each of them is a picture-perfect combination of hills, ponds, buildings and flowers and trees. (Illustration 10: A Glimpse of a Suzhou Garden)

The Surging Wave Garden is located in south Suzhou. A bit wild with winding creeks and lush trees, this is the oldest garden in Suzhou that retains the architectural style of the Song Dynasty. Combining artificial mountains inside it and the landscape outside it, the garden is a masterpiece of "setting off the scene in a garden by borrowing the scene outside."

The lion Grove Garden, constructed in 1342, or the second year of the Zhizheng reign of the Yuan Dynasty, derived its name from the fact that all its artificial mountains are fashioned in the image of lions of different looks. Wandering along the garden's secluded tunnels and paths is an unforgetable experience. In the garden there is a pavilion that houses a stone tablet inscribed in the handwriting of Emperor Qianlong of the Qing Dynasty.

The Humble Administrator's Garden is the largest of its kind in Suzhou. Built during the Ming Dynasty, it is a four-hectare affair that features streams, ponds, bridges and islands of bamboo.

The Garden to Linger In is a famous garden built in the Qing Dynasty. Designed in a way to incorporate the surrounding landscape, it features a 700-meter-long roofed walkway that meanders its way through all the major scenic spots, and dozens of windows that open out to a good variety of scenes and sights. The 9-meter-high Cloud-Crowned Rock is the largest decorative rock collected from the Taihu Lake in south China. The Garden to Linger In, the Summer Palace in Beijing, the Summer Villa in Chengde and the Humble Administrator's Garden are acclaimed as the four leading gardens in China.

Flanked east and west by a mansion, the Net Master Garden is the smallest in Suzhou, being only one-tenth the size of the Humble Administrator's Garden, but it is worth seeing for the single reason that it has the best of all other gardens. In 1981, a duplication of the garden's Ming-style Dianyi Study and all its furniture and palace lanterns were put on permanent display at the Metropolitan Museum of Art in New York City. A miniature model of it was produced especially for a display at the Pompidou Center in Paris in 1982.

The Tiger Hill was reputed as "No.1 Sight of Scenic Beauty and Historical Interest of the State of Wu," where the king, Fuchai, buried the remains of his father, Helü. Three days after his burial, a white tiger was seen perched on the hill; hence the name. The king's father was said to have been buried with a collection of 3,000 swords. Famous historic sites include Sword Pool, Pagoda and One-Thousand-Man Rock. Four big Chinese characters, meaning "Tiger Hill, Sword Pool" are carved on a rock face in the handwriting of Yan Zhenqing, an outstanding calligrapher of the Tang Dynasty.

The Temple of Cold Mountain is at Maple Bridge Town, outside the Changmen Gate of Suzhou. This temple was named after the poet-monk Hanshan (meaning "Cold Mountain") of the Tang Dynasty. A famous poem by Zhang Ji of the Tang Dynasty has won fame for the temple. The poem reads:

> At moonset cry the crows, streaking the frosty sky;
> Dimly lit fishing boats, beneath maples sadly lie.
> Beyond the city walls, from Temple of Hanshan,
> Bells break the ship-borne roamer's dream and midnight still.

This temple is especially popular with the Japanese.

Our seventh stop is Shanghai. To elderly foreigners, Shanghai is probably the most familiar name among China's cities, and other names for this city, like "Paris of the Orient" and "Paradise for Adventurers," are still very much on the lips. After 1949, Shanghai became a municipality directly under the Central Government. In 1990 the Pudong New Area and the Open Areas Along the Yangtze River were established. The local economy is burgeoning, and the city is in the middle of a renaissance. In fact, it is changing so fast that even locals find it a bit difficult to keep pace. Tourist attractions include the Bund, Yuyuan Garden, City God's Temple, Jade Buddha Temple, Oriental Pearl Tower, Pudong New Area, Shanghai Museum and Lu Xun Memorial Hall.

The Bund is symbolic of Shanghai. The buildings of neoclassical 1930s downtown New York style often make the elders recall the flourishing past of Shanghai. Now the whole Bund has been restored as the banking district as it had once been. Nanjing and Huaihai roads in the vicinity of the Bund have long been China's golden miles. Looking over the Pudong New Area across the Huangpu River from the Bund, you will have a strong feeling about the quick tempo of modernization in Shanghai.

A well-known classical garden south of the Yangtze River, Yuyuan Garden is located next to the City God's Temple in Nanshi District and occupies more than 20,000 square meters. Built during the Jiajing reign of the Ming Dynasty, it was the private garden of Pan Yunduan, administration commissioner of Sichuan Province. In terms of architecture, the garden is a hybrid of Ming and Qing styles, for it was destroyed at the end of the Ming Dynasty and rebuilt in the Qing Dynasty. The garden's 40 scenic attractions are divided by five dragon walls into seven areas. The nearby City God's Temple is perhaps the most popular attraction in the bazaar area. Over 100 specialty shops and restaurants jostle shoulders over narrow lanes and small squares. It is a great stop for lunch and some souvenir shopping.

The Jade Buddha Temple is one of Shanghai's few Buddhist temples. It attracts large numbers of visitors — largely overseas Chinese tourists. First built in 1882, the temple got its name from the two jade statues of Sakyamuni, one seated and one reclining, both brought from Myanmar by Huigen, a monk from Putuo Mountain. The temple was destroyed later and rebuilt on the Anyuan Road from 1911 to 1918. The seated Buddha is 1.9 meters tall and was carved out of a single piece of white jade weighing one ton and inlaid with dazzling jewels. The reclining one is 0.96 meter long, with the Buddha sleeping on a padauk bed. (Illustration 11: The Jade Buddha)

The Oriental Pearl Tower stands by the bank of the Huangpu River, at the center of Lujiazui in the Pudong New Area. Completed in 1994, the tower is 468 meters high, the highest TV tower in Asia and the third highest in the world. The Oriental Pearl Tower consists of eleven beautiful spheres of various sizes, including the base, the space module, the upper sphere, the lower sphere etc. The observational deck in the upper sphere is 45 meters in diameter; it is the best place for a bird's-eye view of Shanghai. It has already become one of the symbolic buildings and tourist attractions in Shanghai.

The Pudong New Area, situated opposite the Bund and on the east bank of the Huangpu River and the southwest bank of the Yangtze River estuary, covers an area of 523 square kilometers. Pudong has been developing fast since it adopted the opening-up policy in 1990. The Oriental Pearl Tower, the Yangpu Bridge, the Nanpu Bridge, the Century Avenue, the Lujiazui Banking District, the Central Park, the Waigaoqiao Free Trade Zone and the Tourist Area of Chinese Culture combine to turn Pudong into a modern metropolis.

Shanghai Museum was founded in 1952 and moved to its present site in Renmin Square in 1996. It is a modern architecture with a floor space of 38,000 square meters. Its collection of bronzeware from the Shang and Zhou dynasties, pottery, porcelain, calligraphy works, paintings, sculptures, seals, coins and arts and crafts of various dynasties has won it worldwide fame.

Many eminent personages in modern Chinese history had lived in Shanghai. That is why the city is full of famous former residences and memorial halls, such as Dr. Sun Yat-sen's residence, Soong Ching Ling's residence, Lu Xun's residence and memorial hall, Lu Xun's tomb, the former residence of Zhou Enlai and the site of the First National Congress of the CPC. Other recommendable tourist attractions include Nanjing Road, Renmin Square, Longhua Temple, Grand World Amusement Center, Shanghai Zoo and Shanghai Exhibition Center.

第五课 杭州和黄山

游完上海，我们的中国之旅行程已经过半。第八站是杭州。自古以来杭州就是中国人最喜爱的城市之一。杭州是浙江省的省会，也是中国七大古都之一。马可·波罗在700多年前就形容杭州是世界上最美丽的城市之一。这里也是京杭大运河的终点。杭州的美景很多，像西湖、灵隐寺、岳王庙、六和塔、虎跑泉、钱塘潮等都令人陶醉。

西湖是杭州的灵魂，是中国十大风景区之一。西湖面积为5.6平方公里，周长约15公里。西湖一池碧水，三面环山，湖山映衬，相得益彰。孤山是湖中最大的岛，文化古迹甚多，有浙江省博物馆、中山公园、平湖秋月、楼外楼等。而白堤和苏堤又把西湖隔成外西湖、里西湖和北西湖三个部分。两堤因唐代大诗人白居易和宋代大文豪苏东坡而得名。在湖光山色、花木繁茂的西湖周围，点缀着著名的西湖十景和无数名胜古迹。

图12　六和塔

灵隐寺是中国最著名的佛寺之一，公元326年始建，历史上重建过16次，现存为清代建筑。最前面是四大天王殿，上悬"云林禅寺"匾额，是康熙皇帝的手笔。大雄宝殿高33.6米，是中国最宏伟的佛寺大殿之一。

岳王庙也叫岳坟，为纪念宋朝爱国将领、著名的民族英雄岳飞而建。12世纪时，中国北方被金人所侵占，岳飞将军英勇作战，收复了许多失地，正当节节胜利之时，他却被朝廷召回，又被奸臣秦桧以"莫须有"的罪名处死。1163年孝宗恢复了岳飞的名誉，岳飞被重新安葬在西湖边。

六和塔屹立在钱塘江畔，高60米，是一座八面楼阁式砖木混合建筑，具有中国的传统风格。外观为13层，实际仅有7层。有石阶通往塔顶，可以尽览钱江景色。它的旁边是气势磅礴的钱塘江公路铁路大桥。六和塔始建于970年，是越王为镇钱江潮而建，塔上装灯，为夜航船只导航。（图12：六和塔）

虎跑泉位于西湖西南，它与龙井、玉泉并列为西湖三大名泉。"龙井茶叶虎跑水"历来被誉为"西湖双绝"。你可以在虎跑品尝一杯上好的龙井茶。

其他著名的景观还有钱塘江大潮、富春江千岛湖、宝石山、瑶琳洞、龙井、莫干山以及中国丝绸博物馆、中国茶叶博物馆、胡庆余堂中药博物馆等。

黄山在杭州以西200多公里处，位于安徽省南部，是我们行程的第九站。黄山是中国最美的地方之一，具有五岳的壮丽与秀美。五岳是中国的五座名山，即东岳泰山、西岳华山、北岳恒山、南岳衡山和中岳嵩山。明代著名旅行家徐霞客说过："五岳归来不看山，黄山归来不看岳。"黄山的奇松、怪石、云海和温泉被称为"四绝"。黄山有72座名峰，最高峰是海拔1,873米的莲花峰。景区有玉屏楼、云谷寺、北海、西海、温泉、百丈瀑、天都峰、莲花峰、始信峰等。黄山山顶佳景荟萃，如同仙境，是黄山风景的精华，黄山云海日出尤为脍炙人口。1990年，黄山列入联合国"世界自然与文化遗产"名录。（图13：黄山）

黄山的登山道主要有四条，即南路、东路、北路和西路。南路也称前山路，是多数游客选择的登山道路，这条15公里的登山道上有黄山最雄奇秀美的景色。东路设有登山索道，也是游人上山的主要线路。

图13　黄山

Lesson Five　Hangzhou and Huangshan Mountain

We have finished more than half of this itinerary after our visit to Shanghai. The eighth stop is Hangzhou, one of the most favored cities in China since ancient times. Hangzhou is the capital of Zhejiang Province; it was one of the seven ancient capitals of China. When Marco Polo stopped over at Hangzhou in the 13th century, he described it as one of the finest and most splendid cities in the world. Hangzhou is also the southern end of the Grand Canal. There are many scenic spots there, including the West Lake, Temple of Soul's Retreat, Tomb of General Yue Fei, Six Harmonies Pagoda, Running Tiger Spring and the tidal bore of the Qiantang River.

As one of the 10 best scenic spots in China, the West Lake is the soul of Hangzhou. It covers 5.6 square kilometers with a circumference of 15 kilometers. Emerald hills embrace the picturesque lake on three sides. The largest island in the lake is Solitary Hill with a wealth of cultural relics; it is home to the Provincial Museum, the Louwailou Restaurant, the famous scene of Autumn Moon on Calm Lake and the Zhongshan Park. Two causeways, the Baidi and the Sudi, split the lake into three sections. The names of Baidi and Sudi came from the Tang-dynasty poet Bai Juyi and the Song-dynasty poet Su Dongpo. Around the lake are 10 famous scenic wonders and numerous cultural relics shrouded in lush vegetation.

The Temple of Soul's Retreat is one of the best-known Buddhist temples in China. Built in AD 326, it has been destroyed and restored again and again, altogether 16 times. The present buildings are restorations of the Qing-dynasty structures. At the front of the temple is the Hall of the Four Heavenly Guardians. The four-character name of the temple inscribed on a board was written by Emperor Kangxi of the Qing Dynasty. The 33.6-meter-high Mahavira Hall is one of the most magnificent temple halls in China.

Yue Fei was a national hero and patriotic general of the Southern Song Dynasty. During the 12th century, when north China was overrun by the Nüzhen tribes from the north, General Yue Fei was commander of the Song armies. Despite his success against the invaders, he was framed and put to death by a treacherous court official called Qin Hui. In 1163, Emperor Xiaozong of the Southern Song Dynasty exonerated his name and had his remains reburied at the present site.

The Six Harmonies Pagoda is a 60-meter-high octagonal pagoda by the Qiantang River. Its brick-and-wood structure, a masterpiece of traditional Chinese architecture, appears to have 13 storeys from outside, but actually it has only 7 storeys. A stone staircase leads to the top, where one can enjoy the beauty of the Qiantang River. Close by is an enormous rail and highway bridge, which spans the Qiantang River. The pagoda was originally built by the King of Yue in AD 970 to halt the tidal waves. It was later used as a lighthouse (Illustration 12: The Six Harmonies Pagoda)

The Running Tiger Spring lies in the southwest of the West Lake. Hupaoquan (Running Tiger Spring), Longjing (Dragon Well) and Yuquan (Jade Spring) are the three best-known springs in Hangzhou. Tea leaves from Longjing Village and water from Running Tiger Spring are considered the best for tea brewing. You can savor a cup of delicious tea there.

The other recommended tourist attractions are the tidal bore of the Qiantang River, the Thousand Islet Lake, the Precious Stone Hill, the Yaolin Cave, the Longjing Village, Mogan Mountain, the China Silk Museum, the China Tea Museum and Huqingyutang Chinese Medicine Museum.

Huangshan Mountain is the ninth stop of our journey. Situated in south Anhui Province and more than 200 kilometers west of Hangzhou, it is one of the most beautiful scenic spots in the country. It has all the grandeur and beauty of the five sacred mountains in China: Taishan Mountain (Shandong), Huashan Mountain (Shaanxi), Hengshan Mountain (Shanxi), Songshan Mountain (Henan) and Hengshan Mountain (Hunan). Xu Xiake, a well-known traveler of the Ming Dynasty, said, "After visiting the five mountains, I decided not to see the other mountains, but after my return from Huangshang Mountain I don't care ever to glance at the five holy mountains." Its graceful pine trees, extraneous-looking rocks, sea of clouds and hot springs are its four unique views. Of the mountain's 72 peaks, the highest is the Lotus Flower Peak, 1,873 meters above sea level. Its scenic zones include Jade Screen Tower, Yungu Temple, North Sea, West Sea, Hot Springs, Baizhang Waterfalls, Heavenly Capital Peak, Lotus Flower Peak and Shixin Peak, but none of these can match the beauty of the fairyland-like scenery at its summit where the sunrise over a sea of clouds every morning never fail to captivate its visitors. In 1990 Huangshan Mountain was declared a World Natural and Cultural Heritage Site by UNESCO. (Illustration 13: Huangshan Mountain)

There are four routes leading in all direcrions to the top of Huangshan Mountain. The southern route is also called Qianshan Route, which most tourists take. Along this 15-kilometer route are some of the most spectacular scenes and sights in Huangshan Mountain. The cable car is on the eastern route, which also provides major access to the mountain.

第六课 厦门和广州

厦门是第十站，从黄山可乘火车经江西鹰潭直达厦门。厦门是福建第二大城市，与台湾隔海相望。厦门是美丽的海滨城市，1980年辟设经济特区后，经济贸易迅速发展。有鼓浪屿、南普陀、集美等名胜。

鼓浪屿是一个小岛，位于厦门西南面，与厦门相隔700多米。鼓浪屿常年无霜雪，四季鲜花盛开，楼台屋宇依山而筑，环境怡静幽美，有"海上花园"之称。中国很多著名的钢琴家都出自鼓浪屿。游鼓浪屿，必登日光岩。日光岩是全岛最高峰，由几块大岩石构成，约90米高。山脚下有日光寺。山腰处有个古代发现的避暑洞，洞左有巨石平台，这就是明代民族英雄郑成功当年训练水师的水操台。离日光岩不远，是港仔后海滨浴场和菽庄花园。菽庄花园利用天然地形，借山藏海，巧为布局，其游览主线是九曲四十四桥，蜿蜒曲折，横跨海上。

南普陀寺位于厦门南面，始建于唐朝，规模宏大，已有千余年历史了。明代时曾毁于兵火，清代时重建。寺院的最前面是天王殿，大肚弥勒佛盘坐中央，笑呵呵地欢迎游客。天王殿后有一个院子，左右有钟楼和鼓楼。大雄宝殿内有三座释迦牟尼像，分别代表过去、现在和将来。大雄宝殿左右墙壁上镶嵌的8块石碑上，刻着清朝乾隆皇帝的手迹。

厦门的景观还有万石岩、集美鳌园（爱国华侨陈嘉庚的陵园）、厦门大学等。

广州是第11站，从厦门可乘火车经梅州直达广州。广州简称"穗"，别称"羊城"、"花城"，是广东省省会，华南最大的城市，中国的南大门，中国南方的经济、交通、教育和外贸中心。每年春秋两季举行的广州中国出口商品交易会是中国外贸的最大盛会。广州也是一座历史文化名城，有许多文化古迹和革命纪念地。中国近代史上许多著名人物如洪秀全、林则徐、孙中山、蒋介石、鲁迅、毛泽东、周恩来等都与这座城市有过密切的关系。以广州为中心的珠江三角洲地区是中国改革开放后最先富裕起来的地区。广州的古迹名胜主要有南越王墓、黄花岗七十二烈士墓、孙中山纪念堂、越秀公园、陈氏书院、白云山、沙面、莲花山、香江野生动物园等。

南越王墓的全称是西汉南越王墓博物馆，建在南越国文王赵眛的墓址上，位于中国大酒店南侧。"南越"是汉朝时对广州一带的称呼，南越国始建于公元前一百余年，文王是第二代君主。南越王墓是岭南地区出土文物最多、考古收获最大的一座汉墓。

黄花岗七十二烈士墓是为纪念同盟会在广州起义中英勇牺牲的烈士而建的。这次起义是由孙中山领导的同盟会在1911年4月27日发动的。起义失败后仅过了五个月，清王朝就被推翻，中华民国宣告诞生。黄花岗烈士墓园始建于1912年，由各种石块叠砌的建筑风格象征着自由与民主，顶端还有一座小型的自由女神像。

孙中山纪念堂由海外华侨和广州人民捐资兴建，以纪念孙中山先生的伟大功绩。纪念堂建在1922年孙中山任非常大总统时的总统府旧址上，1929年动工，1931年完成。纪念堂是一座八角形宫殿式建筑，具有浓郁的民族风格。大礼堂可容纳4,700人。在纪念堂前面屹立着孙中山先生的青铜塑像。

图14　五羊石像

越秀公园是广州最大的公园，占地93公顷。公园内的五羊石像是广州市的象征，五只羊口含谷穗，祝愿广州永无饥荒。（图14：五羊石像）广州因此又有了"羊城"和"穗"的别名。

陈氏书院俗称陈家祠，位于中山七路。1888年筹建，1894年建成，是广东省72县陈姓人氏合资兴建的合族祠堂，因接受本族各地读书人来广州应科举考试时居住，又称陈氏书院。书院占地一万平方米，由九座厅堂、六个院落组成。建筑装饰华丽，具有典型的岭南特色。有木雕、石雕、砖雕、陶雕、灰塑、铜铁铸等工艺装饰，现辟为广东民间工艺馆。

白云山在广州市区北部，其最高峰是摩星岭，高382米，在珠江三角洲平原上显得高大挺拔。有山顶公园、山北公园、鸣春谷大鸟笼、广州碑林、云台花园等景点，南侧山脚下有麓湖公园。广州人民十分喜爱登白云山，欣赏自然风光，远眺繁华都市。每逢重阳节（农历9月9日）有二三十万人连夜登白云山。白云山林木茂盛，也被称为广州市的"绿肺"。

沙面是珠江江畔的一个小岛，鸦片战争后成为英法的租界地，岛上分布具有殖民地色彩的欧洲风格的建筑物。这里是外国游客喜欢流连的地方。由中国人设计、建造与管理的五星级大酒店白天鹅宾馆也屹立在沙面岛上。

莲花山位于广州市郊番禺，距广州市40公里，是古代采石场旧址。远在明代以前，人们就在这里大规模地开采石料，遗下无数的悬崖峭壁、奇岩异洞。山上建有亭、塔、楼、廊和40米高的观音佛像，山下是碧波荡漾的珠江。

香江野生动物世界位于市郊番禺，以保护野生动物、自然环境为宗旨。园内分乘车游览区和步行游览区，有动物300多种，约10,000只。设有四个动物表演场。

广州市值得推荐的其他去处还有六榕寺（佛教）、石室教堂（天主教）、怀圣寺光塔（伊斯兰教）、光孝寺（佛教）、清平市场、文化公园、广州世界大观、广州动物园及海洋馆、星海音乐厅、广东省博物馆、广东省美术馆等。

深圳（毗邻香港）、珠海（毗邻澳门）这两个经济特区以及广东最著名的风景名胜肇庆七星岩都在珠江三角洲，从广州乘火车或汽车前往这些地方，只需要一个多小时。这些地方都是广东旅游热点。

Lesson Six   Xiamen and Guangzhou

Xiamen (Amoy) is our tenth stop. You can go there by train from Huangshan via Yingtan in Jiangxi Province. Xiamen is the second largest city of Fujian Province. This beautiful coastal city faces Taiwan across the Taiwan Straits. Xiamen's economy has developed fast since it became a special economic zone in 1980. Main tourist attractions include Gulangyu Island, Nanputuo Temple and Jimei Town.

Gulangyu Island is situated southwest of the coastal city of Xiamen, separated from the latter by a narrow 700-meter-wide strait. Free from frost and snow throughout the year, the island boasts flowers blooming year-round and lush, green trees. In the midst of these are human dwellings nestling at the foot of the natural rises. Dubbed "Garden on the Sea," the island provides an environment where people can enjoy perfect seclusion and peace. Many of China's celebrated pianists come from this island. Sunshine Rock is a must if you visit the island. As the highest point with an elevation of 90 meters on the island, Sunshine Rock is actually a pile of boulders. Underneath the rock is a temple of the same name. Halfway up Sunshine Rock is the Cave to Escape Summer Heat. To the left of the cave is a huge rock platform where Zheng Chenggong (Koxinga), a Ming-dynasty hero, oversaw the training of his navy. Not far from Sunshine Rock is a fine bathing beach known as Gangzihou. Adjoining the beach is the beautiful Shuzhuang Park, which is ingeniously laid out by making full use of the topography. Sightseers to the park usually follow a winding route with nine turns and forty-four bridges that span the sea.

On the southern outskirts of Xiamen stands the Nanputuo Temple, built during the Tang Dynasty more than 1,000 years ago. It was ruined in a battle during the Ming Dynasty but rebuilt during the Qing Dynasty. In the forefront of the temple is the Heavenly King Hall, where the welcoming Maitreya Buddha sits cross-legged, exposing his protruding belly. Behind the hall is a courtyard flanked by the drum and bell towers. The Mahavira Hall houses three statues of Sakyamuni which represent past, present and future. The left and right walls of the hall are inlaid with eight stone tablets with inscriptions in the handwriting of Emperor Qianlong of the Qing Dynasty.

Other tourist attractions include the Wanshiyan Temple, the Turtle Garden at Jimei Town (where the tomb of the patriotic overseas Chinese Mr. Tan Kah Kee is) and Xiamen University.

Guangzhou is our eleventh stop. You can get there from Xiamen via Meizhou by train. The city is also called "Sui (ear of rice)," "City of Rams" or "City of Flowers." Known formerly as Canton, Guangzhou is the south gate of China, the capital of Guangdong Province, the largest city and center of industry, commerce, education and foreign trade in South China. The Guangzhou Export Commodities Fair, held twice a year in spring and autumn respectively, attracts wide attentions from international businesspeople. As one of the famous historical and cultural cities in China, it has many historic sites and revolutionary memorials. Many famous modern historical figures such as Hong Xiuquan, Lin Zexu, Sun Yat-sen, Chiang Kai-shek, Lu Xun, Mao Zedong and Zhou Enlai all had close connections with this city. The Pearl River Delta, taking Guangzhou as its center, has become one of the most prosperous areas in China since China set a course of reforms in economic development. Main historic sites and scenic spots in Guangzhou include Tomb of the King of Nanyue, Mausoleum of 72 Martyrs at the Yellow Flower Hill, Sun Yat-sen Memorial Hall, Yuexiu Park, Chen Clan Academy, White Cloud Mountain, Shamian Island, Lotus Flower Mountain and Xiangjiang Safari Park.

The Tomb of the King of Nanyue, also known as the Museum of the King of Nanyue of the Western Han Dynasty, stands to the south of the China Hotel. Nanyue is a name that the Han Dynasty conferred on the area around Guangzhou. The Nanyue Kingdom was first established more than 2,100 years ago, and what was buried in this tomb was the remains of King Wen, its second king. The Tomb of the King of Nanyue boasts the largest number of unearthed artifacts among Han-dynasty tombs in the area of Guangdong and GuangXi.

The Mausoleum of 72 Martyrs at the Yellow Flower Hill commemorates the martyrs of the abortive Guangzhou Uprising on April 27, 1911, just five months before the Qing Dynasty collapsed, and the Republic of China was established. Built in 1912, this monument is a collection of architectural symbols of freedom and democracy, with a small Statue of Liberty on its top.

Sun Yat-sen Memorial Hall was built with donations from overseas Chinese and Guangzhou citizens. Construction was started in 1929 and completed in 1931 on the former site of the presidential residence where Dr. Sun Yat-sen acted as provisional president in 1922. It is an octagonal structure with a distinct Chinese Style. The auditorium can hold 4,700 people. In front of the hall stands a bronze statue of Dr. Sun Yat-sen.

Yuexiu Park is the biggest park in Guangzhou, covering an area of 93 hectares. The sculpture of the Five Rams is the symbol of Guangzhou. (Illustration 14: The Sculpture of the Five Rams) Legend has it that long ago five celestial beings came to Guangzhou riding on rams. Each ram carried a rice ear, which they presented to local people as well-wish from heaven that the area would be free from famine forever. From this legend the city derived its aliases — City of Rams and City of Rice-Ear.

The Chen Clan Academy, also known as the Chen Ancestral Temple, is situated on Zhongshanqilu Road. Built from 1888 to 1894, with funds raised from the Chen families in 72 counties in Guangdong Province, the temple accommodated young scholars of the Chen clan who came to Guangzhou to take the imperial examinations, hence the name of Chen Clan Academy. Covering an area of 10,000 square meters, the complex consists of six

中国导游

courtyards and nine main halls in a typical south Chinese architectural style, and embellished with a vast collection of wood, stone and brick carvings, clay and porcelain sculptures, and cast-iron or bronze decorations. Now it has been turned into a Provincial Museum of Folk Arts and Crafts.

The White Cloud Mountain is in the northern suburbs of Guangzhou. Moxingling, 382 meters high and the highest peak of the White Cloud Mountain, stands out conspicuously on the plain of the Pearl River Delta. Many scenic sights, such as Shanding Park, Shanbei Park, Mingchungu Birdcage, Forest of Steles and Yuntai Garden, are located here. At the southern foot of the mountain is the Luhu Park. The mountain is popular with the local people, who come here to admire the beautiful scenery and the panoramic view of the city. Every year on the Double Ninth Festival, which falls on the 9th day of the 9th lunar month, over 200,000 people climb the mountain in the evening. The dense forest makes the White Cloud Mountain the "lung" of Guangzhou.

Shamian, a small island by the Pearl River, became a British and French concession after the Opium War. Colonial buildings are still seen today on the island, making it a historical attraction for foreign tourists. The five-star White Swan Hotel, designed and managed by the Chinese, also towers on this island.

Lotus Flower Mountain, located in Panyu, 40 kilometers southeast of Guangzhou, is the former site of an ancient quarry. As early as in the Ming Dynasty, people collected stones at a large-scale in this place, creating many precipitous cliffs, bizarre-shaped rocks and caves. Today, pavilions, towers, corridors and a 40-meter-high statue of Goddess of Mercy decorate the mountain, while at its foot the limpid, surging Pearl River adds more interest to the beautiful landscape.

The Xiangjiang Safari Park, also located in Panyu, the southern suburbs of Guangzhou, aims at protecting wild animals and natural environment. The park is divided into two parts of bus route area and walking route area. It is now home to more than 300 species of animals, altogether about 10,000 head. Four animal performance auditoriums have been set up there.

Other interesting places in Guangzhou include the Liurong Temple, Stone Room Catholic Church, Huaisheng Mosque, Guangxiao Temple, Qingping Fair, Cultural Park, Grand World of Guangzhou, Guangzhou Zoo and Marine Park, Xinghai Concert Hall, Guangdong Provincial Museum and Guangdong Art Gallery.

Shenzhen (next to Hong Kong) and Zhuhai (next to Macao), two special economic zones, and Zhaoqing, which boasts the most famous scenery in Guangdong — the Seven-Star Rock, are all located in the Pearl River Delta. It only takes one or two hours to get there from Guangzhou by train or by bus.

第七课 桂林和昆明

第12站是桂林。桂林位于广西壮族自治区的东北部，是一座山水奇特、秀美的历史文化名城。因此地桂花树多而得名。"山青、水秀、洞奇、石美"是桂林胜景的概括，自古就有"桂林山水甲天下"之称。桂林是著名的风光旅游城市。名胜有独秀峰、伏波山、七星公园、芦笛岩、象鼻山、叠彩山、漓江、阳朔等。

独秀峰兀然屹立在城市中心，有60米高。登上峰顶，四周山水美景尽收眼底。这里原是明代皇帝朱元璋的侄孙靖江王朱守谦的王府，尚有城门遗存，现为广西师范大学的所在地。

伏波山位于漓江西岸，站在山顶可以眺望全市风景。因纪念东汉的伏波将军马援而得名，山上建有伏波庙，山下有还珠洞、试剑石和摩崖石刻像200多尊。

七星公园是中国最美的城市公园之一，位于漓江东岸。七星公园的名称来自园内的七座小山峰，排列得恰似北斗七星。山下有七星岩洞，曲折幽深，能容万

图15　桂林象鼻山

人，是桂林最大的岩洞。洞内的石钟乳、石笋、石柱等形态万千，中国人凭借想象力为它们起了很多优美的名称。

芦笛岩在桂林西北郊光明山南麓，是一个巨大的、神奇的喀斯特构造石灰岩溶洞。在500米长的曲折游程中，石钟乳、石笋、石柱、石幔、石花等石景，瑰丽奇特，好像是法国小说家儒勒·凡尔纳《地心游记》中所描绘的场景。这个绚丽多姿、奇特怪异的芦笛岩被人们称为"大自然艺术之宫"。

象鼻山在桂林市内漓江、阳江汇流处。山的形状恰如大象伸鼻吸饮江水。象鼻山因常常做为桂林的象征而为世人熟知。（图15：桂林象鼻山）

叠彩山在桂林城北漓江边上，山石层层横断，好像层层叠彩，所以得名。最高峰明月峰高223米，半山有"风洞"，长年凉风习习。山上有许多石雕石刻，多为唐宋风格。千百年来，这里一直是吸引游客的地方。

从桂林到阳朔之间的83公里长的漓江水道，两岸景色非常秀丽，是广西最著名的旅游线路。一千多年前一位诗人这样描绘阳朔一带的风光："江作青罗带，山如碧玉簪。"从桂林乘船到阳朔，两岸奇峰林立，江水澄碧，田园似锦，如在画中行。

　　阳朔在桂林东南65公里处，以山青、水秀、峰奇、洞巧著名，素有"阳朔山水甲桂林"之说，胜景有碧莲峰、榕荫古渡、冠岩幽境、九马画山、书僮山等。

　　值得推荐的去处还有南溪山、隐山、老人山、虞山、兴安灵渠、龙胜花坪林区等。

　　从桂林西行约1,000公里，就来到了昆明。昆明是第13站，也是S形中国之旅的最后一站。昆明是云南省省会，中国历史文化名城之一。由于地处海拔1,890米的高原，昆明的气候温和，四季如春，又名"春城"和"花城"。云南是中国少数民族最多的省份（有26个少数民族），昆明因此也具有多民族文化交融的特点。昆明的名胜有滇池、西山、金殿、筇竹寺、世博园等。来到昆明的游客，如果时间充裕，最好去看看云南的几处著名游览胜地，如石林、西双版纳、大理、丽江等。

　　滇池又称昆明湖、昆明池或滇南泽，总面积340平方公里，是中国第六大淡水湖，人称"高原明珠"。滇池雄伟壮阔，很有海的气魄，所以昆明人又称之为海。滇池四周有许多名胜古迹，湖畔的西山龙门是最佳观景点。

　　西山在昆明市西南，滇池西岸，延伸很长。山上有华亭寺、太华寺、三清阁寺院，均建于元代。从三清阁至达天阁之间的悬崖上有一组洞穴、石刻、廊道和亭阁，这是1781年至1835年间一位道士及其合作者把身体悬吊在悬崖绝壁上凿刻出来的，称为龙门石道，有990多级，是西山著名的胜景。龙门是西山的最高处，从这里俯瞰滇池，一览无余。

　　金殿在昆明市东北7公里的鸣凤山上。始建于明朝万历年间，现存为明末吴三桂所扩建。方形大殿的柱子、门窗、檐瓦及神像均用黄铜铸成，故称金殿。

　　筇竹寺在昆明市西北12公里处，始建于唐朝，是中原佛教传入云南的第一寺。全寺依山而建，寺中彩塑五百罗汉像最为著名，塑于清末，高约一米，或栩栩如生，或神态怪异，被称为东方雕塑艺术的明珠。

　　世博园是1999年昆明世界园艺博览会公园的简称。公园常年开放，已成为昆明市著名的新兴景观。

图16　石林

　　来到昆明，不可不去石林一看。石林位于路南彝族自治县，在昆明市东南约100公里处。在方圆2.7万公顷的地区，青色石灰岩被长期侵蚀风化成大片石柱、石芽、石峰，好像石头的森林。进入石林，如入迷宫，奇峰异石，千姿百态，人们根据想象，取了很多生动的名称，如母子偕游、象踞石台、凤凰梳翅、犀牛望月等等。（图16：石林）路南石林村寨是彝族撒尼人聚居区，在附近可以买到彝族手工艺品，有刺绣、荷包、鞋等。

西双版纳傣族自治州在云南省最南部，与缅甸和老挝相接壤。它以美丽的热带风光和浓郁的傣族风情著称于世，是中国西南著名的旅游区。曼飞龙群塔、勐海八角亭、傣族村寨、勐腊热带植物园都是吸引人的去处。如果你在4月中旬去，还能参加泼水节，这是傣族人民最盛大的新年庆祝活动。

大理在昆明以西390公里的苍山洱海边，是一座有2,200多年历史的古城，曾是唐代南诏国和宋代大理国的首都。大理以盛产花纹美丽的大理石著称于世。大理是云南白族自治州的州府，这里的白族民居很有特色。名胜有三塔、苍山、洱海、鸡足山、蝴蝶泉等。民族节庆有三月街和火把节。

到此为止，我们已经走完了这条S形的线路，领略了中国的名山胜水和民俗风情。当然这13站远远不是中国的全部精华，还有许多享誉世界的名胜古迹我们还没去，比如拉萨、莫高窟、张家界、丝绸之路、哈尔滨的冰雪世界、山东巍峨的泰山、孔子的故里曲阜、美丽的海滨城市大连、青岛……如果你迷上了中国的历史文化和自然风光，欢迎你常来看看。中国丰富的旅游资源举世瞩目。你可以尽情地探索、感受和发现。

Lesson Seven   Guilin and Kunming

Guilin is our twelfth stop. Located in the northeast part of Guangxi Zhuang Autonomous Region, it is a famous historic and cultural city with uniquely beautiful landscape. The name Guilin originated from the numerous cassia trees in this area. A tourist city known all over the world for its "green mountains, limpid waters, strange caves and exotic-looking rocks." Guilin has earned itself, since ancient times, the laudatory saying: "The landscape of Guilin is unmatched under heaven." Among its many scenic spots are Duxiu Peak, Fubo Hill, Seven Star Park, Reed Flute Cave, Elephant Trunk Hill, Diecai Hill, Lijiang River and Yangshuo City.

The Duxiu Peak, 60 meters high, is situated in the center of Guilin. Once on the top, you can have a panoramic view of the beautiful scenery down below. This place used to be the residence of Prince Jingjiang, the son of a nephew of the Ming Emperor Zhu Yuanzhang. Today, only a gate remains. It is now part of Guangxi Normal University.

The Fubo Hill stands on the west bank of the Lijiang River. Ascending its top, one can have a panoramic view of the city. The hill derived its name from the Eastern Han-dynasty General Ma Yuan, who was confered the title of General Fubo. On the hill is the Fubo Temple; at its foot are the Returning Pearl Cave, Sword Test Rock and over 200 Buddha statues.

Seven Star Park, one of China's nicest city parks, is on the east side of the Lijiang River. The park derives its name from its seven peaks, which appear to be patterned after the Big Dipper constellation. Its Seven Star Cave is the biggest and the most fascinating cave in Guilin, which can hold as many as 10,000 people. Inside the cave are winding paths lined with a gallery of stalactites and stalagmites in the most spectacular shapes and forms, which have inspired the imagination of the Chinese people, who have given them many beautiful names.

Reed Flute Cave is situated at the southern foot of the Guangming Hill in the northwestern suburbs of Guilin. It is a huge and fantastic karst limestone cave. Along a 500-meter-long zigzag path are stalactites and stalagmites that are spectacular and remind people of the description in Jules Verne's novel *Journey to the Center of the Earth.* This fantastic cave has been widely acclaimed as an "Art Gallery of Nature."

Elephant Trunk Hill is situated at the confluence of the Lijiang and Yangjiang rivers. It looks very much like a giant elephant drinking water with its trunk, hence the name. Elephant Trunk Hill is the symbol of Guilin. (Illustration 15: Elephant Trunk Hill)

Diecai Hill or Hill with Many Splendid Hues, is located by the Lijiang River in north Guilin. The name is derived from the fact that the hill consists of many layers of rocks in different color tones. The 223-meter high Bright Moon Peak is its highest peak. Halfway up the peak is a Windy Cave, which enjoys cool breeze all year round. On the hill, there are many stone carvings, mostly in the style of the Tang and Song dynasties. For hundreds of years, Diecai Hill has been popular as a tourist attraction.

The scenery along the Lijiang River between Guilin and Yangshuo is one of the main tourist attractions of the area. A thousand years ago, a poet thus described the scenery around Yangshuo: "The river forms a green gauze belt, and the mountains are like jasper hairpins." Touring the stretch of 83 kilometers from Guilin to Yangshuo by boat, you can enjoy the picturesque landscape of towering peaks on the banks, sparkling waters and lyrical scenes all around you.

Yangshuo is located 65 kilometres southeast of Guilin. Famous for its majestic green mountains, crystal-clear rivers, storybook caves, and statuesque peaks — the scenery here is reputed to be Guilin's best. Its well-known scenic spots include the Green Lotus Peak, Old Ferry under the Banyan, Guanyan Hill, Nine Horses on the Picturesque Hill and Shutong Hill.

Other interesting attractions include Nanxi Mountain, Hidden Hill, Old Man Hill, Yushan Hill, Lingqu Canal in Xing'an and Huaping Forestry Center in Longsheng.

Kunming, about 1,000 kilometers west of Guilin. is our thirteenth stop, also the last stop of this S-shaped tour route. Kunming, capital of Yunnan Province, is one of China's famous historic and cultural cities. At an elevation of 1,890 meters, Kunming has a more pleasant climate than most other Chinese cities, and can be visited any time of the year since it is spring all year round. Agreeable humidity and temperature make it a "City of Spring" and "City of Blossoms." No other province in China has as many ethnic peoples as Yunnan, the homeland of 26 ethnic groups. Therefore, Kunming is full of ethnic colors. Interesting sights in Kunming include the Dianchi Lake, West Hill, Golden Palace, Bamboo Temple and the 1999 Kunming Expo Park of World Horticulture . If you come to Kunming and if time permits, you must visit other interesting places in Yunnan, such as the Stone Forest, Xishuangbanna, Dali City and Lijiang City.

The Dianchi Lake, located southwest of Kunming, is also known as the Diannan Pool and the Kunming Lake. The sixth largest fresh water lake in China, it covers an area of 340 square kilometers and is reputed as a "pearl on the highland." Majestic and imposing like the ocean, it is called "sea" by local people. Around the lake are many scenic attractions and historic sites. You can have a best view of the lake at the Dragon Gate in the West Hill.

The West Hill, located southwest of Kunming, extends along the west bank of the Dianchi Lake. In the hill there are three Yuan-dynasty temples: the Huating Temple, the Taihua Temple and the Sanqingge Temple. On the cliff between the Sanqingge Temple and the Datiange Tower a path leads upward, flanked by a group of grottoes, stone carvings, corridors and pavilions, all done by a Taoist monk and his co-workers from 1781 to 1835, who must have suspended themselves in midair to finish the mission. Called Dragon Gate Stone Path with 990 stone steps, it is a famous sight in the West Hill. The Dragon Gate is the highest of the scenic area, where you can have a bird's-eye view of the whole Dianchi Lake.

The Golden Palace is located on the Mingfeng Hill 7 kilometers northeast of Kunming. It was first built during the Wanli reign of the Ming Dynasty but what remains today is an expansion built by Wu Sangui at the end of the Ming Dynasty. Its pillars, windows, gates, tiles and the Buddha statues of the square hall are all made of bronze; hence its name.

Located 12 kilometers northwest of Kunming, the Bamboo Temple dates back to the Tang Dynasty, and was the first Buddhist temple in Yunnan since Buddhism found its way here from central China. The temple, built according to the topography of the hill, was famous for its 500 arhat statues. Sculpted at the end of the Qing Dynasty, each statue is about one meter high. These lifelike figures with different facial expressions are claimed to be the pearl in the art of oriental sculpture.

The 1999 Kunming Expo Park of World Horticulture opens to the public every day. It has become a new landscape in Kunming.

Stone Forest is a must when you visit Kunming. About 100 kilometers southeast of Kunming and located in Lunan Yi Autonomous County, it is a 27,000-hectare land of topographical turmoil wrought by a jungle of weather-beaten monoliths in fanciful shapes ranging from pillars, sprouts and peaks. Once you enter this stone forest, you will feel as if you entered a maze of bizarre-shaped stone pillars and rocks. People have given many descriptive names to them according to their different shapes, such as Mother and Son on a Tour, Elephant on a Stone Platform, Phoenix Combing Its Wings, and Rhinoceros Looking at the Moon. (Illustration 16: The Stone Forest) The natural spectacle is made all the more alluring by its inhabitants — the Sani people of the Yi ethnic group, from whom you can buy works of embroidery, purses and shoes.

Xishuangbanna Dai Autonomous Prefecture is located in the southmost of Yunnan Province, bordering Myanmar and the Laos. It is a well-known tourist destination in southwest China for its picturesque tropical scenery and the Dai ethnic culture. The Manfeilong Towers, the Octagonal Pavilion of Menghai, the Dai villages, the Mengla Tropical Botanical Garden are all popular with tourists. If you come here in mid-April, you will have a chance to participate in the Water-Splashing Festival, a traditional activity to celebrate the Dai New Year.

The historic Dali City, about 390 kilometers west of Kunming and the seat of the Dali Bai Autonomous Prefecture, lies on the western edge of the Erhai Lake and at the eastern foot of Cangshan Mountain. Dali has a history of more than 2,200 years. It was the capital of the State of Nanzhao in the Tang Dynasty and of the State of Dali in the Song Dynasty. Dali is famous for its product of beautiful marble. The local dwellings are full of Bai flavor. Scenic spots include the Three Pagodas, Cangshan Mountain, Erhai Lake, Chicken Claw Hill and Butterfly Spring. The Third Month Fair and the Torch Festival are two famous minority festivals.

By now, we have finished the S-shaped route, visited a great number of scenic attractions, historic and cultural sites, and learned a lot of native customs. These 13 stops, of course, cannot cover all of China's natural and cultural interests. There are more world-famous scenic spots and historic sites in China, such as Lhasa; the treasure of Chinese mural art in Mogao Grottoes in Dunhuang, Gansu Province; the wonderful peaks and waters in Zhangjiajie, Hunan Province; the scenery along the Silk Road in Xinjiang Uygur Autonomous Region; the ice world of Harbin; the lofty Taishan Mountain, and the birthplace of Confucius in Qufu, Shandong Province; and the beautiful seaside towns of Dalian and Qingdao. If you are fascinated with China's history, culture and natural scenery, please visit China often. China's richness of tourist resources have attracted worldwide attention and they are waiting for you to explore, to experience and to discover.

中国特产

NATIVE PRODUCE OF CHINA

中国特产

周 健 编写／翻译

Native Produce of China

Compiled and Translated by Zhou Jian

第一课　中国著名特产

一、茶

在世界三大饮料（茶、咖啡、可可）中，茶的消费者是最多的。

中国是茶的故乡，中国人种茶、饮茶已有几千年历史。茶叶和丝绸、陶瓷一起经由古丝绸之路运往国外，从而享誉世界。世界上几大主要语言中，"茶"一词的发音都来自汉语。

中国的茶叶品种很多，由于产地和加工方式的不同，主要可分为五大类：

1. 绿　茶　绿茶的加工不经发酵过程，保持了茶叶原有的嫩绿色泽。著名品种有：浙江的龙井茶（又以杭州西湖狮峰龙井为最著名）、安徽黄山的毛峰和江苏太湖的碧螺春。

2. 红　茶　西方人叫Black tea，中国人称之为红茶。红茶的制作需要经过全发酵的过程。中国著名的红茶有安徽的祁红、云南的滇红、江苏的苏红、四川的川红、福建的闽红和湖南的湖红。

3. 乌龙茶　乌龙茶是介于绿茶和红茶之间的品种，乌龙茶的制作要经过半发酵的过程。它主要产于我国的东南沿海，如福建、广东、台湾一带。名茶有闽南铁观音、台湾冻顶乌龙茶。

4. 压制茶　通过机械压力，把茶叶压制成一定的形状，如砖状、饼状或碗状，就成了压制茶。由于压制茶便于运输和储存，流行于西南边疆少数民族地区。主要产地有湖北、湖南、四川、云南等。其中云南的沱茶较为著名。

5. 花　茶　用茉莉花等芳香的鲜花熏制的绿茶，也叫香片。福建和湖南生产的茉莉花茶较为有名，在中国北方颇受欢迎，近年来也受到很多外国人的喜爱。

中国特产

二、酒

中国是世界上最早酿造酒类饮料的国家之一。在山东大汶口曾经出土过大批4,000年前的陶制酒器；在河北平山县一座战国时期的古墓里曾出土过两罐保存了2,300年的白酒。

中国人喜欢喝的酒有白酒、黄酒、葡萄酒、药酒和啤酒。著名的有：

1. 白酒

茅台酒	（贵州）	泸州特曲	（四川）
汾酒	（山西）	剑南春	（四川）
古井贡酒	（安徽）	洋河大曲	（江苏）
五粮液	（四川）	酒鬼酒	（湖南）

这些酒的酒精含量多分为高度(50%以上)和低度(40%以下)两种。

2. 黄酒

大多由糯米制成，颜色呈琥珀色，酒精含量一般为15%～20%。人们通常热饮。黄酒也是做中国菜的调料之一。

最著名的黄酒是产于浙江绍兴的老酒，有花雕、女儿红、绍兴加饭酒等品牌。

3. 葡萄酒

中国红葡萄酒	（北京）
烟台红葡萄酒	（山东）
长城白葡萄酒	（河北）
民权白葡萄酒	（河南）
王朝干白葡萄酒	（天津）
王朝干红葡萄酒	（天津）
张裕干红葡萄酒	（山东）(图1)

4. 药酒

通常是在白酒中浸入一味或多味中药材，这种酒具有祛病强身的功效。

著名的药酒有山西的竹叶青酒、吉林的人参酒、黑龙江的五加白等。

5. 啤酒

啤酒是近代从外国传入中国的饮料，很受中国人尤其是青年一代的欢迎。最著名的是山东的青岛啤酒，在世界上也享有一定的声誉。

图1　张裕干红葡萄酒

此外，北京的燕京啤酒、广州的珠江啤酒以及深圳的金威啤酒等都很有名。

三、陶瓷

中国陶瓷的制作至少可以追溯到6,000年之前的新石器时代。中国的陶瓷到了唐代已闻名于世，china 一词成了陶瓷的代名词。中国的陶瓷与丝绸、茶叶一道沿着古丝绸之路源源不断地运到了国外。

中国南方城市景德镇在宋代就成了瓷都，到明清达到全盛，三百多座官窑的制瓷工艺达到炉火纯青的地步。

1．青瓷

早期青瓷出现于三国两晋时期，到了五代时期，技术臻于成熟。它的造型古朴雅致，釉色如青玉，瓷质坚实，风格独特。浙江龙泉县是宋元时期青瓷的著名产地，通常人们又称青瓷为"龙泉青瓷"。

除了青绿色外，龙泉窑又创烧了梅子青、粉青等令人喜爱的釉色。宋代龙泉瓷器胎骨坚硬，制作规整；元代略显厚重；明代的青瓷胎釉更为粗厚，装饰图案丰富，产品远销海内外，是民间普遍使用的一种瓷器。如今龙泉青瓷发展出许多新的品种。

2．紫砂陶器

江苏宜兴在中国被称为"陶都"，这里生产一种棕红色的紫砂陶器。器物成型后经1,200℃左右高温烧成，不上釉，以茶壶为代表作品。这里的茶壶被公认为是最好的茶具。

宜兴紫砂器古朴隽永，耐人寻味，美观实用。紫砂泥经火烧后不仅坚固、不渗水，而且具有透气性能。紫砂茶壶能增加茶叶的色、香、味。用它盛茶，可以隔夜不变味。冬天把小巧的紫砂壶握在手中，可以暖手而不会烫手。中国的鉴赏家们把紫砂壶视为"最理想的"茶壶。

除了茶壶之外，宜兴还生产紫砂咖啡壶、餐具、炊具、花瓶、花盆以及种种艺术品。

3．唐三彩

唐三彩是唐代烧制的一种三色彩釉陶器。称之为"三彩"，主要是因为常用黄、绿、蓝三种釉色。其实唐三彩的颜色并不限于三种，还有红、褐等多种颜色。唐三彩通过丝绸之路运往中亚和西方，在唐代已经闻名海外。

地下出土的唐三彩，常见的有马、骆驼、侍女、龙首杯、武士像、杂技表演人像，以及壶、罐、碗、枕等。唐三彩造型生动，栩栩如生，色彩斑斓。唐三彩在历史上的兴盛时期比较短，贵族们多用唐三彩作为随葬品。（图2：唐三彩）

今天在洛阳、西安等城市，仿制逼真的唐三彩制品，深受旅游者们的青睐。

图2　唐三彩

4．薄胎瓷

薄胎瓷是中国陶瓷的瑰宝，它胎质极薄，洁白无瑕。迎光映照，几乎透明；轻轻敲击，声如钟磬。主要用于制作碗、花瓶、杯、灯罩和书房用品。

薄胎瓷的先驱是北宋时代的"影青瓷"和明代永乐时期的"甜白瓷"。制作薄胎瓷对工艺和技术的要求极高。现在景德镇制作的薄胎瓷无论数量还是质量都远远超过了历史上的最高水平。（图3：瓷器）

图3　瓷器

四、文房四宝

笔、墨、纸、砚是传统的书画工具和用品，它们常常被合称为"文房四宝"。其中每一样都有最佳的品种，即"湖笔"、"徽墨"、"宣纸"和"端砚"，它们一直受到海内外使用者的高度评价。

1．湖笔

中国自古以来就有"蒙恬造笔"的传说。蒙恬是秦始皇时的一位将军，他长期率兵驻守长城。现在从历史记载和考古实物等许多方面都可以证明，在蒙恬以前很早的时候，中国就已经有了毛笔。比如在西安半坡村出土的6,000多年前制作的彩陶上就曾经使用过毛笔一类的软性工具。到了商朝，甲骨文中已经有"笔"字了。但人们仍愿意把毛笔的发明权归于蒙恬，实际上，蒙恬的确对毛笔做了一些改进。

中国的"毛笔之都"在浙江吴兴县（今湖州市）善琏镇，又名"蒙溪"，这是古人为纪念蒙恬而取的名。镇内还有一座蒙恬祠，内有蒙恬的塑像。善琏镇属于湖州管辖，因此这里出产的笔又叫"湖笔"。湖笔是中国最好的毛笔，被称为"笔中之王"。（图4：湖笔）

图4 湖笔

湖州毛笔的原料主要用山羊毛、兔毛和黄鼠狼毛。一流的湖笔具备四大优点，即"尖、齐、圆、健"。制作一枝湖笔，需要70多道工序。例如，仅选毫一项，就需要把羊毫或兔毫根据其长度、粗细、软硬分为几十种，然后用不同的毫毛制成用途不同的毛笔。现在湖笔已经有两百多个品种。笔杆选用当地出产的上等竹子，有时还要用象牙、红木、牛角、兽骨等加以装饰。

2．徽墨

中国的"硬墨"或"墨块"是用来研磨墨汁的，本身也是一种艺术品。

制作墨汁的方法，是先在砚石上加一点儿清水，然后用墨条在上面来回磨动，当液体变得又黑又稠之后，就可以用毛笔蘸着写字了。

在制墨技术产生之前，人们用石墨来书写。到了汉朝，石墨已经不能满足日益增长的需要，人们发明了用松烟或桐烟制作的墨。制墨技术到了明代发展到了高峰，涌现出大量的名墨佳品。

安徽省歙县在明朝成为制墨中心。歙县的墨质地坚硬、油润光滑、漆黑发亮、书写流畅，是墨中的上品。歙县的墨被称为徽墨，是因为歙县在宋代时地属徽州。

徽墨中还掺入了兰麝等高级香料，可以保存很长时间。

普通的墨是一块块出售，但名贵的墨是成对或成套地出售。成套的墨块由名家高手在上面题诗绘画，并盛在衬有锦缎的木匣中，成为人们争相收藏的艺术品。

中国书画家历来非常重视墨的选择。到了清代，一块极品徽墨的价值可以超过同样重量的黄金。

3．宣纸

宣纸适用于毛笔，用它来写字作画，效果绝佳。宣纸的制作，已有1,000多年的历史了。远在唐朝的时候，宣纸就作为"贡纸"，供朝廷使用。由于有了宣纸，中国的书法、绘画艺术才得以表现出绝妙的艺术神韵，我们可以说，没有宣纸，就不会有特色如此鲜明的中国书画。

西方人常把宣纸称之为"米纸"，这是不确切的。实际上，宣纸的主要原料是青檀树皮，还要用一些稻草。它产于安徽泾县，由于在古代属于宣州，加上这种纸又集中在宣城出售，所以被人们称为"宣纸"。

宣纸的制作很费工夫，从选料到成纸要经过18道工序，有100多道操作要求。一张宣纸要经过近一年的时间才能制造出来。

宣纸素有"纸中之王"的称号，纯白、细密、柔韧，经久不变色，还能防虫蛀，可以保存千余年。它吃水性能好，又不纵横浸渗。毛笔在宣纸上可以任意挥洒，既不飘滑，又不滞涩。由于具备这许多优点，除用于书法、绘画外，宣纸现在还用于文献、档案和公文的记录。此外，宣纸还有吸墨、过滤、防潮等特殊用途。

4. 端砚

要用毛笔写字，就必须制备墨汁，为此目的，中国人发明了砚台，又叫砚石。迄今为止，地下出土的年代最久远的砚台是汉代的，证明至少在2,000年前，中国人就使用这种研墨的器皿了。

实际上，砚台就是一块磨石，先在石上放上点儿清水，然后用墨条在上边研磨就制成了墨汁。因此，砚台通常是用细密耐磨的石头制成的。

对于一个讲究的书法家来说，一方好的砚台必须是来自端溪的。端溪在广东肇庆市郊区，肇庆古称端州，端砚因此而得名。端砚的开采至少有1,500多年的历史，一直被称为文房中的珍宝。制作一方优良的端砚需要经过许多艰苦的工序，包括采掘、挑选、雕刻、修饰以及制作外盒等。其中最困难的是采石。肇庆附近有一座斧柯山，采石工匍匐着才能爬进幽深的洞坑，还要先将洞内的渗水淘出后才能采掘出需要的石头。

端砚石质柔润细腻，发墨快，不损害笔毫，砚中墨汁不易干燥冻结，墨色细润生辉。端砚上常有"石眼"，这是端砚的特殊纹理。一方端砚既是写画的用具，也是精美的工艺品。

五、印章

"印章"与"诗、书、画"一起并列为中国传统艺术的"四绝"，一个有高深造诣的艺术家通常四艺皆精。印章是中国文化遗产中一个非常独特的组成部分。钤在书法或绘画作品上的朱红色印章，不仅代表着著者的署名，更为艺术品带来了不可缺少的生动气韵。

中国印章的出现历史悠久。远在3,000多年前的商朝，人们就已经把文字（甲骨文）刻在龟壳上了，这时产生了印章的雏形。随着商品交换的扩大和私有制度的建立，到了周秦时代，人们把自己的姓名刻在器物或文件（竹简或木简）上，作为所有权的标志。此后，人们逐渐把姓名刻在一小块犀角、玉、竹、木等材料上，成为今天意义上的印章。

从印章也可以看出中国文字的发展。秦汉时的早期印章，镌刻的是篆字，因此至今人们仍把刻印章称为"篆刻"，英文则把篆字称为"印章文字"。其实，随着时代的发展，各种字体都被用来刻印章。刻在印章上的字有阳文和阴文两种。印章的材料也越来越多，普通的有木、石或牛角等，贵重的有鸡血石、玉、水晶、象牙等材料。过去君王曾用黄金或美玉来制作金印和玉玺。

治印艺术主要涉及三个方面——书法、布局和刻工。篆刻艺术家必须善于书写反字，更要善于在方寸之地巧妙地安排汉字的大小与位置，因为有的字笔画多，有的字笔画少，恰当的布局能产生气势与和谐。此外，还要熟悉各种材料的性能，熟练掌握各种刀法与技能。观察一位治印大师雕刻印章有如观看一场动人的表演。

如今，人们不仅在印章上刻汉字，也刻外文字母、图案和各种形象。不少外国朋友喜欢在中国为自己或亲友刻上一方质地美观、字体隽永的印章，作为永久的纪念。（图5：石砚、印章）

图5　石砚、印章

六、刺绣

　　刺绣这一具有悠久传统的民间艺术，在中国工艺美术史上占据着重要的地位。中国是丝绸的故乡。随着养蚕、缫丝和纺织技术的成熟，刺绣也逐渐发展起来了。

　　中国是世界上最先生产丝绸的国家，大约5,000年以前，中国人就开始养蚕了。刺绣的发展也相当早，在先秦的古籍《尚书》中就有关于服装与绣花的规定。

　　1958年挖掘的战国楚墓中，有一块丝绸出土，丝绸上绣有龙凤图案。这是迄今出土的年代最为久远的刺绣实物。

　　如今刺绣生产遍及全国，其中最为有名的是四大名绣，即江苏（尤其是苏州）的苏绣、湖南的湘绣、四川的蜀绣和广东的粤绣，它们各具特色。

　　现在的刺绣工艺十分复杂和精湛，以苏绣的代表作——双面绣"猫"为例。刺绣艺人要将头发般粗细的彩色丝线劈开成2股、4股、12股甚至48股，用这么细的丝线来刺绣，能使数千个线头和结点奇迹般地消失得无影无踪。绣成的猫既可爱又顽皮，而且两面完全一样，不分正反。其中最困难的地方是绣猫眼，为使眼睛栩栩如生、炯炯有神，要使用20多种不同颜色的丝线。最近双面绣又有了新的发展，工艺大师们能在同一块丝绸的两面绣出不同颜色、不同类型的形象，使人觉得他们真是无所不能。（图6：中国刺绣）

图6　中国刺绣

七、玉雕

在中国，玉通常是各种珍贵的石料的总称，因此，玉雕在中国工艺美术中占有重要的地位。著名的英国自然学家约瑟夫·尼达博士说，对玉器的钟爱，已成了中国文化的一个特色。考古发现，使用玉制的简陋工具，一直可以追溯到新石器时代。由于玉石坚硬，适宜制造工具和武器，因此他们选择了玉石。渐渐地他们欣赏起玉石的美丽，雕刻、打磨了一些纯粹用于观赏的玉器。（图7：玉雕）

当奴隶社会被封建社会取代后，人们已经只把玉用作装饰品了。在这一漫长的历史时期的出土墓葬中，发现了大量的作为个人装饰品和礼仪用品的玉器。今天人们在博物馆中可以看到那些瓶、香炉、鼎、杯、酒器等。

在中国封建社会中期出现了大型玉器，如在北京北海公园团城上的渎山大玉海，有小浴盆那么大。它是元朝皇帝忽必烈大宴宾客的盛酒用器。另一个大型的玉雕是清朝乾隆时期的"大禹治水玉山子"，它有2.4米高，1米多宽，是世界上最大的玉器。

中国俗语说"黄金有价玉无价"。美玉常常被形容为"价值连城"。古代的秦昭王就曾提出用15座城市来换那块有名的和氏璧。

玉为什么那么贵重？

首先，好玉极其罕见。它们要经过漫长的地质年代才能形成，而且不易获得，尤其是碧玉、白玉和玛瑙。

其次，玉的价值在于它的坚硬。贵重的石头可以分为硬玉和软玉两大类。硬玉具有紧密的纹理，硬度在6度以上（钻石为10度），如绿玉，硬度在8度至9度之间。软玉容易切割和雕刻，但价值低得多。

第三，玉石的宝贵在于其天然的色彩与形态，有的洁白如雪，有的绚丽如霞，有的青翠欲滴。

如今在中国各大城市都有玉雕厂或玉雕车间。昔日完全依靠手工的工艺现在有一部分用上了机械。虽然有些加工借助于简单的机械比过去快多了，但玉雕的工作基本上还是手工艺活。由于玉材越来越稀少，玉器的价格将会保持上升的趋势。

图7　玉雕

中国特产

八、景泰蓝

掐丝珐琅在元代传入中国，到元朝末年逐渐成为富有中国民族特色的著名手工艺品，它在明朝景泰皇帝时期盛极一时。由于这种工艺品大多是蓝色的，因此，人们通称为景泰蓝。

景泰蓝用铜作胎体，上面的图案是用铜线弯成，并用白芨粘在铜胎上。在铜线分割的各个空里填上不同颜色的釉料，放在窑里烧四五次之后，再打磨、抛光，就成了一件五颜六色、光彩夺目的艺术品了。

在明代，景泰蓝制品主要用于宫廷使用，大多制成香炉、花瓶、罐子、盒子、烛台等，形式上完全模仿古代的陶瓷和青铜器。

北京是现代景泰蓝制作中心，如今景泰蓝的发展趋势是在装饰美的基础上更注重实用。现在生产的工艺品有花瓶、盘、罐、盒、筷子、茶具、台灯、宫灯、笔、桌子、凳子、酒具和书桌上的小物件等等。（图8：景泰蓝餐具）

北京景泰蓝厂近年曾经制作了一对大型景泰蓝马，每匹马高2.1米，长2.4米，重700公斤。数百人花了八个月的时间才得以完成，仅烧制用煤就达60吨之多。它们是自500年前景泰蓝在中国诞生以来，迄今为止最大的景泰蓝制品。

景泰蓝的表面是一层玻璃状的珐琅，正如瓷器一样，要用软布轻轻地拂拭灰尘，如果用粗布硬擦，时间长了就会损坏它的光泽。这是保养景泰蓝必须注意的。

图8 景泰蓝餐具

九、漆器

漆器是中国传统的工艺品。作为天然原料，漆要从漆树上获取。中国是漆树的故乡，原料很丰富。很多地方都适合漆树生长，但生漆产量最多的是陕西、湖北、四川、贵州和云南五省。

漆器在中国有悠久的历史。从目前出土的文物来看，中国制造和使用漆器的历史可以追溯到新石器时代。

在墨被普遍使用以前，人们用漆来书写，在河南信阳就出土过战国时期的二十八片竹简，上面用漆写明了随葬品的品种。

北京、福州和扬州是中国漆器生产的中心。

北京漆器用铜或木作胎体，定型、抛光以后，涂上几十道甚至上百道漆，漆膜的厚度可以达到5毫米～18毫米，然后雕刻工在变硬的漆层上雕刻出山水、人物、花鸟等图画，再经烘干、装饰，一件漆雕作品就完成了。传统的北京漆器多为椅子、屏风、茶几、花瓶等等。（图9：涂中国漆的传统家具）

福州以"脱胎漆器"闻名于世，常被称为中国手工艺品"三绝"之一（其他两项为北京景泰蓝和景德镇瓷器）。制作脱胎漆器要先用泥土、石膏或木头做一个胎体，再把亚麻布或丝绸粘贴在上面，再一层又一层地涂上漆，待其凝结固定成型以后，移去胎体，然后用油灰修补并打磨光滑，再涂上若干层漆。最后把彩色图样雕饰上去，一件轻巧别致的脱胎漆器就完成了。（图10：福州脱胎漆器）

图9　涂中国漆的传统家具

图10　福州脱胎漆器

十、中医药制品

传统中医和中药是灿烂的中华文化的一个重要组成部分。中医和中药对于中华民族几千年来的繁衍生息作出了巨大的贡献。中医药由于其显著的疗效、浓郁的民族特色，独特的诊断治疗手段、系统的理论、丰富的历史记录和实物积累而为世界所瞩目，成为人类医疗宝库中的精华。中医药已有几千年的历史，至今依然充满了活力。现代医药技术中，传统的中医中药是一个极为重要的组成部分。（图11：中药材）近年来，用中西医结合的方法已经成功地医治了许多疑难病症。中国的针灸疗法和针刺麻醉已在全世界120多个国家和地区广泛应用。随着自然药物和非药物治疗手段在国外的普及，近年来传统的中医和中药疗法引起了全世界日益广泛的关注。

您来到中国，不妨采购一些久负盛名的中成药，如北京同仁堂生产的牛黄清心丸、乌鸡白凤丸（女性滋补药丸）、六味地黄丸（滋补药）、六神丸等，以及中医保健品、美容品、药膳和依据中医理论设计制造的医疗器械。

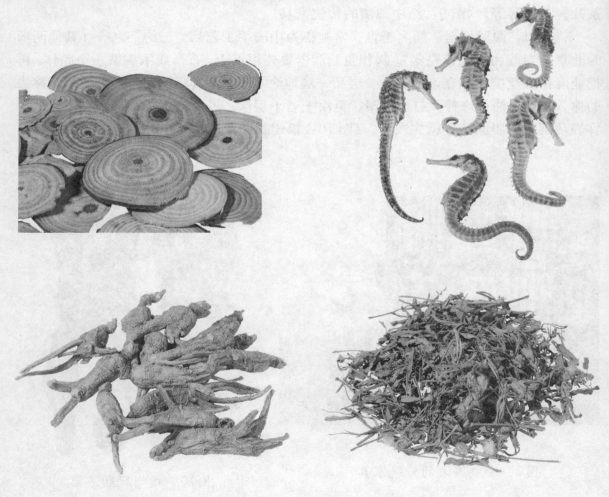

图11 中药材

Lesson One   Famous Specialities of China

1. Tea

Of the three major beverages of the world — tea, coffee and cocoa, tea is consumed by the largest number of people.

China is the homeland of tea. It is believed that the Chinese drank tea as early as five to six thousand years ago, and that human cultivation of tea-plants dates back two thousand years. Tea, along with silk and porcelain, were introduced abroad via the Silk Road. The varied pronunciations for tea in the world's major languages are based on the Chinese pronunciation.

There are various kinds of tea in China, which may be classified into five different categories according to their different processing methods and different places of production.

1) Green tea Green tea retains its original tender green color because no ferment is used during its processing. Longjing tea from Zhejiang Province (especially the Shifeng Longjing of West Lake from Hangzhou), Maofeng tea from Huangshan Mountain in Anhui Province, and Biluochun tea from Taihu Lake in Jiangsu Province are extremely well-known.

2) Black tea Black tea, known as "red tea" in China, is fermented before "baking." The best brands of black tea are Qihong of Anhui, Dianhong of Yunnan, Suhong of Jiangsu, Chuanhong of Sichuan, Minhong of Fujian, and Huhong of Hunan.

3) Oolong tea This is a kind of tea between green tea and black tea, which has gone through only half of the fermenting process. It comes from the coastal provinces of Fujian, Guangdong and Taiwan in southeast China. Famous brands include Tieguanyin from the south of Fujian Province and Dongding oolong tea from Taiwan Province.

4) Compressed tea This kind of tea is compressed and hardened to be made into brick, cake and bowl shapes. Because it is convenient for transport and storage, it is popular with ethnic minorities in the southwest border areas of the country. Compressed tea is mainly produced in Hubei, Hunan, Sichuan and Yunnan provinces, among which Tuo tea from Yunnan is the most famous.

5) Scented tea Scented tea is made by mixing fragrant flowers, such as jasmine, with tea leaves in the course of processing. Famous jasmine tea, mainly produced in Fujian and Hunan provinces, is a favorite of northerners in China and of a growing number of foreigners in recent years.

2. Alcoholic drinks

China is one of the first countries to brew alcohol drinks. A large number of 4,000-year-

中国特产

old pottery wine vessels have been excavated in Dawenkou of Shandong Province. From an ancient tomb of the Warring States Period in Pingshan County, Hebei Province, two jars containing spirits with a history of 2,300 years have been brought to light.

The Chinese like to drink white spirits, yellow rice wine, grape wine, traditional Chinese medicinal liquor and beer. The famous brands are as follows:

1) White spirits

Maotaijiu	(Guizhou)	Luzhou Tequ	(Sichuan)
Fenjiu	(Shanxi)	Jiannanchun	(Sichuan)
Gujing Gongjiu	(Anhui)	Yanghe Daqu	(Jiangsu)
Wuliangye	(Sichuan)	Jiuguijiu	(Hunan)

Most of these spirits are classified into two groups according to their alcohol content, either over 50% or under 40%.

2) Yellow rice wine

Made from glutinous rice through a special process, yellow rice wine has an alcohol content of 15% to 20% and is so called because it is amber in color. Traditionally, yellow rice wine shoud be heated before it is served. It is also an important seasoning in Chinese kitchens.

The best yellow rice wine is Laojiu made in Shaoxing, Zhejiang Province. Famous brands include Huadiao, Jiafanjiu and Nü'erhong.

3) Grape wine

China Red Wine	(Beijing)
Yantai Red Wine	(Shandong)
Great Wall White Wine	(Hebei)
Minquan White Wine	(Henan)
Dynasty Dry White Wine	(Tianjin)
Dynasty Dry Red Wine	(Tianjin)
Zhangyu Dry Red Wine	(Shandong) (Illustration 1)

4) Chinese medicinal liquor

The Chinese like to soak certain kinds of traditional Chinese medicine in alcohol, believing that it keeps people strong and healthy.

Famous medicinal liquors are Zhuyeqing Spirits from Shanxi Province, Ginseng Spirits from Jilin Province and Wujiabai Spirits from Heilongjiang Province.

5) Beer

Beer was introduced to China in modern times, and has become a very popular drink now, especially among young people. The most famous brand is Tsingtao Beer of Shandong Province. Other popular brands are Yanjing Beer of Beijing, Zhujiang Beer of Guangzhou and Jinwei Beer of Shenzhen.

3. Ceramics

Ceramics appeared in China some 6,000 years ago during the Neolithic Age. Chinese ceramics became known to the world in the Tang Dynasty, so that the word "china" became the name of ceramics. Chinese ceramics, together with Chinese tea and silk, found their way to other countries via the Silk Road.

The city of Jingdezhen in southern China became the principal center of the porcelain industry during the Song Dynasty. At the peak of its development in the Ming and Qing dynasties, there were over 300 government-operated kilns with superb techniques.

1) Celadon

Celadon, a famous type of ancient Chinese porcelain, appeared in the Three Kingdoms Period and in the Eastern and Western Jin dynasties. The techniques had reached maturity during the Five Dynasties, characterized by simple but refined shapes, jade-like glaze, solid texture and a distinctive style. Because Longquan County in Zhejiang Province produced the most famous celadon ware during the Song and Yuan dynasties, celadon is also commonly called Longquan celadon.

Besides the colors of blue and green, the kilns in Longquan also invented and produced other shades of colors. The porcelain ware produced in these kilns in the Song Dynasty was solid and well-designed. While those in the Yuan Dynasty looked somewhat thick and heavy, those produced in the Ming Dynasty had even thicker glaze and richer decorative designs. They were not only commonly used by the Chinese but also exported to other countries. Today, Longquan has developed many new color varieties.

2) Purple pottery ware

Yixing in Jiangsu Province, known in China as the "pottery-making capital," produces a kind of unglazed purple pottery ware, which is fired in a 1,200-degree-centigrade kiln. Teapots, representatives of this category, are generally believed to be the best among all teapots.

The purple pottery ware produced in Yixing is generally marked with simplicity and exquisite craftsmanship. It is also appreciated for its practical use. A teapot made of the clay called *zisha* (purple sand) is solid and impermeable, yet porous enough to "breathe." It not only enhances the color, aroma and taste of the tea brewed in it, but also can keep the fragrance of overnight tea. The teapot also serves as a hand-warmer in winter. To the Chinese tea connoisseurs, it is an "ideal" teapot.

Besides teapots, Yixing also produces coffeepots, tableware, cooking utensils, vases, flowerpots and various other artifacts.

中国特产

3) Tang tricolor

Tang tricolor pottery refers to the tricolored glazed pottery of the Tang Dynasty. It is called "tricolor" because yellow, green and blue are commonly used, though other colors, such as red and brown are also used. Tang tricolor was exported to Central Asia and the West via the Silk Road in the Tang Dynasty, thus winning itself a great fame in the world.

Unearthed tricolored pottery pieces of the Tang Dynasty are commonly seen in the shapes of horses, camels, maids, dragon-head goblets, warriors and acrobatic performers. There are also jars, pots, bowls and pillows. All the pieces are lifelike and colorful. Tang tricolor pottery flourished for only a short period, and the pottery ware was mostly used by aristocrats as burial objects. (Illustration 2: Tang Tricolor Glazed Pottery)

Today, imitations produced in Luoyang, Xi'an and other cities are well received by tourists.

4) Eggshell porcelain

A gem of Chinese ceramics, eggshell porcelain is remarkable, first of all, for its extraordinary thinness. It is appreciated also because it is spotlessly white, translucent, and sonorous when tapped. Eggshell porcelain wares mainly include bowls, vases, cups, lampshades and various articles for use in a study.

Eggshell porcelain originated from Yingqingci (shadowy celadon) made in the Northern Song Dynasty and Tianbaici (sweet white celadon) of the Yongle reign of the Ming Dynasty. To make such thin porcelain requires excellent techniques and craftsmanship. Present-day products manufactured in Jingdezhen of Jiangxi Province far exceed the best standards in history in both quantity and quality. (Illustration 3: Chinese Ceramics)

4. Four treasures of the study

The writing brush, ink stick, paper and ink-slab are traditional implements and materials for writing and painting and have always been named collectively as the "four treasures of the study."

Each of these items is represented by its "best": the Huzhou writing brush, the Huizhou ink stick, the *xuan* paper and the Duanzhou ink-slab. They are highly valued in the country and abroad as well.

1) The Huzhou writing brush

Legend has it that the first writing brush was made by Meng Tian, a general during the reign of Qinshihuang, the first emperor of Qin. For a long time, he and his troops were stationed along the Great Wall. Archaeological finds and historical documents, however, have proved that China had writing brushes long before the time of Meng Tian. Traces on the painted pottery unearthed at the ruins of the Banpo Village of the Neolithic Age near Xi'an show that the brush in its crude, primitive form was used 6,000 years ago. And the character for brush was found among the inscriptions on bones and tortoise shells of the Shang Dynasty. But people still attribute the patent right to Meng Tian, who had, in fact, improved the brush.

Shanlian Town in Wuxing County (today's Huzhou City), Zhejiang Province, is known as the "writing brush capital in China." It is also known as Mengxi (Meng Stream) in memory of Meng Tian. There is also a Meng Tian Temple in the town, which enshrines a statue of Meng Tian. Hence, the brushes produced in Shanlian Town, which was under the jurisdiction of Huzhou Prefecture, are called Huzhou brushes and supposed to be the best in the country — "king of all writing brushes." (Illustration 4: The Huzhou Writing Brush)

The main materials for producing Huzhou brushes are goat hair, rabbit hair and weasel hair. A first-grade Huzhou brush must meet four requirements: a sharp tip, neat hair arrangement, round shape and great resilience. Its making involves more than 70 steps in a careful process. For example, the step of "hair-choosing" means classifying the hair into dozens of groups according to its length, thickness and softness, and different hair will be used to make different brushes. At present, Huzhou brushes are produced in more than 200 varieties. The shafts of the brushes, made of local high-quality bamboo, are often decorated with ivory, horn, redwood and animal bones.

2) The Huizhou ink stick

The Chinese "solid ink" or "ink stick" is used to produce ink, but it can also be a work of art itself.

The way to make Chinese ink is to put a little water on an ink-slab and then rub the ink stick on it. When the liquid becomes thick and black enough, it is ready for writing with a brush.

Before the ink stick was developed, graphite was used for writing. By the Han Dynasty when the country became more developed, graphite could not meet the growing demand. It was then that ink sticks were produced with pine or tung soot. The art was perfected during the Ming Dynasty, when high-quality ink sticks were made.

The best Chinese ink sticks were first made in Shexian County, Anhui Province, which were generally called Huizhou ink sticks because Shexian was under the jurisdiction of Huizhou Prefecture in the Song Dynasty.

High-quality Huizhou ink sticks contain musk and other precious aromatics normally used in Chinese medicine, which are supposed to preserve the black color for a long time.

Ordinary ink sticks are sold one by one, but costly ones are more often sold in pairs. They are as a rule inscribed with pictures and poems by the hand of celebrated artists. Arranged in pairs in a satin-lined box, they are kept by collectors as works of art.

Accomplished Chinese artists and calligraphers have always been careful about selecting ink sticks. During the Qing Dynasty, the value of a high-quality ink stick could well exceed that of gold of its weight.

3) The *xuan* paper

Xuan paper is the best for writing or painting with a brush. With a history of over 1,000 years, it was a "tribute paper" for the court as early as the Tang Dynasty. What is known today as Chinese painting and calligraphy is, for the most part, done on *xuan* paper, without which one might say there would be no Chinese painting and calligraphy.

Xuan paper is known to some Westerners as "rice paper," which is a misnomer. In fact, it is made from the bark of wingceltis trees mixed with rice straw. Its home is Jingxian County, Anhui Province. As the county was under the jurisdiction of Xuanzhou Prefecture in ancient times and the trading center of the paper was at Xuancheng, it has always been called *xuan* paper.

The making of *xuan* paper is a painstaking procedure involving 18 processes and nearly 100 operations and lasting about one year from the selection of materials to the finished products.

Xuan paper is praised as the "king of paper" and is supposed to "last a thousand years," because it is white as alabaster, soft but firm, and resistant to time and worms. It absorbs but does not spread the ink so that the brush can move freely and comfortably, giving a feeling neither too smooth nor too rough. For these qualities, *xuan* paper is not only used for painting and calligraphy but increasingly used nowadays for important archives and other documents. In addition, it may also be used for blotting, filtering and moisture-proof purposes.

4) The Duanzhou ink-slab

To write with a brush, one should prepare ink. For this purpose, the ancestors of the Chinese developed the ink-slab or ink-stone.

The earliest Chinese ink-slabs unearthed so far date from the Han Dynasty, which show that this kind of utensil has been in use in the country for at least 2,000 years.

In fact, the ink-slab is a sort of millstone on which water is turned into ink by rubbing an ink stick. The ink-slab is generally made of smooth fine stone.

To a rigorous calligrapher, a good ink-slab should be made of the stone produced at Duanxi in the suburbs of the city of Zhaoqing (formerly known as Duanzhou), Guangdong Province. Named after the hometown of the stone, the Duanzhou ink-slab has a history of over 1,500 years and has always been regarded as a valuable item in a study.

The making of an ink-slab goes through several painstaking processes including quarrying, selecting, cutting, polishing and making of the containing box. The most difficult part is the quarrying of the stone, which lies in the Fuke Mountain near Zhaoqing. Quarrymen have to make tunnels at the foot of the mountain, drain them of water and creep in to dig out the right kind of stone.

Duanzhou ink-slabs are valued for their fine and glossy texture. Ink can be easily and quickly made on them and the ink produced this way can wet the hair of a writing brush evenly without doing any damage to it. They are also good for keeping leftover ink. A well-chosen piece of stone may also bear fine veins, and an ink-slab made of this kind of stone is not only a good piece of stationery but also an exquisite work of art.

5. Seals

Seal-carving, poetry, calligraphy and painting are claimed as the "four arts" expected to be grasped by an accomplished scholar. Seal-carving is a unique part of traditional Chinese culture. A red seal stamp on a painting or a piece of calligraphy is not only the signature of the artist but an indispensable touch to add vividness to the work of art.

The art of seal-carving dates back to the Shang Dynasty more than 3,000 years ago and has its origin in the inscriptions on tortoise shells. It flourished in the Qin Dynasty about 2,200 years ago when people engraved their names on utensils and documents (of bamboo or wood) to show ownership. Out of this grew the carving of personal names on small blocks of horn, jade or wood, namely the seals as we know them today.

Seals reflect the development of written Chinese. The earliest seals of the Qin and Han dynasties bear inscripions in the *zhuan* script (curly script style), which explains why the art of seal-carving is still called *zhuanke* and why the *zhuan* script is also known in English as "seal characters." As time went on, the other script styles appeared one after another on Chinese seals. Characters on seals may be carved in relief or in intaglio. Materials for seals vary from common wood, stone and ox-horn to precious materials like precious stone, jade, crystal and ivory. Monarchs in the old days used gold or fine jade to make their imperial seals.

The work of carving a seal involves mainly calligraphy, composition and carving skill. The artist must be good at writing Chinese characters in a reverse style. He should know how to arrange within a limited space a number of characters — some compact with many strokes and others sketchy with only a few — to achieve a vigorous or graceful effect. He should also be familiar with the materials and skillful at using his carving knife. Watching a master engraver at work is like watching an excellent performance.

Today, seals bear not only Chinese characters but designs, various images and even foreign letters. Many foreign friends like to have some pretty Chinese-style seals either for their friends or for themselves as permanent souvenirs. (Illustration 5: The Ink-Slab and Seals)

6. Embroidery

Embroidery, a folk art with a long tradition, occupies an important position in the history of Chinese arts and crafts. China is the hometown of silk. The development of embroidery is inseparable from the development of silkworm-raising, silk-reeling and weaving techniques.

China is the first country in the world that discovered the use of silk. Silkworms were domesticated as early as 5,000 years ago. The production of silk thread and fabrics gave rise to the art of embroidery. *Shangshu*, a pre-Qin classic, records the regulations on costumes and embroidery.

In 1958, a piece of silk was excavated from the tomb of the State of Chu of the Warring States Period, which is embroidered with a dragon-and-phoenix design. It is the earliest piece of Chinese embroidery ever unearthed.

Today, embroidery is practiced almost all over China. The most famous Chinese embroidery comes into four major shools: Su-style embroidery from Jiangsu Province (notably Suzhou), Xiang-style embroidery from Hunan, Shu-style embroidery from Sichuan and Yue-style embroidery from Guangdong, each with its distinctive feature.

Embroidery works have become highly complex and exquisite today. Take the two-side embroidery work of "cat" for an example. It is a representative work of Su-style embroidery. The artist splits the hair-thin color silk thread into filaments — half, quarter, 1/12 or even 1/48 of its original thickness — and uses them in embroidering, concealing in the process thousands of ends and joints so perfectly as if by magic. The finished work is a cute and mischievous-looking cat on both sides. The most difficult part of the job is the eyes of the cat. To give them luster and life, silk filaments of more than 20 colors have to be used.

Recently, new development has been made in the field of two-side embroidery. Master embroiders can make a two-side embroidery with different images in different colors. It seems that they are so capable that they can make the impossible possible. (Illustration 6: Embroidery Works)

7. Jade carving

Jade is the collective name for most precious stones in China, and jade carving in this sense constitutes an important part of Chinese arts and crafts. The love of jade ware, according to Dr. Joseph Needham, a noted British naturalist, has been one of the cultural features of China. Crude jade tools have been found among the archaeological finds dating back to the Neolithic Age. The Neolithic people chose jade only because it was hard and good for making tools and weapons. As time went on, people came to appreciate the beauty of the stone, which after carving and polishing might be turned into things not only useful but also nice to look at.

(Illustration 7: Jade Carving)

When the slave system was replaced by the feudal system, people started to use jade only as ornaments. Among the burial objects unearthed from tombs of this period are many jade articles used as personal ornaments or ceremonial vessels. The jade exhibits in today's museums are normally comprised of vases, incense-burners, tripods, cups and wine vessels of various descriptions.

Large-sized jade articles began to appear in the middle of the Chinese feudal period. Today, in the Round City of the Beihai Park in Beijing, there is a large jade jar the size of a small bathtub. It was used as a wine container by Kublai Khan of the Yuan Dynasty when he feted his followers. Another large piece worth mentioning is a jade sculpture dating from the reign of Qing Emperor Qianlong in the 18th century, entitled "Jade Mountain Showing Yu Taming the Flood." Standing 2.4 meters high and over 1 meter wide, it is the largest jade sculpture in the world.

An ancient Chinese saying goes, "There is a price for gold but no price for jade." Jade ware is often described as "worth a string of towns." An ancient story tells how King Zhao of Qin once offered 15 towns in exchange for the famous Heshi Jade.

How is it that jade is so valuable?

First, pure jade is rare. Precious stones are formed over long geological years and hard to get, especially emeralds, white jade and agate.

Second, jade is solid and hard. Precious stones are divided by their hardness into two major groups: jadeites and nephrites. Jadeites are of a solid texture and a hardness of degree 6 or above (on the basis of 10 for diamond). Valuable varieties, such as the emerald, may be as hard as degree 8 or 9. Nephrites are easy to cut and polish, but their value is much lower.

Third, precious stones have natural colors and forms. Some are as white as snow, others are brightly red, and still others alluringly green.

Today, there are jade workshops or factories in all major Chinese cities. What used to be done purely by hand has been partially mechanized. Although some of the processing work can be done quickly with the use of simple machines, jade carving remains basically a handicraft art. And as raw materials are getting scarcer, the price of jade ware will keep on going up.

8. Cloisonné

After cloisonné found its way to China at the end of the Yuan Dynasty, it reached its peak of development during the reign of Ming Emperor Jingtai. And as cloisonné objects were mostly blue (*lan* in Chinese), cloisonné came to be called Jingtailan, a name still used today.

A piece of cloisonné has a copper body. The design on it is formed by copper wire, which is glued onto the body. Colored enamel is filled in the spaces framed by the wire. After being fired four or five times in a kiln, the piece is polished and gilded into a colorful and lustrous work of art.

In the Ming Dynasty, cloisonné ware was mainly supplied to the imperial palace, like incense-burners, vases, jars, boxes and candlesticks — all imitating the forms and patterns of antique porcelain and bronze wares.

Beijing is the cloisonné production center today. While paying attention to the function of decoration, people start to stress more the practical side. Present-day products include vases, plates, jars, boxes, chopsticks, tea sets, lamps, lanterns, pens, tables, stools, drinking vessels and small articles for the desk in a study. (Illustration 8: The Cloisonné Dishware)

A pair of big cloisonné horses have been made in recent years by Beijing Cloisonné Factory, each measuring 2.1 meters high and 2.4 metres long and weighing about 700 kilograms. It took several hundred people eight months and up to 60 tons of coal to finish them. They represent the largest cloisonné object ever made in the 500 years since the art was brought to China.

Cloisonné ware bears on the surface a layer of vitreous enamel. Just as we remove dust from porcelains, we should whisk the dust off a piece of cloisonné with a soft cloth. A rough cloth will wear off the sheen on the surface in the long run.

9. Lacquer ware

Lacquer ware is a traditional art in China. Lacquer is a natural substance obtained from the lacquer tree which has its home in China, a country still leading the world in lacquer resources. Many places in China are suitable for growing the tree, but most of the output comes from the five provinces of Shaanxi, Hubei, Sichuan, Guizhou and Yunnan.

Lacquer ware has a long history that can be traced back to the Neolithic Age, as lacquer articles already unearthed in China prove.

Before the invention of the Chinese ink, lacquer had been used for writing. Twenty-eight bamboo slips found in a Warring States tomb at Xinyang, Henan Province, bear a list of the burial objects with the characters written in lacquer.

Beijing, Fuzhou and Yangzhou are the leading cities in the production of Chinese lacquer ware.

The making of Beijing lacquer ware starts with a brass or wooden body. After polishing, it is coated with dozens up to hundreds of layers of lacquer, which amounts to 5 to 18 millimeters thick. Then, engravers will cut into the hardened lacquer, creating "carved paintings" of landscapes, human figures, flowers and birds. It is then finished after drying and decorating. Traditional Beijing lacquer objects are in the forms of chairs, screens, tea tables, vases etc. (Illustration 9: Traditional Chinese Lacquer Furniture)

Fuzhou is well-known for its "bodiless lacquer ware," one of the "Three Treasures" of Chinese arts and crafts (the other two being Beijing cloisonné and Jingdezhen porcelain). The bodiless lacquer ware starts with a body of clay, gesso or wood. Linen or silk is wrapped around it before lacquer is applied on to it layer upon layer. After the lacquer is dry, the original body is then removed. The remaining part is then mended with putty and polished, before more lacquer is applied on to it. Finally, colorful designs are engraved on it. Now, a light and exquisite bodiless lacquer ware is done .(Illustration10: Fuzhou Bodiless Lacquer Ware)

10. Products of traditional Chinese medicine

Traditional Chinese medicine and pharmacology are important parts of China's splendid culture. Chinese medicine and pharmacology have made tremendous contributions to the Chinese nation throughout the history of several thousand years. They are noted worldwide for their outstanding curative effects, strong national characteristics, unique method of diagnosis and treatment, systemic theories and vast accumulation of historical records and materials. Chinese medicine and pharmacology have shown great vitality for several thousand years and is still full of vitality today. They are also a valuable complement to modern medicine and pharmacology. (Illustration 11: Traditional Chinese Medicinal Materials) In recent years, great success has been made in treating difficult and complicated cases by combining Chinese and Western medical techniques. Acupuncture treatment and acupuncture anesthesia are now used in more than 120 countries and regions throughout the world. Following the increasing use of natural medicines and non-medicinal treatment in foreign countries, people all over the world have become more interested in traditional Chinese medicine and pharmacology in recent years.

Now that you are in China, you might as well buy some patent Chinese medicines such as Niuhuangqingxin Wan, Wujibaifeng Wan (a tonic pill for women), Liuweidihuang Wan (a tonic pill) and Liushen Wan made by Tongrentang, a famous Chinese pharmacy in Beijing. You may also buy some traditional health products, cosmetics, food and medical apparatus, all based on the theories of traditional Chinese medicine.

第二课　各地土特产及风味食品

1．北京市

汇集了全国各地的风味菜肴、工艺品和土特产品。北京的著名食品有宫廷点心、北京烤鸭、蜜饯果品。北京的刺绣、景泰蓝、玉器、京剧服饰、绢人等久负盛名。

2．天津市

传统手工艺品有天津地毯、棉毯，泥人张的泥塑，杨柳青年画、风筝等。风味食品有灌肠、狗不理包子、十八街麻花等。

3．河北省

唐山和邯郸的陶瓷、曲阳石雕、秦皇岛的贝雕画、武强年画、蔚县剪纸、衡水内画鼻烟壶、张家口蘑菇、赵州雪花梨、宣化葡萄、深州水蜜桃全国有名。风味食品有秦皇岛的海味、保定的酱菜、石家庄的烧鸡等。

4．山西省

手工艺品有太原的刀剪、大同的艺术陶瓷。著名特产有汾阳杏花村的汾酒、竹叶青酒，清徐、陵川、榆次等地的老陈醋。清徐葡萄，原平梨，稷山、临汾、太谷、运城的枣，永济的柿子都很有名。风味食品有刀削面、并州火锅、太原的全羊席、平遥的牛肉等。

5．内蒙古自治区

工艺品有呼和浩特的毛纺织品，包头、阿拉善左旗的仿古地毯，蒙古族银器、皮靴。畜产品有羊毛、驼绒、皮毛、皮革。土特产品有蘑菇、鹿茸、河套蜜瓜等。风味食品有烤全羊、烤羊腿、奶皮子、奶豆腐、马奶酒、奶茶等。

6．辽宁省

辽东如大连、营口等地的苹果，辽西如绥中、北镇的梨，大连的黄金桃、海产、贝雕、刺绣和玻璃制品，丹东、营口的海产，岫岩玉雕，锦州的玛瑙制品，抚顺的琥珀工艺品，沈阳的雪花啤酒等颇有名气。风味食品有东北火锅、沈阳老边饺子、沟帮子的熏鸡等。

7．吉林省

俗话说"关东有三宝：人参、貂皮、鹿茸角"，这三宝都出在吉林。珲春的木耳，延边的圆蘑、白蜜和苹果梨，吉林市的三宝酒，朝鲜族的冷面、泡菜等。

8．黑龙江省

大马哈鱼、鲟鱼是黑龙江和乌苏里江的著名特产，山区盛产六十多种蘑菇，还有黑木耳、松子以及貂、水獭、人参、鹿茸等。大庆和齐齐哈尔的牛奶制品，哈尔滨的大红肠、酒心糖、太阳岛啤酒，五大连池的矿泉水均享有盛名。风味食品有赫哲族的风味杀生鱼、鄂伦春族的烤肉串等。

9．上海市

上海是中国最大的工业城市，上海的轻纺工业和手工业产品包括服装、毛呢、化纤、皮鞋、领带、化妆品、钟表、玩具、耐用消费品、文娱运动器材、家具、照相机、奶糖、食品等。手工艺品包括金银饰品、舞台服装、雕刻、刺绣、假花等。上海的中西餐馆很多，同时，上海菜和各种糕点、奶糖、五香豆等小吃品种齐全，风味独特。

10．江苏省

传统工艺品有苏州的刺绣、草编、檀木扇，宜兴的紫砂陶器，无锡的泥塑，扬州的漆器，常州的毛笔、梳篦等等。土特产有连云港的大对虾，阳澄湖的大闸蟹，长江的鲥鱼，太湖的银鱼、碧螺春茶叶、莲藕，南京的板鸭，无锡的酱排骨，如皋火腿，太仓肉松，高邮的双黄鸭蛋，镇江的醋、洋河大曲、双沟大曲，苏州、无锡、扬州的糕点等。

以淮扬风味为主的江苏菜在中国八大菜系中占重要地位。

11．浙江省

浙江的工艺品很多，如杭州的丝绸、刺绣和织锦，宁波真丝绣衣，温州刺绣，萧山花边，杭州、乘县的竹编和竹器，余姚、慈溪、黄岩的草编，东阳的木雕，青田的石刻，杭州的印章篆刻、绸扇绸伞，绍兴的金银首饰、毛笔、张小泉刀剪等都很有名。土特产有杭州西湖龙井茶，黄岩蜜橘，温州蜜橘，衢州红橘，奉化水蜜桃、枇杷，诸暨香榧，义乌枣，金华火腿，绍兴黄酒，杭州西湖藕粉等。风味食品有西湖醋鱼、东坡肉、叫花鸡、嘉兴粽子、宁波汤圆等。

12．安徽省

传统的手工艺品有文房四宝即宣纸、泾县的毛笔、徽墨和歙砚，芜湖的刀剪、铁画等。土特产有砀山酥梨、怀远石榴、宣州枣、歙县枇杷、祁门红茶、黄山毛峰、亳州的古井贡酒、淮北的口子酒等。风味食品有符离集烧鸡、定远的桥尾（用猪臀肉制成）、泾县的琴鱼干、寿县和安庆的糕点等。

安徽菜是中国八大菜系之一。

13．福建省

传统手工艺品有福州脱胎漆器、寿山石刻、厦门和泉州的木雕、德化陶瓷、漳州五彩泥塑、安溪竹编、平潭贝雕等。土特产包括闽南乌龙茶、安溪铁观音、福州茉莉花茶、橘子、福安红茶、南安绿茶、莆田橘子、晋江龙眼、漳州橘子、香蕉和水仙、笋干、香菇、银耳等，还有平潭紫菜、同安文昌鱼、沿海水产等。风味食品有福州鱼丸、厦门南普陀素菜、泉州葫芦鸡等。

14．台湾省

台湾是祖国美丽富饶的宝岛，特产丰富。工艺品有澎湖的珊瑚，花莲的翠玉，北投的艺术陶瓷，台北的风筝、玻璃器皿，新竹的圣诞灯饰，绿岛的贝雕画，桃园的家具，大甲的草编，台中和台北的竹艺品等。岛上盛产香蕉、菠萝、龙眼、荔枝、木瓜、柑橘、橄榄、甘蔗、茶叶等。盐酥海虾、火把鱼翅、当归鸭、烧酒鸡、台中凤梨酥、太阳饼、宜兰金枣糕食品和风味小吃也很著名。

15．江西省

传统手工艺品有景德镇瓷器和瓷雕，南昌瓷板画，铅山竹编，萍乡烟花，瑞金、永丰的毛边纸以及木雕、玉雕、石雕和刺绣等。土特产有庐山云雾茶，婺源的茶，井冈山的茶、竹笋和茶油，武宁的红茶，临川西瓜，信丰瓜子，广昌通心莲，南丰蜜橘，鄱阳湖的银鱼，樟树的四特酒等。风味食品有九江的的鱼席菜，庐山的"三石"（石鸡、石鱼和石耳），南安咸鸭，景德镇船板肉等。

16．山东省

传统轻工业和手工艺品有烟台钟表、刺绣，淄博的陶瓷，潍坊的嵌银制品、风筝和年画，青岛的贝雕，胶东的草编等。山东盛产水果，如莱阳梨、烟台苹果、肥城桃、即墨葡萄、乐陵枣、德州西瓜等。土特产有沿海水产，烟台对虾，寿光鸡，菏泽牡丹，东阿阿胶，青岛啤酒，崂山矿泉水，龙口粉丝，烟台果酒、白兰地，曲阜孔府家酒等。风味食品有德州扒鸡、济南糖酥煎饼、青岛高粱饴、济宁酱菜等。

山东菜是中国八大菜系之一。

17．河南省

手工艺品有开封的书画、汴绸、汴绣，禹州的钧瓷，洛阳的宫灯、唐三彩，临汝的汝瓷，南阳的玉器、烙花筷子等。土特产有新郑的枣、孟津的梨、开封西瓜、信阳毛尖茶、黄河鲤鱼、驻马店芝麻油等。风味食品有道口的烧鸡、朱仙镇五香豆腐干、汴京烧鸭、洛阳杜康酒、民权葡萄酒等。

18．湖北省

江陵荆缎，武穴、广济的竹器，沙市丝棉被，宜昌红茶，咸宁青砖茶、桂花，恩施玉露茶，秭归红橘，随州蜜枣，鄂州的武昌鱼，黄梅银鱼。风味食品有孝感麻糖、黄州东坡饼、武汉炸米窝以及多种小吃。

19．湖南省

土特产有岳阳君山银针茶，大庸古丈毛尖茶，长沙银峰绿茶，雪峰蜜橘，浏阳金橘，长沙腊肉，岳阳银鱼、干鱼、辣椒油，邵阳竹笋、生姜，益阳松花蛋等。手工艺品有长沙湘绣、鸭绒被，邵阳竹器，醴陵瓷器，浏阳花石雕、烟花等。

湘菜属中国八大菜系之一。

20．广东省

广东地处热带、亚热带，物产丰饶。其中东莞的香蕉，潮州柑橘，增城、从化荔枝，潭州甘蔗最为有名。英德红茶、潮州水仙茶、沿海水产十分畅销。手工艺品有广州的粤绣、牙雕、玉雕，肇庆的端砚，佛山石湾的陶瓷、木雕、剪纸，深圳的艺术陶瓷，潮州、汕头的抽纱、刺绣等。

广东菜在中国八大菜系中占有重要地位。广东的茶点，在全国最负盛名。

21．海南省

土特产有文昌菠萝、椰子，五指山芒果，琼山荔枝，西沙群岛的燕窝，海口的椰子盅、椰子奶、椰子糖以及万宁的咖啡、胡椒、槟榔等。手工艺品有椰雕、贝雕、珊瑚饰品等。

22．广西壮族自治区

手工艺品有靖西、宾阳的壮锦，都安的瑶绣，坭兴的陶瓷，钦州的陶器，桂林的艺术陶瓷、竹杖，梧州的竹丝挂帘，北海的贝雕，柳州的石雕、柳砚，合浦的珍珠等。土特产有蓉县沙田柚，南宁菠萝，柳州柑橘，玉林桂圆以及荔枝、香蕉、罗汉果、茴香等。风味食品有桂林腐乳、米粉、三花酒，梧州三蛇酒等。

23．重庆市

手工艺品有重庆竹帘画、花丝首饰、漆器等，土特产有重庆锦橙、脐橙、血橙、柑橘，万县桐油、红橘，涪陵榨菜，合川红橘，江津柑橘等等。重庆的麻辣火锅极富特色。

24．四川省

又称"天府之国"，物产十分丰富。手工艺品有成都蜀绣、蜀锦、漆器、瓷胎、竹编，南充的竹帘画，自贡、宜宾的竹艺，荣昌、会理的陶瓷，自贡的剪纸等。土特产有中药材、川红花、沱茶、峨眉毛峰茶等。名酒有宜宾五粮液、泸州特曲、绵竹剑南春、古蔺郎酒等。成都小吃远近闻名，如龙抄手、赖汤圆、担担面、西昌板鸭等。

川菜在中国八大菜系中占有重要地位。

25．贵州省

手工艺品有遵义丝绸被面、安顺蜡染、恩州石砚、大方漆器、玉屏箫笛等。土特产有威宁黄梨，兴义红袍橘，安顺的毛尖茶、毛峰茶、青毛茶、绿茶，仁怀的茅台酒，遵义的董酒。风味食品有威宁火腿，绥阳空心面，镇宁波波糖，独山泡菜，镇远道菜，三穗板鸭，贵阳野刺梨汁、天麻蒸鸡、恋爱豆腐果等。

26．云南省

"云烟"全国著名，主要产于玉溪、曲靖、昆明等地。产于大理、思茅、西双版纳的普洱茶、沱茶、滇红闻名中外。土特产还有云南白药，中药材，西双版纳的香蕉、芒果，昆明的梨和食用菌。大理的云石雕刻，剑川的木雕，昆明、个旧的斑铜和锡制工艺品，腾冲玉器，通海银饰品，昆明的少数民族器物，昭通版纳地毯，西双版纳的傣锦、哈尼族刺绣、孔雀毛饰品，丽江"披星戴月"服装等等。风味食品有宣威火腿、路南腐乳、云南汽锅鸡、过桥米线以及少数民族食品等。

27．西藏自治区

传统手工艺品有拉萨和日喀则的地毯，江孜的藏毯，泽当、拉萨的氆氇（藏毛呢）、花围裙、藏靴、藏族服装、金器、银器，山南地区的木碗等。风味食品有酥油茶、"卡色"（面粉、清油、牛奶、白糖、椰油制成）等。

28．陕西省

水果名产有汉中、城固的柑橘，临潼的石榴、柿子和红枣，彬县的枣，陕北的苹果，华县的杏。土特产有商洛的核桃、洋县的香米和黑米、韩城的大红袍辣椒、紫阳的毛尖茶等。风味食品有西安的腊羊肉、羊肉泡馍、饺子宴、长安八景宴、三原蓼花糖、西乡牛肉干、凤翔的腊驴肉。名酒有凤翔的西凤酒、眉县太白酒等。

29．甘肃省

土特产有白兰瓜，醉瓜，兰州的黑瓜子和百合，康县黑木耳，庆阳黄花菜，文县花椒、中药材等。手工艺品有酒泉的夜光杯、嘉峪关的石砚、天水的雕漆、华亭的陶瓷、临洮的仿古地毯、兰州的毛纺织品。风味食品有敦煌的清炖全羊，敦煌驼掌，陇西腊肉，兰州的烤小猪、牛肉饼，甘肃西部的烤肉等，名酒有西凉大曲、马奶酒。

30．青海省

西宁羊毛、长毛绒、皮张、地毯、奶酪、奶粉，青海湖的湟鱼，青海东南部的长把梨，玉树的麝香、虫草等。食品有西宁的涮羊肉、马杂碎，果洛的牛肉干等。手工艺品有西宁和湟源的银器、饰物和藏刀等。

31．宁夏回族自治区

中宁、中卫的枸杞，盐池、同心的甘草，贺兰的砚石，平罗的滩羊皮，同心、海原的发菜并称为宁夏红、黄、蓝、白、黑"五色宝"。传统手工艺品有银川仿古地毯、贺兰石刻、石嘴山民族陶瓷等。风味食品有清真奶油糕点、牛羊肉酥、手抓羊肉、清蒸羊羔肉、马三白水鸡等。

32．新疆维吾尔自治区

盛产优质瓜果，如吐鲁番的哈蜜瓜、西瓜、白葡萄，伊宁的苹果，库尔勒香梨，叶城的石榴，阿克苏的核桃，阿图什的无花果，伽师的甜瓜等。新疆的细毛羊、和田玉、桑蚕，南疆的长绒棉，北疆的雪莲等土特产远近驰名。手工艺品有和田地毯，乌鲁木齐的维族服装、饰物、铜器、玉雕，喀什的民族乐器等等。风味食品有维吾尔族和回族的烤全羊、烤羊肉串、烤鱼、馕、抓饭、烤包子、奶茶，吐鲁番和鄯善的果酒、葡萄酒等。

33．香港

香港特产主要有珍珠、玩具、香港茶花、蝴蝶、石斑鱼等。美食有海鲜、烧烤、虾酱、烧鹅等。

34．澳门

澳门名特产品有金制品、葡制葡萄酒、陶器、瓷器、象牙制品、玻璃串珠制品等。澳门特别有名的一种美食是用十多种香料烧烤而成的全鸡——非洲鸡。还有澳门鲜蚝、红豆猪手、老婆饼等。

Lesson Two   Local Specialities and Flavors

1. Beijing Municipality

Beijing offers an array of delicacies, handicrafts and specialities from all over the country. Famous foods include diverse snacks of the palace, Beijing roast duck, and candied fruit. Beijing embroidery, cloisonné ware, jade carvings, stage costumes of Beijing opera, silk figures etc. are also very famous.

2. Tianjin Municipality

Traditional products include Tianjin carpets, cotton blankets, painted clay figures by Master Craftsman Zhang, Yangliuqing New Year pictures, and kites. Local flavors include sausages, Goubuli stuffed buns, Shibajie fried dough twists etc.

3. Hebei Province

Porcelain and pottery products from Tangshan and Handan, stone carvings from Quyang, shell mosaics from Qinhuangdao, New Year pictures from Wuqiang, paper-cuts from Yuxian, inside-painted snuff bottles from Hengshui, mushrooms from Zhangjiakou, pears from Zhaozhou, grapes from Xuanhua, peaches from Shenzhou etc. are all famous in China. Local flavors include seafood from Qinhuangdao, pickles from Baoding, roast chicken from Shijiazhuang etc.

4. Shanxi Province

Famous handicrafts include knives and scissors from Taiyuan and artistic pottery and porcelain ware from Datong. Local products include Fenjiu Liquor and Zhuyeqing Liquor from Xinghuacun in Fenyang, vinegar in Qingxu, Lingchuan and Yuci, grapes from Qingxu, pears from Yuanping, Chinese red dates from Jishan, Linfen, Taigu and Yuncheng, and persimmons from Yongji. Local dishes and snacks include knife-cutting noodles, chafing dish from Bingzhou and mutton banquet from Taiyuan, beef from Pingyao etc.

5. Inner Mongolia Autonomous Region

Handicrafts include wool fabrics of Hohhot, carpets of Baotou and Alxa Left Banner, and Mongolian silver ware and boots. Animal by-products include wool, camel's hair, fur and leather. Local products include mushrooms, pilose antlers and sweet melons in the Hetao area. Local flavors include roast whole lamb, roast lamp leg, skin of boiled milk, milk bean curd, kumiss, buttered tea etc.

6. Liaoning Province

Apples produced in Dalian and Yingkou in the east of Liaoning, pears from Suizhong and Beizhen in the west of Liaoning, peaches, seafood, shell carvings, embroidery and glassware from Dalian, seafood from Dandong and Yingkou, jade carvings from Xiuyan, agate carvings from Jinzhou, amber handicrafts from Fushun and Snowflake Beer from Shenyang are well-known. Local flavors include chafing dish in the Northeast China style, Laobian dumplings from Shenyang and smoked chicken from Goubangzi.

7. Jilin Province

"Three Treasures of Northeast China" — ginseng, marten pelt and pilose antler — all can be found in Jilin. Among native produce are black edible fungus of Hunchun, round-shaped mushrooms, honey and apple pears of Yanbian, Sanbao Liquor of Jilin, Korean cold noodles, and pickles etc.

8. Heilongjiang Province

Famous products include chum salmons and sturgeons from the Heilongjiang and Wusuli rivers, more than 60 species of mushrooms, black edible fungus, pine nuts, marten pelts, otters, ginseng, pilose antlers, and dairy products from Daqing and Qiqihar, sausages, candies and beer from Harbin and mineral water from Wudalianchi. Local dishes include raw fish of Hezhen ethnic group, and shish kebabs of Oroqen ethnic group.

9. Shanghai Municipality

Shanghai is the largest industrial city in China. Its light industrial and textile products include costumes, woolens, poplin, leather shoes, neckties, cosmetics, clocks and wristwatches, toys, durable goods, sports and entertainment gear, furniture, cameras, toffee, foods etc. Art and craft articles include gold and silver ornaments, theatrical costumes, carvings, embroidery and artificial flowers. At the same time, Shanghai has a large number of Chinese and Western restaurants. Shanghai cuisine and special snacks and refreshments, such as cakes, toffee and spiced beans, are available, too.

10. Jiangsu Province

Famous handicrafts in Jiangsu Province include silk, embroidery, straw-woven articles and sandalwood fans of Suzhou, purple pottery ware of Yixing, clay figurines of Wuxi, lacquer ware of Yangzhou, and writing brushes, combs of Changzhou. Local products include prawns of Lianyungang, crabs of Yangcheng Lake, reeves shad from the Yangtze River, and whitebait fish, lotus root and Biluochun green tea from the Taihu Lake area. Local delicacies include salted duck from Nanjing, braised pork spareribs from Wuxi, ham from Rugao, dried meat

中国特产

floss from Taicang, twin-yolked duck eggs from Gaoyou, vinegar from Zhenjiang, Yanghe Daqu Liquor, Shuanggou Daqu Liquor and cakes from Suzhou, Wuxi and Yangzhou.

Jiangsu cuisine, based on the Huai'an-Yangzhou style, is one of the eight major schools of the Chinese culinary art.

11. Zhejiang Province

Handicraft articles include silk, embroidery and brocade of Hangzhou, silk embroidered clothes of Ningbo, embroidery of Wenzhou, laces of Xiaoshan, bamboo-woven articles of Hangzhou and Chengxian, straw-woven articles of Yuyao, Cixi and Huangyan, wood carvings of Dongyang, stone carvings of Qingtian, metal and stone seal engravings, silk fans and umbrellas of Hangzhou, Zhang Xiaoquan brand knives and scissors, writing brushes and gold and silver ornaments of Shaoxing. Local products include Longjing tea of the West Lake, sweet oranges of Huangyan and Wenzhou, red oranges of Quzhou, sweet peaches and loquats of Fenghua, Chinese torreya nuts of Zhuji, dates of Yiwu, ham of Jinhua, yellow rice wine of Shaoxing and lotus root flour of the West Lake of Hangzhou. Local delicacies include vinegar fish of the West Lake, Dongpo pork, begger's chicken, *zongzi* (glutinous rice wrapped in bamboo or reed leaves) of Jiaxing and sweet boiled rice dumplings made of glutinous rice flour of Ningbo.

12. Anhui Province

Traditional handicrafts include the "four treasures of the study": *xuan* paper, writing brushes of Jingxian County, Huizhou ink sticks and ink-slabs of Shexian. Besides these, knives, scissors and iron pictures from Wuhu are also very famous. Local products are pears of Dangshan, pomegranates of Huaiyuan, dates of Xuanzhou, loquats of Shexian County, black tea of Qimen, and green tea of Huangshan. Famous spirits include Gujing Gongjiu Liquor from Bozhou and Kouzijiu Liquor from Huaibei. Local delicacies include roast chicken from Fuliji, Qiaowei pork from Dingyuan, dried fish from Jingxian County, and refreshments from Shouxian and Anqing.

Anhui cuisine is one of the eight major schools of the Chinese culinary art.

13. Fujian Province

Traditional arts and crafts include bodiless lacquer ware from Fuzhou, stone carvings from Shoushan, wood carvings from Xiamen and Quanzhou, porcelains from Dehua, colored clay sculptures from Zhangzhou, bamboo articles from Anxi, and shell carvings from Pingtan. Local products include Oolong tea from south Fujian, Tieguanyin tea from Anxi, jasmine tea and oranges from Fuzhou, black tea from Fu'an, green tea from Nan'an, oranges from Putian, longans from Jinjiang, oranges, bananas, narcissus, dried bamboo shoots, mushrooms and white fungus from Zhangzhou, laver from Pingtan, Wenchang fish from Tong'an and other seafoodes.

Local delicacies include fish balls from Fuzhou, vegetable dishes from Nanputuo of Xiamen, and Hulu chicken from Quanzhou.

14. Taiwan Province

Taiwan is China's treasure island with abundant products. Handicrafts include coral from Penghu, green jade from Hualian, artistic pottery and porcelain articles from Beitou (Peitou), kites and glassware from Taibei (Taipei), Christmas ornaments from Xinzhu (Hsinchu), shell mosaics from Lüdao (Luato), furniture from Taoyuan, straw-woven articles from Dajia (Tachia), bamboo articles from Taizhong(Taichung) and Taibei (Taipei).

This locality abounds in bananas, pineapples, longans, litchis, papayas, oranges, olives, sugarcanes and tea etc. Local delicacies include salty crisp shrimps, torch-shaped shark's fin, duck stewed with Chinese angelica, spirits chicken, pineapple shortbread and Sun cakes from Taizhong (Taichung), jujube cakes from Yilan (Ilan) and other local snacks.

15. Jiangxi Province

Traditional handicrafts include porcelain ware and porcelain engravings from Jingdezhen, porcelain plates from Nanchang, bamboo-woven articles from Yanshan, fireworks from Pingxiang, bamboo paper, wood carvings, jade carvings, stone carvings and embroidery from Ruijin and Yongfeng. Local products include Yunwu tea from Lushan, green tea from Wuyuan and Jinggang Mountain, black tea from Wuning, watermelons from Linchuan, melon seeds from Xinfeng, lotus seeds from Guangchang, bamboo shoots and tea oil from Jinggang Mountain, oranges from Nanfeng and whitebait from the Poyang Lake and Site Liquor from Zhangshu. Local delicacies are fish dishes from Jiujiang, "Three Stones" (stone chicken, stone fish, stone fungus) from Lushan, salty duck from Nan'an and deck meat from Jingdezhen.

16. Shandong Province

Traditional light industrial products and handicrafts: clocks, watches and embroidery from Yantai, porcelains from in Zibo, silver-inlaid products, kites and New Year pictures from Weifang, shell carvings from Qingdao and straw-woven articles from Jiaodong. Shandong is abundant in fruits, such as Laiyang pears, Yantai apples, Feicheng peaches, Jimo grapes, Leling dates and Dezhou watermelons. Local specialities are seafood, Yantai prawns, Shouguang chicken, Heze peonies, Dong'e donkey-hide gelatin, Tsingtao Beer, Laoshan mineral water, Longkou bean noodles, Yantai fruit wine and liquor, Confucius Family Wine in Qufu. Local delicacies include Dezhou stewed chicken, Jinan crisp sweet hot cakes, Qingdao sorghum syrup and Jining pickled vegetables.

Shandong cuisine is one of the eight major schools of the Chinese culinary art.

17. Henan Province

Handicrafts: painting and calligraphy, Bian silk and Bian embroidery of Kaifeng, Junci porcelain from Yuzhou, palace lanterns and Tang tricolor pottery of Luoyang, Ruci porcelain from Linru, jade ware and pyrographic chopsticks from Nanyang are all very famous. Special local products include dates from Xinzheng, pears from Mengjin, watermelons from Kaifeng, Maojian tea from Xinyang, carp from the Yellow River and sesame oil from Zhumadian. Local delicacies include roast chicken of Daokou, spiced and dried bean curd of Zhuxianzhen, roast duck of Bianjing, Dukang Liquor of Luoyang and Minquan Wine.

18. Hubei Province

Jiangling satin, Wuxue and Guangji bamboo ware, Shashi silk-floss wadded quilts, Yichang black tea, Xianning brick tea and osmanthus flowers, Enshi green tea, Zigui oranges, Suizhou preserved dates, Ezhou blunt-snout bream, and Huangmei whitebait. Local delicacies include Xiaogan sesame candy, Huangzhou Dongpo cakes, Wuhan fried rice cakes and many other snacks.

19. Hunan Province

Local specialities include Silver Needle tea of Junshan in Yueyang, Guzhang Maojian tea of Dayong, Yinfeng green tea, Xuefeng oranges of Changsha, cumquats of Liuyang, cured meat in Changsha, whitebait, dried fish, and spicy oil of Yueyang, bamboo shoots and ginger of Shaoyang, and preserved eggs of Yiyang. Handicrafts include embroidery and eiderdown quilts of Changsha, bamboo articles of Shaoyang, porcelain ware of Liling, and pattern stone carvings and fireworks of Liuyang.

Hunan cuisine is one of the eight major school of the Chinese culinary art.

20. Guangdong Province

Guangdong is located in tropical and subtropical areas and abundant in fruits. Bananas from Dongguan, oranges from Chaozhou, litchis from Zengcheng and Conghua , sugarcanes from Tanzhou are claimed to be the most famous fruits in Guangdong. Black tea from Yingde, narcissus tea from Chaozhou and seafood are very popular. Handicrafts include embroidery, ivory carvings, jade carvings, ink-slabs from Zhaoqing, porcelain ware, wood carvings, and paper-cuts of Shiwan in Foshan, artistic porcelain products of Shenzhen, and drawnwork and embroidery of Chaozhou and Shantou.

Guangdong cuisine occupies an important position among the eight schools of the Chinese culinary art. Guangdong snacks are the most famous in the country.

21. Hainan Province

Special local products include pineapples and coconuts of Wenchang, mangoes of Wuzhi Mountain, litchis of Qiongshan Mountain, edible bird's nests of Xisha Islands, coconut goblets, coconut milk and coconut candies of Haikou, and coffee, pepper and betel nuts of Wanning. Handicrafts include coconut shell carvings, shell carvings and coral ornaments.

22. Guangxi Zhuang Autonomous Region

Native arts and crafts include Jingxi and Binyang brocade, Du'an embroidery, Nixing pottery and porcelain ware, pottery of Qinzhou, artistic ceramics and bamboo sticks of Guilin, bamboo hanging screens of Wuzhou, shell carvings of Beihai, stone carvings and ink-slabs of Liuzhou, pearls of Hepu etc. Fruits include Shatian pomelos from Rongxian County, pineapples from Nanning, oranges from Liuzhou, and longans, litchis, bananas, mangosteen, and cassia aniseed from Yulin. Local delicacies include preserved bean curd, rice noodles, Sanhua Liquor from Guilin, and Sanshe Liquor from Wuzhou.

23. Chongqing Municipality

Handicraft products include paintings on bamboo curtains, filigree jewelry, and lacquer ware. Local specialities are Chongqing navel oranges, red oranges, mandarin oranges and tangerines, tung oil and red tangerines from Wanxian County, Fuling pickled mustard tuber, oranges of Hechuan and Jiangjin etc. Chongqing's chili oil hot pot is a well-known local flavor.

24. Sichuan Province

Rich in native produce, Sichuan Province wins the title of "Nature's Storehouse." Handicrafts include Chengdu embroidery, Shujin brocade, lacquer ware, porcelain roughcasts, bamboo-woven ware, Nanchong paintings on bamboo curtains, Zigong and Yibin bamboo artifacts, Rongchang and Huili pottery and porcelain, Zigong paper-cuts etc. Local specialities include Chinese medicinal materials, Sichuan safflower, Tuo tea, Maofeng tea of Emei Mountain and so on. Liquors include Wuliangye of Yibin, Luzhou Tequ, Jiannanchun of Mianzhu and Gulinlang Liquor. Chengdu is famous for its snacks, such as wonton soup with pepper sauce, glutinous rice dumplings, street vendor's noodles and duck from Xichang.

Sichuan cuisine is one of the eight schools of the Chinese culinary art.

25. Guizhou Province

Handicrafts include Zunyi silk quilt covers, Anshun batik, Enzhou stone ink-slabs, Dafang lacquer ware and Yuping bamboo flutes. Local special products include pears from Weining, red robe oranges from Xingyi, Maojian tea, Maofeng tea, Qingmao tea, green tea from Anshun, Maotai Liquor from Renhuai, and Dongjiu Liquor from Zunyi. Local delicacies include ham from Weining, empty noodles from Suiyang, Bobo candies from Zhenning, pickled vegetables from Dushan, Dao dishes from Zhenyuan, pressed salted duck from Sansui, wild pear juice from Guiyang, steamed chicken from Tianma and Love Bean Curd.

26. Yunnan Province

Yunnan Province is famous for its tobacco products — Yunyan cigarettes, mainly produced in Yuxi , Qujing and Kunming. Pu'er tea and Tuo tea from Dali, Simao and Xishuangbanna as well as Yunnan black tea (Dianhong) are well-known at home and abroad. Local special products include Yunnan white medicine, Chinese medicinal materials, bananas and mangoes from Xishuangbanna, pears and edible fungus from Kunming, marble sculptures from Dali, wooden sculptures from Jianchuan, copper and tin handicrafts from Kunming and Gejiu, jade ware from Tengchong, silver ornaments from Tonghai, articles with ethnic flavors from Kunming, carpets from Zhaotongbanna, brocade of the Dais, embroidery of the Hani ethnic group, peacock feather ornaments from Xishuangbanna, and unique dress from Lijiang. Yunnan famous foods: Xuanwei ham, fermented bean curd of Lunan, steamed chicken, rice noodles and delicacies from ethnic minorities.

27. Tibet Autonomous Region

Traditional handicrafts: carpets from Lhasa and Xigaze, Tibetan carpets from Gyangze, woolen fabric, pattern aprons, boots, costumes, gold ware and silver ware from Lhasa, Zetang, and wooden bowls from Shannan area. Local delicacies: buttered tea (made from butter, milk, tea and egg), "kase" (made from wheat flour, vegetable oil, milk, white sugar, and coconut oil) etc.

28. Shaanxi Province

Famous fruits include oranges and tangerines from Hanzhong and Chenggu, pomegranates, persimmons and red dates from Lintong, dates from Binxian County, apples from north Shaanxi and apricots from Huaxian County. Local special products include walnuts from Shangluo, fragrant rice and black rice from Yangxian County, red-robe hot pepper from Hancheng and Maojian tea from Ziyang. Local delicacies include cured mutton, mutton soup with steamed bun, dumplings, and Feast of Eight Sights in Chang'an from Xi'an, knotweed candies from Sanyuan, dried beef from Xixiang, and cured donkey meat from Fengxiang. Famous liquors include Xifeng of Fengxiang and Taibai of Meixian County.

29. Gansu Province

Local special products: Bailan melons, wine-sweet melons, black melon seeds and lilies from Lanzhou, black edible fungus from Kangxian County, day lily flowers from Qingyang, Chinese prickly ash and valuable Chinese medicinal materials from Wenxian County. Traditional handicrafts include phosphorescent jade cups from Jiuquan, stone ink-slabs from Jiayu Pass, carved lacquer ware from Tianshui, pottery and porcelain from Huating, imitation ancient carpets from Lintao and wool fabrics from Lanzhou. Local delicacies include boiled whole lamb and camel hooves from Dunhuang, cured pork from west Gansu, roast suckling pig and beef pie from Lanzhou, roast meat from west Gansu and so on. Famous local beverages are Xiliang Daqu Liquor and kumiss.

30. Qinghai Province

Local special products: fleece, plush, hide, carpets, cheese and milk powder from Xining, Huang carp from Qinghai Lake, pears from southeast Qinghai, and musk and Chinese caterpillar fungus from Yushu. Local delicacies include instant boiled mutton, chopped entrails of horses from Xining and dried beef from Guoluo. Handicrafts include silver ware, ornaments and Tibetan-style knives from Xining and Huangyuan.

31. Ningxia Hui Autonomous Region

Local special products, in five colors and known as the "Five Treasures of Ningxia," are: red Chinese wolfberry from Zhongning and Zhongwei, yellow licorice root from Tongxin and Yanchi, blue ink-slabs from Helan, white sheepskins from Pingluo, and black hair-like flabelliform nostoc from Tongxin and Haiyuan. Handicrafts include carpets knitted after ancient designs from Yinchuan, stone carvings from Helan, and porcelain objects from Shizuishan. Local delicacies include Muslim's cream cakes, crisp beef and mutton, mutton eaten with fingers, steamed lamb mutton and Masan chicken boiled in clear soup.

32. Xinjiang Uygur Autonomous Region

Xinjiang is abundant in melons and fruits, such as Hami melons, watermelons, and stoneless white grapes from Turpan, apples from Yining, fragrant pears from Korla, pomegranates from Yecheng, walnuts from Aksu, figs from Atux, and sweet melons from Jiashi. Other agricultural and animal-husbandry products include fine wool, jade from Hotan, silkworms, cotton of fine staple from south Xinjiang, and snow lotus from north Xinjiang. Handicrafts include carpets from Hotan, Uygur-style costumes, ornaments, bronze ware, jade carvings from Urumqi and musical instruments of ethnic flavor from Kashi. Local foods include Uygur-style and Hui-style roast whole lamb, kebabs, roast fish, baked buns, *shouzhuafan* (a rice and mutton speciality traditionally eaten with fingers), buttered tea and roast buns with meat stuffing. Local beverages are wines made of grapes and other fruits from Turpan and Shanshan.

33. Hong Kong

Local special products: pearls, toys, camellias, butterflies, groupers etc.

Local delicacies: seafood, barbecue, shrimp paste, roast goose etc.

34. Macau

Local specialities include gold ornaments, Portuguese sherry, pottery ware, porcelain ware, ivory goods, glass beads etc.

One of Macau's famous cates is the African chicken, a whole chicken barbecued with more than 10 spices. The others are fresh oysters, red bean pettitoes and wife-cakes.

附录　主要城市购物地点介绍
Appendix：Shopping in Major Cities

1．北京

　　商业中心：王府井大街、西单商业大街

　　工 艺 品：北京友谊商店、北京古玩城、华夏工艺品商店

　　古玩旧货：朝阳区潘家园旧货市场、琉璃厂、红桥市场

　　服装批发市场：朝阳区秀水东街、万通新世界

　　丝　　绸：北京丝绸商店、元隆丝绸公司、国际丝绸商店

　　风味小吃：东安市场、全聚德烤鸭店

　　书　　店：中国图书进出口总业务大楼二层(在使馆区)、王府井外文书店、西
　　　　　　　单图书大厦、海淀图书城

2．上海

　　商业中心：南京路、淮海路、四川路、豫园商城、徐家汇、张扬路、不夜城

　　工 艺 品：上海工艺美术品服务部、城隍庙、友谊商店

　　古玩旧货：东台路、济河路

　　服　　装：南京路、淮海路、四川路、徐家汇、华亭路服装街

　　丝　　绸：老介福呢绒绸缎商店

　　风味小吃：云南路美食街、黄河路、乍浦路、豫园、马泳斋熟食店、邵万生南华
　　　　　　　店

　　书　　店：福州路外文书店、南京路新华书店、上海书城

3．天津

　　商业中心：滨江道、和平路

　　工 艺 品：古文化街

　　古玩旧货：沈阳道旧物市场

　　服　　装：服装街、劝业场、吉利大厦

　　风味小吃：南市食品街、滨江道小吃

　　书　　店：佟楼外文书店、东北角新华书店、方舟图书销售中心

4. 重庆

商业中心：解放碑、杨家坪
工 艺 品：重庆市文物商店、工艺品商店、工艺美术商场
古玩旧货：重庆民间文物收藏馆、渝中区
服　　装：解放碑、朝天门
风味小吃：八一路、民权路、民族路、沙坪坝
书　　店：重庆外文书店、重庆市新华书店、重庆书城

5. 成都

商业中心：春熙路
工 艺 品：四川省工艺品商场、省文物商店、四川美术馆
丝　　绸：春南商场、四川省工艺品商场、成都蜀绣厂、汉皇绣庄
服　　装：成都地下商业街、展览馆时装批发市场、火车北站
风味小吃：总府街赖汤圆、夫妻肺片、北大街郭汤圆、春熙路龙抄手、提督街钟
　　　　　水饺、东风路一段珍珠圆子、红星南路韩包子、后子门担担面、顺城
　　　　　街口古月胡三合泥
书　　店：成都外文书店

6. 广州

商业中心：北京路步行街、上下九路步行街、天河城、正佳广场
工 艺 品：文德路、大新路、一德西路
古玩旧货：清平市场、长寿路
服　　装：白马商场及附近、北京路、上下九路、沙河服装城、东山口
风味小吃：泮溪酒家、广州酒家、北京路、上下九路、赛马场
书　　店：广州外文图书旗舰店、广州购书中心

7. 南京

商业中心：新街口
工 艺 品：北京东路工艺美术大楼、夫子庙
古玩旧货：朝天宫
服　　装：新街口、湖南路夜市
风味小吃：夫子庙
书　　店：江苏省外文书店(中央路)、南京市外文书店(中山东路)、南京市新
　　　　　华书店

8. 西安

商业中心：东大街、南大街、西大街、解放路

工　艺　品：碑林区书院门古文化街、西安市文物商店、三学街

古玩旧货：新城区化觉巷、书院门古文化街

丝　　　绸：西安锦江刺绣厂、秦绣阁商店、西安凤凰刺绣厂

服　　　装：碑林区骡马市、唐城、李家村

风味小吃：大麦市清真饭食街、解放路饺子馆、东新街、同盛祥泡馍馆、西安饺子宴饭店

书　　　店：陕西省外文书店

9．武汉

商业中心：武汉广场、上海商城、亚贸广场

工　艺　品：湖北省工艺大楼

古玩旧货：武胜路文化市场

服　　　装：汉正街、六渡桥、江汉路夜市场

风味小吃：老通城豆皮、四季美汤包、五芳斋汤圆、无名氏烧烤

书　　　店：湖北省外文书店、武汉市新华书店

10．杭州

商业中心：延安路、湖滨、武林、吴山

工　艺　品：解放路天工艺苑、众安桥

古玩旧货：岳王路花鸟市场、湖墅南路收藏品市场

服　　　装：国货路、航海路四季青服装市场

风味小吃：湖滨路知味观、吴山路

书　　　店：浙江省外文书店、杭州市新华书店

11．哈尔滨

商业中心：中外民贸市场、人和地下商业街、中央商业步行街

工　艺　品：秋林公司、中外民贸市场

古玩旧货：道外区市场

服　　　装：以秋林公司为中心的南岗购物中心、以中央大街为中心的道里购物中心

风味小吃：老都一处

书　　　店：黑龙江省外文书店、黑龙江省新华书店、学府书店、哈尔滨购书中心

12．长春

商业中心：和平路、滨江道

工　艺　品：重庆路雅美斋、人民大街友谊商店

古玩旧货：清明街吉发古玩城
服　　装：人民大街长春百货大楼、光复路服装市场
风味小吃：重庆路北方风味一条街、新发路东方饺子王、嫩江路唐人街饭店
书　　店：吉林省外文书店、长春市新华书店

13. 厦门

商业中心：中山路、思明南路、鼓浪屿龙头路、夏禾路、白鹭洲购物娱乐中心、
　　　　　免税店
工 艺 品：中山路、厦门工艺美术厂、工艺美术服务部
古玩旧货：厦门文物店、中山路
服　　装：华联商厦、厦门第一百货商店、中山路
风味小吃：好清香酒店、新南轩酒店、吴再添小吃店、黄则和小吃店、南普陀素
　　　　　菜馆
书　　店：厦门市外文书店、厦门对外图书交流中心

14. 青岛

商业中心：中山路、台东、李沧
工 艺 品：中山路工艺美术商店、即墨路小商品市场
古玩旧货：中山路文物商店、中山路古旧书店
服　　装：中山路、即墨路
风味小吃：中山路劈柴院、春和楼饭店、青岛饭店、汇泉商业广场小吃街
书　　店：青岛外文书店、青岛市新华书店